PERGAMON GENERAL PSYCHOLOGY SERIES

Editors: Arnold P. Goldstein, *Syracuse University*
Leonard Krasner, *SUNY, Stony Brook*

CLIMATE FOR CREATIVITY
PGPS-9

Climate for Creativity

Report of the Seventh National Research Conference on Creativity

Editor
CALVIN W. TAYLOR

Supported jointly by
The National Science Foundation (Grant No. GR-24)
and
The Smith Richardson Foundation, Inc.
Held in Greensboro, North Carolina

PERGAMON PRESS
NEW YORK · OXFORD · TORONTO · SYDNEY · BRAUNSCHWEIG

Pergamon Press Inc.
Maxwell House
Fairview Park
Elmsford, N. Y. 10523

Pergamon of Canada Ltd.
207 Queen's Quay West
Toronto 117, Ontario

Pergamon Press Ltd.
Headington Hill Hall, Oxford

Pergamon Press (Aust.) Pty. Ltd.
19A Boundary Street
Rushcutters Bay, N.S.W.

Vieweg & Sohn GmbH.
Burgplatz 1,
Braunschweig

Library of Congress Catalog No. 70-112399
PRINTED IN THE UNITED STATES OF AMERICA

08 016329 7

CONTENTS

ACKNOWLEDGEMENTS

OUR SEVENTH creativity research conference, reported herein, had the special feature in this series of focusing on the topic of "Climate for Creativity." Yet it was only a decade ago that the subject was discussed for the first time by a subgroup at our second (1957) conference. The conclusion then was that a subgroup report could not be produced because so little was known, especially through research. In 1959, a subgroup brief, primarily pleading for pioneer research on "Environmental Conditions Affecting Creativity," was produced in our third conference report (Kuhn and Kaplan, 1959). Chapter 4 in the fourth (1961) conference book, *Creativity: Progress and Potential,* included "Environment and Training for Creativity" (McPherson, 1964). Only a small portion of the last Part V of the *Widening Horizons in Creativity* book on the fifth (1962) research conference was on climate and settings for creativity. The entire proceedings of the sixth (1964) research conference pertained to questions and challenges about the instructional media surrounding a person, as presented in the volume, *Instructional Media and Creativity* (Taylor, 1966), though practically no research-based answers were yet available across this pair of important topics.

It was time, therefore, not only to hold the next research conference in this series, but also to give special emphasis and attention through it to the problems of a climate or climates for creativity. In keeping with our previous methods of focusing on a particular subtopic, we deliberately included several leaders who were already attending to problems on the climate for creativity in their own organizations. They would thereby be effective reactors to and potential users of any research findings in this area, as well as reporters on their existing programs.

Happily, it was possible again to attract financial aid for this next research conference in the series. The National Science Foundation has given invaluable financial and moral support from the very beginning of this national-international creativity research conference series. Robert Cain of NSF, who was a most understanding monitor for earlier conferences, continued in his role for this seventh (1966) conference of the series.

The Smith Richardson Foundation also gave very timely financial support to the conference. Alex Schenck and members of the Richardson family were local hosts who observed the highest degree of southern hospitality, and Smith

Richardson, Jr. chaired one session of the conference at the Sedgefield Inn, Greensboro, North Carolina. Robert Lacklen served in a most excellent manner throughout the project as the Foundation's monitor, and he and other staff members of the Foundation were of great assistance in the preparation for the staging of the conference.

I also want to acknowledge the most helpful contributions of Frank Barron, J.P. Guilford, Joe McPherson, and Paul Torrance in their vital roles on the steering committee. Their efforts in the initial organizing, planning, selection of participants, and chairing of different sessions of this conference are most appreciated.

Again, let me state that the participants are the heart of a conference and that all the important research and thinking they had done before the conference, their reports and contributions at the conference, plus their afterwork have been most central to the production of this book.

Charles Bish, the talent expert of the National Education Association, commented briefly; Elizabeth Starkweather of Oklahoma State University gave an interesting presentation of her preschool studies which is to be published in our book, *Creativity Across Education;* and Alexander Matejko, visiting Polish sociology professor at North Carolina University, gave a short talk on the current creativity research in his Eastern European region.

For various reasons, the contributions of a few others to the conference have not been included as chapters in this book. We were most fortunate to have William Shockley, Nobel Laureate for his transistor work, speak and review his classroom demonstrations on the talents and potential high level capabilities of a sample of high school students from Greensboro. Because of the complexity of his demonstrations, they could not be captured easily for reproduction in manuscript form. We also had the good fortune the following year to have Dr. Shockley as a guest speaker at our Sixth Annual Summer Creativity Workshop on the University of Utah campus.

We are greatly indebted in many ways to Lester Beck who showed us fascinating films on creativity, but these were also not feasible for presentation in book form. He, too, came to our Summer Creativity Workshop and displayed his ingenious instructional media materials that always excite the imagination of viewers.

William J. J. Gordon, renowned for his work in synectics, was unable to come to the meetings, but he sent Gunther Weil who gave an informative and provocative report on synectics. We thank him for enlivening the conference sessions in a number of other ways also.

Thanks is extended to Robert L. Ellison and Elwin Nielsen for helping to coordinate the conference in Greensboro and for being my valuable co-workers in creativity for several years. Many observers came to the conference at their own expense, contributing their observations and ideas during portions of the discussions and in small sessions. These included William Torpey of the White

House staff and his sister, Dorothy Torpey of the Virginia school system; Seth Payne of the Washington, D.C. office of McGraw-Hill; and Howard Lewis of *Business Week*. Robert Brooks of the Perkin-Elmer Corporation; John Meyers, President of the Foundation for Research on Human Behavior; Vernon Shogren, Architect of North Carolina State University; and Edward Tompkins, Associate Director, U.S. Naval Radiological Defense Laboratory, also attended as observers. Two of the three trustees from the Institute for Behavioral Research in Creativity were present: Leroy Robertson from the University of Utah, and Mrs. L. L. Thurstone from the University of North Carolina.

Finally, I wish to acknowledge the labors of my own staff during the entire project. A strong voice of thanks has been well-earned by Connie Jensen, who gave invaluable assistance in the preparation of the final report. My full appreciation is hereby given to her and to the following persons who assisted in the typing, mimeographing, and collating of this report to its present status: Beverly Smith, Steven Brim, Paulette Vernieu, Ilene Ewell, Sally Strong, and Julie Russel.

Behind the scenes, my wife and family have given me welcomed and needed support throughout this conference and the entire research conference series.

Calvin W. Taylor

Part I
Organizational Settings for Creativity

CHAPTER 1

Can Organizations Be Creative, Too?

Calvin W. Taylor*

ON THE IMPORTANCE OF CREATIVITY

Arnold Toynbee (1964), the historian, describes the value of creativity to a society in a provocative chapter entitled "Is America Neglecting her Creative Minority?" Therein, Toynbee declares that *"To give a fair chance to potential creativity is a matter of life and death for any society.* This is all-important, because *the outstanding creative ability of a fairly small percentage of the population is mankind's ultimate capital asset. . . ."*

Then he warns that "Potential creative ability can be stifled, stunted, and stultified by the prevalence in society of adverse attitudes of mind and habits of behavior. What treatment is creative ability receiving in our Western World, and particularly in America?" He states that any society "has a moral duty to ensure that the individual's potential ability is given free play. If, on the contrary, society sets itself to neutralise outstanding ability, it will have failed in its duty to its members, and it will bring upon itself a retribution for which it will have only itself to blame." He says it is ironic and tragic that America herself should have become the archconservative power in the world after having made history as the archrevolutionary one and that she turned her back on the very same creative and pioneering characteristics which had led her to attain her position in history.

With a note of hope that America can reverse herself concerning her creative potentials, Toynbee states that "America's need, and the world's need, today is a new burst of American pioneering, and this time not just within the confines of a single continent but all round the globe." Toynbee adds a final challenge to our nation by saying that "America's manifest destiny in the next chapter of history is to help the indigent majority of mankind to struggle upwards towards a better life than it has ever dreamed of in the past." And if she is to embark successfully upon this mission, he concludes that *"America must treasure and foster all the creative ability that she has in her."* In sharp focus after receiving Toynbee's warning is the concern of some that today the slogan for many Americans may be: *"I came, I saw, I concurred!"*

---

*Calvin W. Taylor is Professor of Psychology, University of Utah, Salt Lake City.

1

NEEDED: ORGANIZATIONS THAT FACILITATE CREATIVITY[1]

Studies on Environments for Creative Scientific Work

In general, the research on this most challenging topic indicates that what exists and has been studied to date falls far short of being an ideal environment. Consequently, we will struggle with the problem of the need to search for a creative climate (or climates).

At our third (1959) research conference, we reported three by-product studies on the work environment for scientists at the Air Force Cambridge Research Center (Taylor *et al.*, 1963, p. 67-70). For example, Smith, our field researcher in one study, found a long list of negative things that scientists felt were wrong in their environment and a short list of positive features. Nearly every scientist had some complaints when asked specifically if there were any factors hindering his publishing. Shortly thereafter, we had the experience of reporting this first-hand to the head of the Air Force, at the invitation of the Air Force Basic Science Advisory Panel (which included William Shockley and Charles Townes, two Nobel Laureates). Apparently this led to the activation of a work committee in the Air Force which, in turn, then led to another committee at the Department of Defense level, with each committee producing its own report. It appeared that a lot of important action occurred until one checked back with the research centers where there were hints that almost nothing specifically had been changed at the levels where the scientists worked. This last point has greatly bothered me, of course.

Then the Air Force Office of Scientific Research held a meeting between behavioral scientists and lab directors, including William Price with whom we had worked at Wright Patterson Air Force Base. The first day, the lab directors described their problems to the behavioral scientists and the next day, the researchers told of the pertinent research they had done. The third day, the behavioral scientists met by themselves. One of the things I immediately recommended was that some behavioral scientist should attach himself to a top scientific director—William Price was my best example—as one of the regular members of his "working family." By working on these management problems of scientists and research managers, day by day, month by month, and year by year, I urged that some real changes in climate variables could then be expected from the kind of leads we had heard of before. I argued that the effects of these

---

[1]We have an exciting venture in a new field called "Architectural Psychology" in which we are learning to design better physical environments for man. We recognize that the design of the physical environment can affect the social environments therein. Consequently through architectural design, both the physical and the human part of the environment can potentially be constructed so they will lead to more creativeness in the people functioning in that environment. The awareness of this possibility is indicated by a recent description of the new Salk Institute in La Jolla, California, the distinctive building which is depicted as an architectural experiment in creativity.

changes could be studied to see if the climate really improved in the sense of affecting positively the fruitfulness of the scientists.

Later, I gave a speech to research administrators of the nation at Estes Park and, after bringing together the research evidence of ourselves and others, decided to call my report "A Search for a Creative Climate." The past year, I have been thinking and working in this area and have given over 40 speeches on the need to search for a climate or climates that are more favorable for creative work than the ones we now have. These speeches have struck responsive chords in all audiences of all types. The evidence, to date, indicates that the climates we have are far from ideal or optimal for creativity. We need to start searching for something different and we don't know in which direction to go but, at least, we will need to be moving away from what we now have.

Fortunately, in 1965, Dr. Tompkins looked me up and asked me to help him on his management problems at the U.S. Naval Radiological Defense Laboratory. Here was another opportunity to move further into this vital area of research. During that year, he and I were in two different parts of the Navy's comparatively large organization. However, neither his program nor our program called for this new opportunity to be suddenly and unexpectedly arising. Practically everything to be done during that year had been planned and programmed at least two years earlier, so that this new emerging opportunity could, "logically," only be considered for research action two or three or four years hence. But we both decided this opportunity was too important to miss and that it should somehow be cultivated without delay since I would only be there that year. It must have been a good study because we got together and pooled our "lack of official resources," and initiated what we have called "a matching unfunded project." Anyway, we initiated and completed an unofficial project. We felt that this was much more alert behavior than the following type, considered unpardonable in the magazine industry: "He followed the pattern right out the window."

Unfortunately, but not entirely unexpectedly, we still found some of the same kinds of results we had found several years earlier at our previous military research center. In certain respects, we replicated the three by-product studies mentioned above (Taylor et al., 1963, p. 67-70) with similar types of results though, overall, we found a somewhat healthier situation.[2]

We again found that as a person is promoted upward in the scientific organization, the higher he goes, the more activities he becomes responsible for. In our first study, the beginner was responsible for about three or four activities and they increased as he rose in the organization until, at the highest levels, he was responsible for 14 or 15 activities. In this latest lab studied, it wasn't as bad—i.e., the trend wasn't as steep.

---

[2] Recently, a chief scientist in the Air Force claims some effective corrective steps on climate for scientists have been taken, which is, of course, news in the right direction.

We have raised the question as to whether such a system promotes most people out of an opportunity to focus and concentrate very much on anything. Instead, we strongly suspect that it spreads them so thin that they don't have too much chance for creativeness and they can't expect to function much in that way. At this latest lab, we interviewed the scientists and established rapport by hearing their thoughts about needed changes. They had many complaints and many suggestions. Through a sequence of techniques, we had a series of communication exchanges with the scientists and then obtained their recommendations and their suggestions for specific corrective action. They also voted and assigned priorities to each of these suggestions, as guides for management changes. We then reported all these things in thorough, complete fashion to top management, who listened seriously to everything. One of the strong things that came through again in this study—in fact, the scientists assigned their highest single priority vote to it—is that scientific work has been plugged into an existing type of organization without nearly enough thought that this might not be a good organization, let alone anything resembling an ideal organization, for creative scientific work.

In one of our own creativity conferences, Frank Barron made an interesting observation. He said, "As I am hearing these things and as I reflect upon people who have done something that has truly reshaped the world, nearly all of them have gotten outside of existing organizations to do so." Maybe there is something we don't know about these existing organizations that make them far from ideal for the most highly creative workers.

Although we were unable to work at their lab but for three or four very brief periods of a day or two, the scientists made many suggestions as to what might be tried and top management promptly took certain easily implemented actions in line with their suggestions. We have been delighted at the receptiveness of the latter and their eagerness to receive these suggestions and to try to do something about them, even though the suggestions may prove to be merely treating symptoms rather than real causes. But at least management is willing to consider treating these symptoms as a starting point.[3]

We hope management somewhere will make such changes one at a time and have at least crude check-ups to see what differences, if any, in the work of the scientists that each change makes. I believe studies even more potent than the famous Hawthorne studies can be done in scientific centers, since there one certainly deals with potential "psychological uranium" which may have fascinating and untold kinds of possibilities. Some studies should be done by comparing the problems found at different levels in research organizations.

---

[3]Another environmental study emphasizing many measurement approaches has been completed at the same Navy research center, entitled *An Investigation of Organizational Climate* (Ellison *et al.,* 1968). A large number of unexpectedly high relations were found in this first thorough-going measurement approach, which provides high hopes for future studies and organizational changes based upon these findings.

What we find in military labs may be found, to some degree, in other government labs and in industrial labs and, probably, in university labs, too, even though universities are thought by some to be greener pastures (at least they usually are surrounded by green grass). But I have a strong suspicion that there are a lot of skeletons in the closets of universities, too.

I salute this Navy lab not only for having the courage to be studied, but also for seeking our research help on its management problems. We have produced these materials anonymously so that they could be used as management and supervisory training case study materials in developing better R and D supervisors and managers. They are fascinating materials to read. Since the study, one thing management has already found is that some of these corrective changes had already been made in the organization, but the scientists still recall only their strong previous negative experiences and either do not know, or still do not believe, that corrective changes have truly occurred. So, to them, the organization is still the way it used to be—that is the way it still is in their experience—which poses a very challenging communication problem to management and reminds us of certain problems in our own basic research studies on communication abilities.

A really striking lead emerged when the scientists focused upon supportive personnel. Although those in supportive roles are supposed to give all the help they can to the scientists, some of them are seen almost universally to be "can't-doers." When the scientists take anything to them for help, they indicate it can't be done and spend a lot of time telling why it cannot be done. But, at the same time, there are other supportive people around who function in just the reverse manner. No matter what you take them, they are "can-doers" and they will invariably find some way to help you. They have somehow attained this image and will do everything possible to live up to it.

We are very interested in trying to study the psychological differences between these contrasting kinds of supportive personnel. Later, we may move to the scientists with the notion that, at one extreme, a few scientists are almost always "can-doers" and, at the other, there are a few who are too frequently "can't-doers." We are curious to see whether management, through climate changes, can help the "can't-doer scientists" become more "can-doers" or whether it might take some kind of an intensive "psychological overhaul" before these "can't-doer scientists" can become productive and, hopefully, even creative scientists. We see an analogy between the "can't-doer" types here and the "it's impossible" responders in our Peace Corps research project (see Chapter 12).

Before ending this section about specific environmental factors, let me describe a technique used by James Gallagher initially in the educational setting. Anyone can try this with a group of teachers by saying:

Join me in showing certain creative characteristics by thinking flexibly and toying with a problem. Let's flip things over 180 degrees to see how they look from the opposite angle. We are to build the best class-room program possible to accomplish a broad goal. The task is to name each of the *specific features* that you would build into a classroom in order to make it the *best* possible program for the broad goal of *stifling* or *killing* creativity.

After they have thought up 15 or 20 specific features, then innocent-ly ask: 'What do all these add up to?' One or more of them is likely to respond that, 'It sounds a lot like the program I had when I was in school.'

If you are willing to go through a painful learning experience, I challenge you to go back to the workers you supervise and call them all together and say: "Let's have a session of toying with ideas and let's flip a problem over 180 degrees. If we were to establish an organizational structure and working environment and climate that are most ideal for making creativity wilt or for stifling or killing creativity, what would we do?" If you dare to try it, your people will probably be ready and happy to join you in this—we have certainly found scientists very eager to pour out their hearts to us on such matters. But you should be forewarned that, after awhile, they may conclude that they have just about been describing your present organization.

I argue that we urgently need to undergird our management practices with research, meaning management in all fields, especially in science. There is very little excuse for managers of research not to be interested in research on manage-ment of research. Since very few studies have ever held up creative criteria of performance, there is very little yet known through research about environ-mental settings that are ideal for creativity, so such studies are sorely needed.

Other Evidences of Anti-Creativity Climates

In studies at the elementary school (Torrance, 1963), it was found that among youngsters, if someone is producing too many ideas, too unusual and unexpected ideas, the youngsters will say, "We've got to get organized here." It happens early in life. And then they form a little organization with a few rules, and these are usually rules against (sanctions against) certain kinds of behavior. These rules can become very lasting straitjackets because when someone wants to get someone under control he says, "We've got to get organized; we've got to have a chairman; we've got to have a recorder." Guess what they might do to the most creative? Make him a recorder, for example. Then he is kept so busy in recording other people's ideas that he is well taken care of (unless he writes up the wrong set of minutes).

There is an interesting finding at the high school level. Jex (1963), on our campus, tested some high school science teachers who came back to get a master's degree in science. He tried a written creative test on them and they differed widely in their scores. He then determined how they had done the previous year as teachers, when judged by their immediate supervisor or principal. The answer was that the creative scores correlated negatively with all ten ratings by their supervisors. Apparently the system may not want creative teachers. What effect this has on students is an open question.

Another striking result in our own study dealt with how many ideas were submitted through the suggestion box as one of the kinds of contributions of each scientist to the research organization. The answer came out this way: if a person submitted an above average number of ideas which were accepted and rewarded (often with a minor award of $50 or less), he also got another form of reward, namely, a slowed-down promotion rate. If he had submitted an above average number of good ideas through the suggestion box, his promotion rate was slow. Can you explain that one? (This troubling result has been found again in the new study cited in footnote 3.)

We also had another surprising finding. If a person had finished his research and decided to go the extra mile and publish it, to write an article for publication for the larger audience, he got a below average rating on cooperation from his supervisor. Does this result make sense? When we studied hindrances to publishing, the supervisor was one of those persons who had more hindrances to his publishing and wasn't able to publish as much as the people under him. Maybe jealousy or other kinds of things were going on. At least, if you feel that the person who is creative and productive and so on has "an easy row to hoe," it isn't always so. He might be in deep trouble with others around who are threatened by him and his ideas and who may try to get him more and more under their own control.

From a field of dealing with patients, I learned that when a professional person goes in to deal with a patient, if the professional worker suddenly gets into a problem that is over his own head, that is, something for which he has not been trained and is not yet ready to cope and has no natural ways of coping with it, the professional worker is likely to come out of that situation somewhat upset, saying, "The patient is uncooperative." Isn't that an interesting notion? Blaming someone other than himself and blaming the patient for having had some ill symptom or for behaving in some fashion with which this professional person could no longer perform in his usual smooth professional ways. So the trouble is blamed, not on the professional, but on the patient who somehow got the "pro" out of his own ball park and put him in trouble; therefore, the patient is uncooperative. Isn't that interesting? Like the creatives, the patient who communicates too accurately and effectively about his problems may end up in worse straits.

More than once we have been asked, by persons who have sensed the need, whether anyone has tried a new training course for those either in or being considered for leadership positions. They want the course to develop the ability to tolerate ambiguity, especially in current so-called "leaders," where it is not already present as a natural characteristic.

I learned this next point from one of the industrial researchers in the field of creativity. I asked him, "Why don't you ask the most creative people what kind of management they should have, instead of getting new ideas from other management people about how to manage researchers? But why don't you ask the researchers, especially those who have been most creative, what kind of management they would like to have?" He said, "As a matter of fact, we did check on those who had produced the best ideas within our company, the big ideas that had really made the cash register ring. We found that the organization was ready to fire most of them just before they produced their big idea. But someone arose as a protectorate, not from the official organization but from the unofficial organization, and said, Don't you dare do it. Leave him alone. And that buddy, you see, was working for the organization better than the official administration was, and so was this creative scientist because he produced what the organization really needed and wanted. But the official organization somehow couldn't take what he was doing and became impatient or uneasy or something and wanted to fire him."

To summarize these findings about negative features of climates for the creatives, upon request, I have created 12 Golden Rules on How to Kill Creativity, stated primarily for classroom settings.

1. Assume there is only one academic (or intelligence) type of talent.
2. As science teachers, ignore scientific research results about creative talents.
3. Teach the best and shoot the rest!
4. Keep doing what was done to your ideas—and even do it more.
5. Be very human—react quickly and negatively to new ideas.
6. If you don't understand it, OPPOSE it!
7. Keep the rule going: "The more creative the idea, the more likely in trouble."
8. Have a deadly negative incentive system for creative persons and ideas.
9. Fail to try opportunities (which is better than to try opportunities and maybe fail).
10. Organize creatives in (under your controls)—or organize them out.
11. Design all possible features into organizations that stifle or kill creativity.
12. Jealously guard and keep prerogatives only to yourself to plan, think, and create.

AGING CYCLES AND IDEA RECEPTIVENESS OF ORGANIZATIONS

In this section, I will try to keep one foot on the solid ground of research findings available in the young research field. With the other foot, I am reaching out as far as possible to speculate about climates that might be more ideal for creativity.

There will also be a consideration of the characteristics of creative people, together with the bridging efforts needed to modify managements and organizational practices to be in line with these findings. I am very impressed by H. S. Richardson's central idea. He recognizes that corporations and other organizations are continually faced with the problem of surviving and thriving versus growing old and dying. In order for them to be an "Enduring Enterprise" and to move in the direction of "Corporate Immortality"—instead of having an average life span of seven years and dying—the essence of the matter to him is that they must take steps to ensure that creative minds continually rise to the top of the organization. In this way, he believes that *the total effective creative mindpower of the organization will never decrease.* Otherwise, he feels that corporations will show the effects of time in the form of aging and in the form of diminishing total effective creative mindpower, so that they will grow old and die as many corporations do each year. The alternative to these negative effects is to seek ways to be sure that creative minds continually rise to the top.

I have given numerous speeches recently on aging cycles of organizations and their receptiveness to new ideas. At one extreme, I talk about organizations being old and dying and, at the other extreme, the Peace Corps is an example of a young alert organization. Armstrong Cork commented to me over a decade ago that they continue to be a thriving organization on the American scene largely because of two small groups of creative people in their organization. One group produces new products and the other small group creates effective new advertising of these products.

In the beautiful Jefferson Memorial building are the famous words, "I have sworn upon the altar of God eternal hostility against every form of tyranny that binds the mind of man." On the same walls are other Jefferson quotations, including one about how institutions need to keep up with man's increasing insights:

> But . . . institutions must go hand in hand with the progress of the human mind. As that becomes more developed, more enlightened, as new discoveries are made, new truths discovered. . . institutions must advance also to keep pace with the times. We might as well require a man to wear still the coat which fitted him when a boy as civilized society to remain ever under the regimen of their barbarous ancestors.

George Washington also stated brilliantly that the difficulty in bringing about reforms in an organization is that one must do so through the persons who have been the most successful in that organization, no matter how faulty it is. So these people would tend to say, "Look how good an organization it must be because look who succeeded in it," and they are unfortunately the ones through whom one must work to bring about reforms. A syndicated newspaper adviser, Abigail Van Buren, makes the same point in her unique style: "Reforms always come from below. No man with four aces ever asks for a new deal."

Let me try to stir your thoughts about a thing called "creative leadership." There are a lot more unknowns by far about creative leadership than known and we have just barely started to scratch the surface about this. Let me tell you about an extremely creative leader, one who is blazing new trails, taking huge strides ahead, and doing remarkably unexpected things. He may be one who is so creative that he does not yet have any followers; he's way out there all alone. He may have a disciple or two or a handful in his lifetime, but after a decade or a generation or a century or so he may have almost the whole world following him. If you look back in history you will find there have been such people who in their day didn't appear to be creative leaders, but history tells a different story.

There is another behavior quality that I have labeled "trailership." This is, typically, to find out what most people are doing or thinking and jump right into the middle—the safest possible position. Such persons always remain farthest from the fringes or risky areas, particularly where daring innovaters may be thinking ahead and trying to create a better world for tomorrow. But as this circle moves to some degree towards the changes brought about by creative leadership, the trailers must move, too. They must always try to find just where the middle ground is now and jump back into the safe protected area of today's realities, avoiding being near the edge and becoming "edgy."

At times we might become so concerned with what may be called the "efficiency" of this day that we find and reward the most efficient people possible and they put all their focus on today's efficiency so that tomorrow is forgotten. The new ideas that would lead us to a better tomorrow don't have much of a chance because of the press for efficiency. While they might be very effective in this short-range sense, in the broader sense it would be better to be sure there are some people who are good at producing a future for this organization. Some organizations, in looking five years ahead, feel that what they will then be doing will be about two-fifths of the things that they are now doing, and three-fifths will be new things they are going to be doing five years ahead, but they do not yet know what these new things are going to be. If your organization's field is moving fast, you may have to learn to be a producer of the mainstream of tomorrow, or else ask yourself, "Where did the mainstream go?" as your organization ends up on dry land.

There has been remarkable agreement in one very general research finding across several studies. All of the findings lean in the same, though unexpected, direction in terms of an idealistic world. The general finding is that *the more highly creative idea a person has at any stage in his life, the more likely he is in trouble*—that is, the more likely that he and his ideas are in trouble (because they are troublesome). In the first place, he is likely to be alone, because he is the only one in the world with his idea when he first gets it. If it is highly creative, it won't square with what is currently accepted as common sense and so he will probably be alone and lonely. This general finding of being in trouble for creative ideas can be well-documented as a general trend (see previous section) though, if you search hard enough, you can find an occasional instance that is an exception to this usual trend. These results suggest that there can be a lot of conflict in organizations, especially if a person comes up with a new idea that is both unexpected and, potentially, very important. The question is that when new ideas do occur in an organization, what are the chances that the organization will be receptive to them?

Most organizations are triangular in shape because there are a lot more people down at the bottom than up at the top. It would be difficult to argue that most organizations have promoted people highly because of their creativeness. Generally, promotions are based upon a large number of things, so creativity usually is a challenging unknown, not highly focused upon in either selection or promotion. As a consequence, the more creative people may be found all over the organization. And everyone in the organization does have a brain, so ideas may be hatching and can emerge from any mind in the organization. On a sheer probability basis, there is a greater chance that there is more creative talent at the bottom, where there are more people, than at any other level.

One of the crucial questions is that if a new idea does occur in the organization—one of these ideas that will keep the organization alive and thriving—where will the new idea occur? It might happen any place—in anyone's mind. The stage is set for trouble, however, if the new idea doesn't occur in the right place, for it still hasn't been received and officially accepted in the organization. It must often travel across and upwards until it gets to the right place in the organizational chart and it must be received and transmitted and kept alive without major negative distortion, to bring about its impact. The chances may be remarkably slim that a newborn idea can make the full journey necessary without being killed, or so diluted as to lose its vital spark.

One of the almost impossible things for a supervisor to do is to listen to a new idea, especially from someone below him and especially if the idea is highly creative. An estimate from a preliminary investigation shows that a very small percentage of first level supervisors are psychologically capable of giving a good hearing to a new idea from below them. At higher levels, the percentage who can truly listen is greater, though still considerably less than half. Therefore, according to this early evidence, a new idea would have a very low probability of being "listened to" through two or more levels upwards. A really good new idea, a strikingly new and unexpectedly appropriate idea, may be very threatening. So we may need a good technique for selecting supervisors, emphasizing their ability to listen to new ideas.

A person from the audience at one of my speeches had done some research along this line. She found that among the lowest level supervisors in a non-educational organization, only about one out of 20 was psychologically capable of really listening to a new idea from one of his workers. At higher levels, the results were more promising with something like one out of four being capable, psychologically, of listening to new ideas from below. Let's say you are the worker and have a new idea which you want to have accepted into the system because you feel it is just what the organization needs. You decide to submit it to your boss and you hope that he will then submit it to his boss and that the two bosses will accept it wholeheartedly and install it into the system. What are the odds of this happening, considering these estimates? If these are independent, by multiplying them together, you get one chance out of 80 of acceptance versus 79 chances out of 80 that the idea will die en route. This is only a rough order-of-magnitude estimate, but it is certainly a disturbing one. Thus the problem is: what is the chance that an organization can be alert and sensitive and wise, so that it will align itself, adjust itself, to a good new idea emerging from its grassroots?

One of the great difficulties that an organization may face is that it is not alert or sufficiently ready or responsive whenever new ideas or new movements begin to emerge from within. The more slowly that an organization awakens to the new idea or movement, the more difficulties there will be for them eventually to align themselves with it and, therefore, be a party to the new movement if the latter is not killed but continues to emerge and flourish. Such new movements, unhappily, too often find they must seek more favorable environments elsewhere in order to have a chance to thrive or survive—unfortunately for the organization that had the first chance. Many instances where this has happened can be cited.

If you are a supervisor, you may have difficulty in keeping aligned with new ideas. But all ideas are not necessarily good because they are new, and all attempts to change do not necessarily yield progress, so this may pose a tough problem. If all your men are "yes men," you have no problems except that the whole group of you might die together. That's one big problem.

In a sizable percentage of cases, new actions can be initiated and changes occur as a result of the informal organization. In other words, the creative individuals and the creative characteristics in the organization are not located in the official, formal part of the organization, but are in the informal part. New things are started and carried out by informal teams that may cut across and not follow the official organizational pattern. Those in the official positions can sense this as an organizational strength, and keep the formal and informal organizations in a working adjustment with each other. On the other hand, they could feel greatly threatened, or at least upset, whenever things happen this way without being "initiated by their hands in it." Strong reactions of gaining more control, of tightening up the rules, or of opposition may occur in the strained situation.

A similar conflict situation may occur when the official organization has spent a lot of its best effort in mapping out an organizational plan of action that may become highly crystallized and then, suddenly, an unexpected idea emerges from someone who had not been much of a party to formulating this organizational plan. There is a good chance that this unexpected idea will run headlong into the officially approved plan and this intrusion will potentially threaten to unsettle or uncrystallize the plan. The authors of the plan will then be tested as to whether they and their plan have sufficient flexibility to allow new emerging ideas or even new additional information to come into consideration. In some cases, the planners and decision-makers may jealously guard their prerogatives and their plan and thereby cut off this flow of new ideas and new information—they may estrange those who produced the new ideas or discovered the new information which they innocently felt would be of interest and value to the official organization. These "internal threats" may, at times, be reacted to more strongly than competitive threats external to the organization, so that the tensions and even some infighting can greatly consume the attention and energies of the organization away from productive efforts.

Do you want your people to be thinkers and do you want your organization to be a lively communicating and thinking situation? Are you trying to increase the livewood and make thinking contagious in your organization, or is it a situation in which deadwood rests comfortably while livewood is "encouraged out." One person, who had worked in two different organizations, said that the crucial difference between them was that if a person truly did something, one of the organizations backed him up, whereas the other did not.

One way of saying much of this is that organizations may not have seriously looked at the problem of incentive systems for creativity because research, to date, strongly indicates that there are many organizational situations in which there are negative rather than positive incentives for truly creative work. The question an organization could ask of itself is whom they back up? Are they standing behind and reinforcing those moving ahead and doing creative work or are they giving them difficulties so they will not feel like doing anything? Another way to state the question is to ask, "With which workers is the organization keeping itself lined up?" Is it aligned with the more creative persons and ideas, even though such ideas may tend to have a greater breadth of applicability and, therefore, may call for more restructuring and a greater span of change and thereby threaten the status quo the most? On whom does the shoe pinch? Is it pinching on the livewood, that is, the more creative persons, more than on the less livewood (more deadwood) persons? Has some leader had the courage to reverse this unfortunate but almost natural tendency so that he has produced, instead, a situation in which the creative persons are solidly backed up and supported so that they can function full time at their best and highest level of creative work? It may first be necessary to break away from typical patterns even though it may be more painful for many persons than going along with the usual habit patterns and typical plans to avoid encountering reactions and resistance.

Would your organization be considered ideal either by persons who have distinguished themselves and their society in the past by their works or by some of

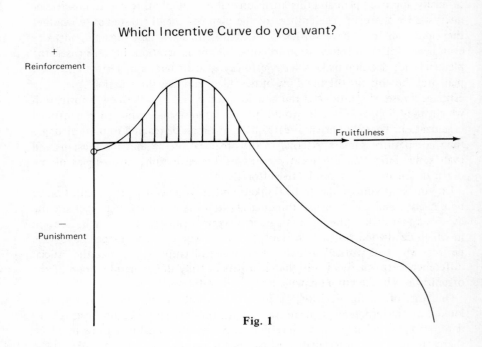

Fig. 1

the truly creative persons of our day?[4] How would they like to come and work in your organization?

Figure 1 shows one general shape of an Incentive System Curve. An incentive system yielding this type of curve is well-designed to keep persons from being highly creative and productive, punishing them more and more severely as they go beyond allowable controlled limits of fruitfulness. In some organizations, this curve could be stretched farther to the right before dipping below the horizontal line, and perhaps in others, the range of tolerable and supportable fruitfulness could be narrowed even more to the left—a truly high controlled-output situation.

Rather than a continuously upward-sloped incentive trend, as described in the Parable of the Talents, we suspect that the most frequent incentive curve is of

---

[4] The following largely unanswered question can provide a stimulus for much thought and discussion. A group could be asked to respond by finishing this sentence in many pertinent ways: "A creative organization is one in which (or one where)...." An eminent chief scientist wrote the following five answers while reflecting on this question: a creative organization is (1) one where people enjoy what they are doing; (2) one where people are considered often to be working on the wrong thing; (3) one with a poorly defined program; (4) one where the mission is always changing or not clear; and (5) one that is considered to be relatively unresponsive to management.

the general shape shown in Figure 1. A highly fruitful person faced with such an "optimal-curve" incentive situation must either submit to be controlled to limited fruitfulness, or endure the pains of being fully fruitful, or find one or more additional organizations as outlets for subportions of his total fruitfulness so that no single organization has more fruitfulness from him than "its psyche" can stand. To pursue the latter pattern successfully, though, a creative subordinate must be highly talented in the ability to keep each of the organizations from trying to own him 100 percent and thus keep full control over him.

I suspect that so-called "leaders" are not always and perhaps not often leading. An enterprising exploratory spirit is needed in more of these leadership spots. Too often they may be giving quick negative reactions of resistance in which they may be honestly indicating that the new suggestion would entail more work than they want to undertake. Too many of the people sitting in leadership spots, as John Gardner recently said, are spending all their energies tending the old system, so that little or no leadership of any type is being displayed—let alone creative leadership. Perhaps many people in leadership positions are afraid of something better and are willing to settle for some thing less with which they are more familiar. It is said that some are much more interested in control than progress, i.e., in tranquility and control than in potential progress; some are so afraid of committing an error that they don't try when an opportunity would permit. Instead of risking making errors when doing certain things, they make "errors of omission," which may ultimately have greater negative consequences than if they had made "errors of commission."[5]

The challenge here is to learn how to continue to run an efficient system while somehow learning also to implement new, sorely-needed things into the system. It may take real devotion to attempt to do both of these. It may especially require *courage to encourage* creativity.

Can Organizations Show Creative Characteristics?

During recent years, I have given numerous speeches on whether organizations can show creative characteristics. Should we ask organizations to display the same creative characteristics that are found in creative individuals? For example, should organizations be alert and responsive to opportunities? Should they sense

---

[5] The role taken by some persons in leadership positions is that of being "a judge." In it, they take no action on their own so that the initiation of new action is left entirely up to their subordinates, who must be sufficiently motivated personally to initiate and prepare their case and present it to "the judge." This non-leader role of judge is contrary to what many scientists expect of their supervisor; they feel he should take the outwardly active, enterprising role of being the scientist's "agent." The "judge" feels little responsibility for and pays little attention to searching and sensing on his own, but needs only to be aware of the cases brought before him by others (the squeaking wheel cases). He can, therefore, be blind and remain blind to emerging ideas until such a case is brought to him, *the power-that-be.*

problems that haven't been sensed before and face up to these problems and try to do something about them, especially in the way of a diversity of fresh attempts toward better solutions, rather than ignore or postpone them for future generations?

Can an organization learn to set the climate so that the inner resources of its people may be more fully developed and utilized? Can an organization have the characteristic of welcoming long strides of progress instead of only being able to tolerate inching ahead? Can an organization learn to adjust to ideas from its people so that both will work together, or will they tend to pull in different directions with the result that many of the good ideas may get killed and, as a result, the organization may also show signs of dying?

As an organization grows older, does it lose some of its potential by building into itself certain self-imposed restrictions and limitations in the process of developing its own set of intellectual and personality characteristics? Or does it develop creative characteristics so that it retains its creative potential and even increases its effective creative mindpower? Does it develop the characteristic and principle that its system is made for man, or is its guiding principle that man is supposed to be made for the system? Does it require its workers to adjust to its organizational environment, or does it allow and even encourage workers to adjust their own environment and build a better climate and organization for creative work?

I have often wondered who were the greatest killers of creativity. At present, my strong conviction is that the person himself is the greatest killer of his own ideas. But if he doesn't kill his own brain-child and sends it out into the world, there will be plenty of other people ready to finish the job by killing it for him. One also wonders which is more effective in destroying ideas *within* itself: an individual or an organization?

The new-idea man may have to exert pressure and strain on the system in order for the system to change enough to allow the new idea in; otherwise, inertia will tend to cause the system to settle back into its old rut. I was fascinated to hear that an organization was planning a meeting to learn how to avoid settling into ruts and, instead, to keep itself young and alive and thriving. They have dubbed this proposed meeting as a "dry rot" conference.

Since the crucial part of organizations are the people in them, one of my recent hunches is that an organization will be no more flexible than its least flexible link (of importance), and that it will be no more creative than its least creative link (of importance). In other words, one inflexible person in the right (?) place can level the entire organization down toward his low degree of flexibility. Likewise, one uncreative person in a key position will tend to lower the creativeness of the organization to his own level.

During one speech, I was describing certain examples of difficulties encountered by creatives and several people in the audience were pondering and then nodding agreement on each point made. Afterwards one of the audience told me, "I have had problems in my organization like the ones you described and I realized that most of my supervisors were in the audience, too. As you brought up each new point, I would look around for the supervisor with whom I had had that problem. After I located him, I noted that he was 'nodding and agreeing' with the point being made—the same point on which he had earlier given me trouble." So there can be a form of understanding and agreement by supervisors on a verbal discussion level, but back in their shop, many of them may still function in the same old way. This may be the real unsolved problem, the heart of the challenge ahead. The warning is that we must all be careful about how we deal with our workers. Even though we may nod in agreement at the points in this report, our real behavior, as seen by our subordinates, may predominantly have a stifling effect on their new ideas and creativeness.

One person suggested that a forward step would be to make creativity a responsibility of leaders, just like safety is, and to back this assignment up with a check system to ensure that supervisors are fulfilling this responsibility. In the case of safety, some supervisors probably tell their workers that "you had better keep it safe around here or I will have to do it for you." With the added responsibility of creativity, supervisors might similarly be put in a position of saying: "You had better create some good new ideas around here or else I will have to do that for you, too."

Richardson's idea, mentioned earlier, about keeping an organization alive and thriving, is that you must have a system which will spot and cultivate and insist upon having creative minds continue to rise to the top. One of his staff reported that there are four stages in the life of an organization as it starts out like a newborn baby with all the potential in the world. It is formed by (1) a group of leaders who could be called "innovators," who, in turn, tend to be replaced by (2) a group of leaders called "developers," who, in turn, make their contribution and tend to be succeeded by (3) a group of leaders called "consolidators," who, in turn, tend to prepare the organization and deliver it into the hands of (4) a group called "undertakers." The last dying gasps of a corporation are when its leaders decide to write "a bigger and better rule book." Under the reign of consolidators, what chance do creative minds have of giving the organization the "lifeblood of tomorrow" and of helping the organization not only to stay in the mainstream today, but even create the mainstream of tomorrow? That is, when an organization is in the hands of consolidators, "what chance does a creative mind have to rise to the top?" And what chance would anyone ever have of reversing the above trend across leader types?

In case a person encounters some hindering features in the organization that were built-in earlier by someone else in order to get control over other creative individuals, he may encounter resistance in trying to get these restricting rules or features removed. He can inquire as to when they were built-in and how did it all happen? He could ask what would be necessary to restore the organization to its earlier state where it still had potential to do all these things? But if he can get rid of the hindrances, the workers might be able to do even better work than at present. To bring about the changes he may have to keep a strain on the system that will only relax when he leaves or when it changes—and it will sometimes bitterly resist the latter. Some key people, unfortunately, may see this pressure as a power struggle, rather than a struggle for ideas to get a chance. A struggle between people for power is distinctly different from a struggle "for ideas to have a hearing." This is like the difference between a person in revolt and a revolutionary. One is after power and the other is after having his ideas heard. If the ideas are given a good hearing, the latter one, but not the former may relax the pressure.

To show the various reactions of leaders to different types of workers, I have sometimes described persons in leadership positions as falling into one of four types. The first type I call a "creative leader," in the sense that he has all the creative characteristics and is blazing new trails and opening new fields so many people can follow into these new fields to work—he is really a pioneer. A second type is not quite this kind, but at least he might be called a creative leader in the sense of being a catalyst and thus being somewhat of a party to, though not the real creator of, the new ideas generated in others. So he does enter into the process as a catalyst and deserves credit for an assist. The third type is a creative leader in another sense; he can at least allow or tolerate or even encourage creativity in others around him and thereby create a more favorable climate. and the fourth type, I call "none of the above".

I also classify workers into four types to set the stage for another point. One type may be a worker with hardly any ideas, so that what he does is almost entirely what he is told to do. The second one may be someone with lots of ideas and he tries them out but quickly realizes that ideas are not "welcome here." So he goes underground with his own ideas and becomes, in effect, a "yes man." A third type is one who tries his ideas out and, when he finds that they aren't welcome, explodes and quits. But the question is where does he go or where can he go? He goes someplace else and great creativity may occur when the administration explains why he left. He probably leaves some psychological scars behind, so that thereafter the chances are reduced for idea persons like him ever being hired into that organization again. The fourth kind of worker is one who has ideas that he believes are needed for the organization to survive and thrive. He, therefore, stays and fights for his ideas.

If a supervisor cannot always say "yes," to whom will he say "no?" Will he be saying "no" very often to the first type of worker who doesn't have any particular ideas of his own? Of course not. Will he say "no" to the second worker who tries suggesting his ideas, but then soon decides to keep them to himself. Again, the supervisor will generally not be saying "no" to a "yes man". Or is he likely to be saying "no" to the third man? Yes, once maybe—but not afterwards. So to which type will he probably be saying "no?" To the fourth type of worker, the one who has decided to stay and push his own ideas. If the supervisor says "no" more often to this type, he may then be creating an opposition party in the company, a neglected minority, even a creative minority of the kind that Toynbee warned us should be fostered rather than neutralized or opposed. Yet supervisors and other administrators, by their own behavior, can be producing a creative minority against which they are lined up in their own organization.[6]

I've given a lot of thought about ways for supervisors to avoid this undesirable predicament. A crucial incident occurs whenever any supervisor senses that his own initial reactions are tending to be strongly negative; this may mean that the idea is highly unexpected and doesn't fit in with his plans—meaning that he has already planned and fully organized and crystallized his own programs ahead. What should a supervisor do if his anxieties are aroused and he gets a strong emotional reaction to kill the new idea? Instead, he should try to go into a cooling-off period, a moratorium, so that he will be able to figure out, unemotionally, what it was that brought about this strong reaction within himself. During this period he should try to analyze his situation and look at the unexpected features and the merits in the idea. This initial emotional reaction may be a sign that something is so unusual that it should be studied and understood. This behavior can be much more sensible than following the slogan, "If you don't understand it, oppose it!"

I have thought of having sessions in which management is asked to tell all the reasons why a new idea is impossible or difficult, or all the ways in which they themselves might be in difficulty and not able to live through the effects of the new idea if it were accepted, or all the ways in which the new idea might require too much work or pose too much trouble. They should be allowed to go fully through a session to produce and carefully think over these "points of threat."

After finishing with that first session, then have them hold a second session in which to think of all the reasons why the idea might be possible. Also have them consider what they would do if the idea were accepted, have them think of all the ways in which they might make their own personal adjustment to it and be able to live through its acceptance and thereby successfully survive it. By various attempts, sound techniques may be discovered which will speed up this process of "reaction to emerging ideas" so that persons in leadership spots will be more receptive, more rapidly adjustable, and more positively responsive to good new ideas emerging from their workers or from elsewhere. By then giving them thinking time, you can give them adjustment time, face-saving time, survival adjustment time. Later they can be assembled together again and asked what they are going to do—move ahead or not?

---

6 Recently I heard a challenging radio talk entitled "Are We Watching America Die?" According to Toynbee, if we are party to enough situations like the one described above, the question should be "Are We Helping America Die?"

Allow me to be sarcastic for a paragraph. If you, as a supervisor, really do want to stop something, be alert, be sensitive very early to the problem. *Nip it in the bud* because not many people will see you kill it—just the person with the idea and you. But if you let it grow into a branch you will have to saw it off, or if you allow it to become a tree, you will have to chop it down. Then many people will hear you sawing and chopping and hear it fall, and they can easily find out who chopped it down. Also, if you let the idea alone to grow on its own and postpone your decision for a while, but later desert it, you may have a problem. Or if it really flourishes, and you try later to join, you may have a hard time having the idea person welcome you and find room for you on the band-wagon. Psychologically, he may not be eager to have you if you failed to back him up when he really needed it.

Can Organizations Facilitate Creative Processes?

I have not yet attempted to write serious suggestions on what management might try to do to develop a more creative climate. However, I have done some analogous writing about educational situations in a series of ten articles, honestly described as merely "Clues to Creative Teaching," (Taylor 1963-64). Since teachers and supervisors have some analogous supervisory roles, I believe that most of the points in these ten articles might be readily paraphrased so that they could appropriately be called a series of "Clues to Creative Supervising."

I like the notion in education that students can be an alive, reactive, responsive environment. The teacher can be, too, thus making a total responsive classroom environment that will be exciting for all.

Students have suggested that they are the ones most ready to be taught about creativity if they can give feedback to teachers and provide a guide as to whether teachers are eliciting the internal processes and responses in students, such as creative processes, desired at that time. Likewise, supervisors could consider their workers to be a responsive environment against which they can check to see if they are supervising more for creativity. The workers might say, "Now you're getting the idea of how to supervise for creativity." Or, alternately, "Now you're moving away, so don't go any farther in that direction because you're making it more difficult for us to do creative and productive thinking." Any supervisor at any level in any organization can hoist an umbrella and thereby create a different climate in that part of the organization from that in any other part. Admittedly it would take a lot of human effort on the supervisor's part and he may have to spend considerable extra energy to maintain the umbrella against the customary organizational climate. But I believe that while he is running an efficient system, he also can still try for new things and can be building a better climate in his part of the organization.

Through serious efforts to acquire greater insight into creativity and to implement these findings in their schools, principals may be able to improve the creativeness of the climate by hoisting unbrellas as buffers against outside forces, including forces from other parts of the system. Under these umbrellas, they can provide climates largely of their own making, in which staff and students can function better than in those already established. They may become not only more creative leaders but also greater leaders for creativity in others. They can thus become more effective catalysts so that their teachers can teach for creativity. The catalytic effect might also work through two levels so that the creativeness in the students, too, can be more effectively displayed and cultivated.

Managers and supervisors can function in analogous ways to facilitate creativeness in their workers. Yet it appears as if organizations are frequently at their very best on routine things, and too often at their very worst on creative things, especially when the creativity has occurred at the grassroots level in the organization.

Malfunctioning in leaders and organizations may have a high probability of occurring when creativity is involved. A time when leaders may be most defensive is when creative ideas are emerging from subordinates within the organization. In such cases, who is there to troubleshoot such malfunctioning behavior of those in leadership positions? In turn, it can be truly difficult for such *creative subordinates* to know what to do or how to feel when they experience such defensive management and leader malfunctioning, especially the first time—and almost always thereafter, too.[7]

Parnes: Cal, isn't it your feeling that things are improving tremendously for creativity? Don't you have more optimism than that?

S: I can talk on both sides of this. From one viewpoint, tremendous progress is occurring but, on the other hand, some of us are quite impatient. In terms of world events, we don't know how much time we have or how rapidly we must go. We may have to run much faster to keep up with competing activities which could have effects counteracting our efforts. Part of the problem, then, is to try to speed up the lag or speed up the processes as rapidly as we know how.[8]

McPherson: But too much impatience is an enemy to creativity.

S: Maybe it could be. But we're impatient about getting things implemented.

---

[7] There is a need for a provocative and insightful report on troubleshooting the malfunctioning of organizations and leaders when creative ideas are emerging from within the organization. Another article that could be of major importance would be on the plight of, or the dilemmas of, the creative subordinate. Our suggestion for a title would be "The Perils of the Creative Subordinate."

[8] To indicate when the discussion changed from one person to another, two symbols have been utilized in this book. These appear at the beginning of a paragraph; appearance of a new symbol signals a change of person.

   S: The speaker giving the report is doing the talking; *S* is also the author of the chapter.

   C: A participant, otherwise unidentified, is making a comment or raising a question; *C* refers to any discussant. Occasionally, it was possible to name the discussant, as above.

C: But our thinking is relative to what? What is the basis of our comparison?

S: You raise a good question. Let me close this topic on it. Richardson has said that creative organizations live longer than other organizations. Richardson believes that creative minds should continue to rise to the top. A note very similar to this is that organizations should be able to listen to things both within and without so that it is very alert to new ideas and new developments from whatever source. If organizations or societies do not have this vital alertness, it will only be a matter of time until their day has passed.

A fascinating hunch of Navy Captain Campbell is that creative persons may live longer. This is analogous to Richardson's idea that creative organizations will live longer. This notion suggests that creative processes might be healthier processes within an individual. The creative individual who can listen and draw effectively upon available resources, both from within himself and from outside, and who can utilize these inner and outer processes effectively, may be a much healthier person and may live longer and more abundantly as a consequence.

As a general closing comment, I want to make the observation that from all the research results I have seen, *it is a rare day when a highly creative person is surrounded by much understanding.* This is, unfortunately, a sad comment, though I am confident it is too frequently a true one. As many have noted, the creative person is likely to find himself in a lonely role, and also in the role of an underdog. This latter role, however, may provide an avenue of hope. If, in America, we can somehow learn to turn this underdog role to an advantage and capitalize upon America's empathy and sympathy for the underdog, we may be able to accomplish a successful switch and bring about better treatment of the creatives because of their usual underdog predicament.

CHAPTER 2

Managing for Creativity in the Organization

Jack R. Gibb*

ONE EVENING, as part of an organizational study of creativity within a church setting, the author was preparing to observe a church teachers' session in the home of one of the teachers. Waiting for others to arrive, she showed us on the wall of her kitchen what she had labeled a "Peacemaker Chart". She had placed on it the names of her four children arranged by age. Each child's name had stars under it, representing times that the mother had judged that the child had "made peace". She told us of an incident in the morning when she had by chance overheard the two pre-schoolers in the room next to the kitchen doing some whispered strategic planning. One said to the other: "Why don't you go into the kitchen where Mommy is and start a fight with me and I'll stop it. Then I'll get a gold star. This afternoon we'll go in and I'll start a fight. Then you can stop me and you can get a gold star. And we can beat this game." The mother said that when they came in to "pull the trick" on her she spanked each of them and sent them out of the kitchen. They weren't going to "pull that on her." If for some perverse reason a parent were to come to me and want to hire me as a psychologist to teach his child to lie and cheat, I would, if I were agreeable to the contract and were inventive enough, recommend a "Peacemaker Chart" and the whole management strategy implied in the above illustration. If the implicit strategy and theory were applied with adequate expertise, the children would inevitably channel their bursting creativity into circumventive and adaptive "lying and cheating".

Later observation of the mother, her children, and her teaching strategies corroborated the initial impression that this vignette embodied all of the essential "management" conditions that tend to depress creativity in organizations. The four factors are:

1. Latent fear and distrust.
2. Restricted flow of communication.
3. Attempted imposition of motivation.
4. Attempted control of behavior.

In the above account, the mother exhibits her latent distrust of the children

---

*Jack R. Gibb is an Organizational Consultant in La Jolla, California. He was formally with the Western Behavioral Sciences Institute in La Jolla.

and her latent fear of the natural processes of growth by attempting to manipulate the motivations and behaviors of the children toward an imposed behavioral standard—a standard which grows out of her own rationalized and projected fears of human confrontation. She impedes communication flow by devising a "management strategy," a closed or camouflaged way of communicating her intentions and impositions to the child. In a sense, she sneaks up on the child and tries to trick him into being peaceful. She then sets up a system of extrinsic rewards and punishments (gold stars and spankings) that she administers in the attempted implementation of her devious behavior. An examination of Table I will indicate that the mother, however unintentionally, fulfills the four basic and definitive conditions for the management of constraint of creativity in groups and organizations. This mother was similar in several ways to many other mothers, teachers, and administrators that we encountered in our studies. She perceived her own motivations as sincere and was indeed proud of her system. She was largely unaware of the unintended effects of her management theory and style. Her theory was fairly consistent and pervasive in her home and classroom managing, but she was only minimally aware of the implicit "theory" that guided her decisions at choice points. Creativity in the system went underground.

Table I presents the major rubrics of a theory of creativity in the organization. Because organizations are so significant a part of life in a complex society, organizational forces that impede or increase creativity are significant elements in any social theory of creativity. What we have called "defensive management" (Gibb, 1965) is an all too prevalent form of management in the schools, businesses, homes, and churches of our culture. Defensive management mobilizes the defenses in the social system and either impedes creative behavior or forces the channeling of creative responses into circumventive and displaced organizational behavior. Managers, teachers, and parents do not intend to impede creativity. Once a consultant clarifies the situation, makes the essential relationships visible (e.g., that closed strategy produces retaliative strategy; that control restricts diversity, etc.) and gives direct and immediate feedback, it is fairly easy for competent management to see these determiners of low creativity. The change of these dysfunctional management behaviors is, of course, a greatly different matter.

Column two in Table I describes the four related patterns of behavior which define and exhibit defensive and low-creativity management. Low-creativity management thus tends to be fearful, strategic, persuasive and controlling. Administrators and parents exhibit fears and distrusts in many ways. Fears manifest themselves in various manners. People who are distrusting lack confidence in subordinates, feel that they must supervise and control so that work will be done correctly, are suspicious of the motivations and loyalties of employees, are afraid that people on their own will get into trouble, and lack confidence in the natural processes of growth and human interaction. The fearful management style is buttressed with a cluster of interlocked attitudes: people need to be led; people respect strong discipline; evaluation and rewards must be carefully administered because people work hard only when appropriately

TABLE I
Managing for the Constraint of Creativity

Basic Organizational Factors	Management Behavior and Attitudes	Typical Effects of Management Behavior and Attitudes
Emotional climate	Fears Distrusts	Fear of criticism, derision, and disapproval Censoring of others' ideas Response inhibition Behavior "goes underground"
Communication flow	Distortion of communication Restriction of communication Closed strategy	Protection of and hoarding of ideas Creativity directed toward circumvention, contraorganization goals, and facade production Restraints on impulsive, unconscious acting out Attempts to appear rational and reasonable
Goal formation	Imposition of motivation Persuasion Manipulation of extrinsic rewards	Creativity deflected toward "neurotic" acts Creativity directed toward extrinsic goals Apathy, stereotypy, and routine performance Resistance
Control	Tight controls on behavior of people	Restricted range of behavior and ideas Conforming and dependent behavior Priority of conformity over creativity Control over own and others' behavior and impulsive, spontaneous behavior

rewarded by good leaders; people need training and counseling because without such help they don't get along too well; creativity and morality must be taught to subordinates by authorities who are creative and moral; people on their own tend to be relatively lazy, irresponsible, conforming, pedestrian, and passive unless these tendencies are contravened by strong responsible leadership.

The fearful manager tends to be a strategist. He plans *for* others rather than *with* them. He protects people from themselves. He programs communications to the troops. He tends, when he can afford it, to build massive communications programs to regulate and control the messages that go through the organization. He is conscious of public relations, impressions, perceptions, and appearances. The strategic manager manages by directing the flow of communications.

As indicated in the table, fearful and strategic management tends to have predictable effects, which are listed, in part, in column three. Fear breeds fear in others. The general atmosphere is one of restraint, control, reaction, camouflage, conformity, and dependence, rather than one of invention, spontaneity, creativity, and independence. The strategy-circumvention model of organization is a familiar one in government, industry, school systems, and all forms of organization.

We worked with one large government agency which tried out the system of giving monetary rewards to workers for ideas that were judged by a management committee to be worth a specific amount of money to the agency. This program seemed to work well because a continuingly greater number of good ideas came in through the idea committee and people were paid increasing amounts of money for ideas that were genuinely creative and constructive. We studied the effects of the system, however, and found through systematic interviews that people were hoarding good ideas and turning them in for monetary rewards rather than giving them to co-workers or supervisors during the process of work. When a worker found that he could get $171.20 for an idea, say, he would carefully preserve his next good idea and turn it in through the mail to the idea committee. It might take five or six months for the idea to be processed. At best, the implementation of the idea was delayed. At worst, the primary function of the idea sharing process was muted and the process was deprived of the accelerating effects of social interaction. People were not sharing their ideas with each other and thus stimulating each other to further excitement, zest, and creativity, but were carefully avoiding this process. Not infrequent was the phenomenon of a supervisor giving an idea to a subordinate and saying: "You turn this in to the idea committee and we'll split the reward." Supervisors were forbidden by agency policy to turn in ideas. It was assumed that supervisors would be creative without special incentive. It seems clear that there are many ways of circumventing organizational processes.

More costly to the organization, however, are the more covert processes that tend to close the person to open and transparent communication with his people environment. The person who lives in high-strategy social environments for a long period of time tends to carry over this closed behavior to all phases of his life. The oft-quoted admonition shared by military personnel over the years to "keep your mouth closed, keep your bowels open, and make six copies of everything" is more than casual humor, and contains the gist of the low creativity, high defense, and muted communication of the traditional organization.

The fearful manager tries to manage motivations. He uses soft sell, gentle persuasion, and subtle ways of influencing the motivations of workers and subordinates. In earlier times, such managers were more apt to use direct coercion, the whip rather than the carrot, the command, the hard sell. One of the effects of education and the greater awareness of democratic management is that autocracy has gone underground, as it were. Autocrats cover up their coercive tendencies by nudging, suggesting, pushing, persuading, counseling, mothering, and by the use of a variety of camouflaged forms of imposition. In some ways, this gentle persuasion is more insidious in its effects upon creativity reduction than are the more direct and clear forms of coercion. Coerced people develop resistance. People who live on a general diet of soft sell tend to be relatively unaware of the manipulations of the "hidden persuaders" and possibly may not develop the resistance that builds strength.

Fearful managers exhibit their creativity by inventing forms of camouflaging manipulations of others' motivations. The mother barters her warmth and affection for conformity. The manager subtly approves the loyal conformist. The minister appoints committee chairmen who reflect the minister's morality. The therapist unconsciously approves the patient by certifying as "well" the person who reflects his own values. The creative act lives a precarious existence, goes relatively unrewarded, is basically threatening to the manager or leader who unconsciously accepts behavior with which he is more empathic, which better fits his values, and which is more congruent with his style and theory.

As indicated in Table I, the effect of persuasional management is to reduce creativity. Subordinates develop either a pattern of muted behavior or one of displaced behavior. Subordinates may become passive, apathetic, resistant, and seek protective stereotypy. Routine, conforming behavior is one form of protection. More aggressive people may deflect their creativity into behavior that is more inventive but is equally unproductive from the organizational standpoint. Performance is directed toward making money rather than toward solving problems. A conforming worker tries to get approval rather than an inventive solution. People work for rewards outside of the act itself.

We found illustrations of this in studying school systems. We interviewed students about motivations and grades. Extrinsic reward systems tend to produce behavior that is oriented toward getting grades rather than toward learning. Students worked for approval, grades, course credits, mention on the honor roll, "getting out of doing a term paper," "getting a free cut from class," and a whole variety of terminal products that have little to do with learning. Creative energies were directed toward these rewards rather than toward personal or learning goals. Even the formal "how to study" guides direct attention to this process of thwarting the intrinsic-reward-for-learning-*qua*-learning processes. We examined one guide which could be paraphrased like this: "Try to figure out what the teacher will think, as she makes out a multiple-choice question. Now if you can figure out what she is likely to think, then you can search through the chapter and seek out the type of multiple-choice phrases that she is likely to use. You can thus avoid wasting time learning things that are not likely to be asked in an examination." Busy and inventive students can thus direct their talents toward what really counts—winning the grade game.

The fearful manager tends to try to control the behavior and attitudes of people in the system for which he is responsible. Controls tend to be subtle, indirect, camouflaged, and extrinsic, rather than to be implicit and emergent in the processes themselves. Control tends to restrict the range of behavior of those controlled, puts a premium on conformity rather than creativity, and tends to produce dependent behavior, on the one hand, and rebellious behavior, on the other.

The current American scene is filled with examples of the ineffectiveness of the defensive control style of management. School administrators spend energy trying to figure out how to get girls to wear longer dresses and how to get boys to wear shorter hair. Students devote their creative impulses to figuring out ways of circumventing the rules. Girls wear skirts with belts that can be lowered for teacher inspections and raised when inspection is over. Boys figure out ways of getting haircuts that will precisely meet standards but still look long. Police figure out ways of making parade restrictions, and demonstrators devise ways of shading the regulations. Creativity is directed toward the making of useless rules and the circumventing of them.

Table II presents a general statement of the managerial conditions that might release creativity. Managers release creativity by trusting, open, allowing, and interdependent actions. Our consulting and research activities in a variety of organizational settings indicate that creativity can be increased in the organization by a gradual process of change of the defensive managerial behaviors described above.

TABLE II

Managing for the Release of Creativity

Basic Organizational Factors	Management Behavior and Attitudes	Typical Effects of Management Behavior and Attitudes
Emotional climate	High trust Low fear	More impulsive, uncensored behavior Greater risk taking, more error Greater creativity and range of response Trust in own impulse and unconscious life
Communication flow	Free flow of communication Clarity Open strategy and planning	Greater spontaneity in response and feeling Greater expression of foolish, irrelevant, and seemingly meaningless ideas and behavior Greater emotionality More feedback up and down Interaction and "piggy-backing" of ideas
Goal formation	Allowing self-determination Allowing self-assessment	Reward for risk-taking Sharing and mutual stimulation of ideas Greater diversity and non-conformity More sustained creativity
Control	Interdependent, emergent and intrinsic controls residual in life processes	Experimentation with work and structure Open expression of conflict and disagreement Greater innovation Priority of diversity and creativity over conformity

Creativity in the organization has been increased in a variety of ways. Changing the formal public relations-oriented communications program to a more informal group-centered program increases the productive creativity of the industrial organization (Gibb, 1964). The use of T groups and sensitivity training in the organizational setting results in greater openness, more free communication, the sharing of creative ideas, and interpersonal confrontation (Miles, 1965). The evidence is indirect and inconclusive, but highly suggestive, that this increased openness has an accelerating effect upon productive creativity within the organization (Gibb et al., 1968).

One of the most promising efforts toward increasing creativity in organizations has been directed toward increasing trust by working through the relatively unconscious manifestations of distrust fears in non-verbal forms of bodily and facial communications (Gibb, 1968). People learn to relate their latent fears to bodily manifestations, and to experience how their fears influence the behaviors of others around them. Effort is directed toward helping people to get in touch with the unconscious and physiological wellsprings of creativity, to translate their impulse life into creative and inventive behavior, to trust their spontaneous impulses, and to communicate more spontaneously and directly their primitive and natural feelings and perceptions. There is some evidence that people who are more spontaneous are more creative. The organizational problem is to translate spontaneous and impulsive behavior into constructive organization action. One approach to improving productive creativity is to work on the problem of understanding and building more creative groups. It is not enough that groups be spontaneous. Decisions must be made about creative ideas and ideas must be translated into organizational action. Organizations, to be creative, must learn to make decisions and to plan actions in such a way that creative ideas can be translated into improved organizational life (Gibb et al., 1967).

The high-creativity manager has a high trust of himself and of those with whom he works. Table II indicates some of the effects of increased trust. People who are trusted take more risks, or may not see trying out inventive or new behavior as risky. The manager who communicates genuine trust produces a relatively risk-free macro-environment for the subordinates. The high-creativity manager is likely to make a number of self-fulfilling assumptions about people with whom he works. He is likely to have attitudes such as these: people are likely to be highly motivated and responsible when left on their own; people will be creative if restraints are removed; people work best when they set their own goals; people have amazing potential when allowed to flower.

The high-creativity manager is likely to participate freely in giving and receiving communication of feelings and ideas. The author has a vivid memory of one manager who revealed something in a sensitivity training group to his fellow executives. He said that he had been kicked out of college when he was a junior for faking a transcript, and that he had kept this a secret for some 26 years.

Keeping the secret had made him tense, secretive, suspicious, and wary of advances from fellow, workers. Revealing this in the group started processes which during the following two years after the sensitivity training group helped him to be more open and communicative. His openness led directly to his being seen and rated by his fellow workers as more creative and productive. When organization and team members become more open they are likely to show more emotionality, seem more erratic, be less predictable, take more risks, and express more seemingly irrelevant ideas. Openness and creativity are mixed blessings in the organizational setting. Managers and workers alike do not always welcome creativity. In order for creative responses to be integrated into organizational life, it is necessary for changes to take place in the total macro-environment of the organization. The evidence is clear that groups and organizations must *learn* to be creative. Short term programs of sensitivity training and team development show little continuing improvement in creativity in the organization. Contra-creativity forces are strong within the stable environment of most families, schoolrooms, companies, and work groups.

The high-creativity manager is likely to allow more self-determination and more self-assessment. He is likely to attempt to form healthy groups and encourage group goal determination and group assessment of progress toward group goals. This process of optimal self-determination is central to the process of realizing the creative potential within the person. The growth of creativity is probably cumulative in some way. Assertive and free individuals *create* their goals out of an integrated process of self-search, seeking new and challenging experiences, risking new behavior, testing limits, and exploring the boundaries of the person. The more the manager or leader creates conditions in which persons *initiate, feel responsible* for this process, and *feel free* to create their own goals, the more the person creates the internal conditions which maximize the growth of creativity potential. The most promising training method for developing self-determination is a performance appraisal and goal-setting program which is completely centered in the employee rather than in the supervisor. This inventive program is being tried successfully in one of the author's client companies. There is some preliminary evidence that employees are judged to be more creative. This increased creativity is attributed by the company to the increased feelings of responsibility on the part of employees for their own goals and own careers. The conventional appraisal programs originate in the supervisor, are carried out by management, and are "owned" by management. This kind of training program is supplemented by "team development" programs, a form of sensitivity training in which natural planning and decision-making units or teams in the organization are given depth sensitivity training and follow-up consulting. Goal setting is an interdependent process. Functional and productive creativity is a highly interdependent activity and is far from the individual and personal matter that it has been traditionally thought to be.

The high-creativity manager tends to be interdependent, to allow freedom, to create very few arbitrary controls over people, and to rely upon the natural, emergent processes of growth to create residual controls upon participants. There is some independent evidence that low creativity is associated with dependence and unresolved authority problems. Tight controls, especially those perceived as arbitrary, often exacerbate the dependency-authority syndromes of the worker, student, or child, and either impede creative responses or channel creativity into rebellion. It may be true that creativity is occasionally associated with counter-dependent rebellion, but this form of creativity is not easily integrated into the complex functions of modern organizations. Rebellion-motivated creativity sets up self-defeating counterforces that impede the productive integration of the inventive response into organizational effectiveness.

One promising form of creativity training focuses upon the rule-making propensities of supervisors. These tendencies are self-sustaining and seem to be based upon deep-seated needs for control. These tight control, need-action sequences are easy to rationalize and indeed are supported by popularized psychology and psychiatry (e.g., children need and respect firm discipline, etc.). Intensive sensitivity training easily makes visible the relation between control needs and the rule-making habits, and somewhat less readily makes clear the self-defeating quality of rules and the relationship between creativity and the rule-free social environment.

The basic learning of the sensitivity training group is the effectiveness of the emergent group control system. The most effective controls are those which are residual in the processes of interdependence, processes which emerge in all joint inquiry, shared problem-solving, group planning, and participative group learning. The effective T group is the most readily available model for seeing this phenomenon in its full clarity.

To return to our original statement about the constraints to creativity, let us now look again at the basic theory that is being illustrated. It is assumed that human beings are, under normal conditions of growth, creative. They contain within themselves the propensity for novel and inventive solutions to problems and choices that confront them. Novel and creative solutions are more apt to appear when the person is trustting and is trusted, when he is in communication in depth with his interpersonal environment, when he is growing along lines that he has determined himself and is thus deeply committed to, and when he feels free to work in true interdependence with others on common tasks and in mutual play. These, then, are the organizational determinants of creativity: trust, openness, self-determination, and interdependence.

The blocks to the integration of productive creativity into organizational activity are the converse of the above four factors: fear, restriction of communication, imposition, and control. Managers who are distrustful, strategic, impositional, and controlling tend to impede creativity within the organization. An organizational development program that wished to optimize creativity would focus upon barrier removal: the reduction of the four restraining forces listed above. Creativity is there; it grows; it nurtures itself. One cannot produce creativity, only nurture it.

CHAPTER 3

The Innovational Revolution
(Necessity Has Too Often and for Too Long
Been the Mother of Invention)

Warren Wiggins*

THE PURPOSE of this report is to advocate that the time has come for our society to radically alter its approach to creativity and innovation and to increase significantly the amount of resources devoted thereto.

Western civilization has excelled in producing invention and innovation. The second third of this century has been distinguished by the expansion of knowledge, new processes, new products, and new thought. It is said that half of all the scientists since the beginning of scientific thought are living today; that the expansion of technical knowledge in the last decade or so is as great in many quantitative senses as in all prior history; and that the increase in knowledge and understanding of our universe since World War II has been as great as that achieved prior to World War II.

In many fields of endeavor, creativity and innovation are the most distinguishing features of our current epoch. In the United States, many of these advances are dramatic. In each twenty-four hour period, nearly two billion dollars of new goods and services are now produced in our country. We are indeed rich and the most predominant factor which has brought about the present cornucopia here has been the concentration on, and investment in, *innovation.*

The will to invent, the environment in which to innovate, the availability of risk capital for that which is new, and society's willingness to accept change—all these things have produced the American economic miracle.

We are indeed taken with the necessity for change, growth, innovation, invention, and creativity. The United States, for example, spends something like 30 billion dollars on research and development out of a total gross national product of some 600 billion dollars. This allocation of one-twentieth of all our resources to research and development clearly indicates the enormous importance we attach to growth, change, wealth, a better defense system, and a better future.

Nonetheless, this hallmark of distinction of our country has been little studied and is only vaguely understood. Although innovation is the very engine of expansion, the sparking mechanism which ignites production in new and hither-

*Warren Wiggins is President, TransCentury Corporation in Washington, D.C. He was formerly Deputy Director of the Peace Corps in Washington.

to unknown fields, there is only the beginning of scientific investigation of the process of innovation itself and how to change and influence this process.

Equally as important, the degree of innovation in our economic life is not to be found in comparable breadth and intensity in non-economic fields. For example, in international relations the post World War II history of the United States has been characterized by change, but few changes have been of the creative sort in response to a search for better ideas, institutions, organizations or approaches. The Marshall Plan and the Peace Corps are illustrations of exceptional innovation, but in many ways they were clear, direct, limited responses to recognized narrow areas of deterioration.

In the social and political life of domestic America, rapid change has sometimes occurred—but most would agree that when it has come, it has been long overdue and not responsive to a creative seeking out of a better life. The whole arena of the civil rights development in this decade has, in a sense, been a long overdue, tragic sort of change marked by the deep passions of *forced* rapid social adjustment and it has not been guided by creative inspiration. The roles of passive resistance, protest, the student movement, and the legislative and executive responses have evidenced elements of innovation and creativity, but largely they haven't been the outgrowth of the sort of open and systematic search for improvement in the technique and organization that we find in American business or the national program for space exploration. Indeed, we need to be concerned with the extent to which our society conducts its affairs through organizations that seem characteristically to dampen instead of encourage creativity and innovation.

The lives of the people in the United States are generally structured by the federal and local governments, business corporations, trade unions and professional associations, religious institutions, political parties, and a variety of economic and social organizations. With the major exception of business corporations, creativity is *not* a dominant feature of any of these broad institutions. Even the creativity of business corporations relates not to the way in which they organize themselves or examine their own relative role in society, but relates to the narrow—but clearly main—purpose of producing and selling more of a better product at a lower cost to obtain the largest possible profit.

Obviously there are exceptions to these generalizations. Within the federal government, the space exploration and the poverty program are among the clear examples; Job Corps camps, Operation Headstart and the program for landing a man on the moon clearly rank as innovational efforts worthy of note. But such are to be compared with the character of the massive operations and attitudes in most government departments and the rules, procedures, and leading personalities of the legislative branch.

The Civil Service and Congressional seniority systems are two important governing systems of thought and action which stand in contrast to many of the exceptions which have elements of creativity as central features of their being.

In summary, it is becoming increasingly clear that, as we seek to improve our society, we need not only to work on the understanding of the process of innovation and creativity, but we also need to work on the expansion of its application into the fields of endeavor where creativity and innovation are not new characteristics.

It is the postulate of this report that of all the fields in which innovation and creativity are needed, none compare in importance or potential with being innovative and creative in the field of innovation itself. The world has not seen a broad, conscious, well-organized scientific and interdisciplinary attempt to innovate in the process of innovation.

Clearly, such is a next major step for society: innovating in the process of innovation—research and development in the techniques of research and development. It is the thesis of this chapter that such activity on a grand and important scale might lead to an innovational revolution that would dramatically change and improve our total society.

In a realistic sense, necessity has too often and for too long been the mother of invention.

Achievement in the innovational field often is forced by circumstances. Consciously organized opportunity ought to replace necessity as the mother of invention. When we decide that a high priority is to be given to large-scale organized thought and experimentation in the process of innovation itself, we may have begun the innovational revolution.

INTERIM GOALS

Our country needs to examine and modify the whole of the process of innovation, ranging from the formulation of innovational goals, the recognition and mobilization of creative talent, the training and stimulation of such talent, the examination of the techniques of organizing such talent, the procedures and environment in which such talent is used, to, finally, society's acceptance or rejection of innovation. In a broad sense, what is advocated is research in the total process of innovation. This would include "research on research" as a main theme because research is the present central activity that produces organized innovation. "Research on creativity" appears to be a second and overlapping theme. However, research in the process of innovation is broader than both research on research and research on creativity, in that research on innovation is concerned with all the relationships of our total society to the production, application, and acceptance of innovation. "Research in the process of innovation" thus includes seeking to understand the process by which recognition of hitherto unrecognized problems and/or opportunities occur; the study of the process by which new approaches, concepts, techniques, and attitudes are created; and research in the understanding of the ways in which new ideas, concepts, inventions, systems, and organizations are accepted.

However, research in the process of innovation is a true overhead item (in a strict analytical approach, it is "overhead on overhead"). The main branches of institutional life and subbranches within institutions have not considered within their priorities to carry this "overhead on overhead" item at the level needed. Generally speaking, this field of study is not even recognized, let alone given an adequate priority.

Large-scale research in the process of innovation itself opens up views of a new horizon that has been hitherto largely unexplored. It appears possible, for example, to contemplate increasing by more than 1000-fold the intellectual resources devoted to improving the process of innovation. Considering monetary measures of the magnitude of intellectual effort, it is possible to say that instead of such a potential use of one to two billion dollars of talent on research in the process of innovation, our society is probably allocating annually something less than one million dollars.[1] The potential impact on our society of such a quantum jump in the use of resources in the field of research in the process of innovation cannot be approached. The changes in our life in the next twenty years, if we did increase by 1000-fold our resources devoted to improving the process of innovation itself, are most far-reaching. Both qualitative and quantitative[2] change are involved. The industrial revolution compared to such an *innovational revolution* would be like a comparison of the invention of dynamite to the splitting of the atom.

More important than the enormously important increases obtainable in our material wealth, would be the potentially dramatic changes in the character and quality of our social and political life. For example, in the international relations field it is clear that the proportion of resources put into research and development is far, far smaller than on the economic or military front. The present effort to change and improve the process of innovation itself in non-military foreign affairs is so small that it is even difficult to identify. It may even be non-existent.

In summary, as an interim goal we ought to consider devoting something like one one-thousandth instead of one one-millionth of all our talents and resources in the improvement of the process of innovation—and in a few decades our *total* society might be entirely different—and better—as a consequence.

---

[1] This is a guess. No one, to my knowledge, has attempted a refined estimate.

[2] It is *not* inconceivable that if we increased the resources devoted to research in the process of innovation by 1000-fold—say from the guessed present level of less than one million dollars per annum to one billion dollars per annum (a clearly attainable goal given our $600 billion economy)—we might double or quadruple the basic growth factor in our economy due to innovation. Our economy might produce an extra 5, 10, 20, or 30 billion dollars a year from an investment of one billion dollars per annum in changing and improving the process of innovation.

RESEARCH IN THE PROCESS OF INNOVATION

Research in the process of innovation appears to include the following broad categories:

Identification of Need for Innovation

Clearly, our country has a requirement to seek out, to find, and to identify those areas where innovation is needed. Some foundations, for example, approach this concept. But recognizing the "unfelt" opportunity is a most difficult task. Seeing the voids and inadequacies in our life that are not now seen is a prime requirement for which we ought to organize. This is as true at the corporate business level as at the national social organizational level.

However, the initial requirement discussed here is *not* the requirement to identify such unfelt needs—it is the requirement to think through the theory, the process, and the approach by which such needs can be identified.

A. Identification of Unfelt Needs in the Private Sector. The closest approach to this theory on discovering unfelt needs is found in the writings about research management in the private corporate sector. For example, James R. Bright, in *Research, Development, and Technological Innovation* (1964), considers at some length, in case studies as well as theoretically, the choice of research and development alternatives as they are seen from general management's viewpoint. However, this textbook's design does not include material on the approach to the discovery and recognition of opportunity by systematic search that would flow *from* general management as an *initiative* to the R&D departments, rather than as management responding to stimuli that come in the course of business inside and outside R&D endeavors. Perhaps this will be taken up in a subsequent work. Bright says:

> Other students will notice that I have not included anything from the extensive literature on the mathematics of decision making in research. After some experimentation in my classes and exploration with a number of leading research men and scientists, it seemed that relatively little material of value to management had yet emerged. I reluctantly passed by this material. My conclusion is not intended to disparage this effort, but only to point out that 'research on research' largely is still 'in the laboratory.' In another five years the story should be different. (Preface, p. ix)

What appears to be missing in the private firm is the recognition of the need for generalized exploration in a systematic way with *research techniques* of target opportunities to which one applies applied research. Somewhere in the flow and production of ideas between and among top corporate executives, research directors, and the researchers, there is a void in that no one is charged with the responsibility for a systematic scientific search for the "unfelt need."

Another way of understanding this void is to say that in the field of "research on research," the work available to corporations is "basic research on research," not *"applied* research on research." For example, many, many studies have treated the variety of patent statistics seeking to understand some limited aspects of the innovative process. "Knowledge" has been developed about when, where, and under what institutional environments patents emerge. Numerous case studies have been prepared on the lives and environments and motivations of successful inventors.

The history of innovation for individual corporations has been detailed. In many ways, nearly all of this work could be classified as "basic research on research" as they expand knowledge about how a prior unfelt need or opportunity was discovered. They do not present theoretical understanding in a form that can be exploited by the business corporation.

What appears generally to be true is that major corporations have not had available to them theoretical and practical results of "applied research on research" to enable them to recognize the need for and elaborate the techniques of systematically discovering the "unfelt" profit opportunity.

B. Identification of Unfelt Needs in the Public Sector. Considering the Office of the Presidency with particular reference to the White House Special Assistants, the government departments, as organized, and the Bureau of the Budget, there is a general inability to fully develop innovational possibilities and to pursue their implementation if they do not spontaneously arise from the working of the normal government structure. In recognition of this inadequacy, "task forces" have been created to produce innovations following the recognition of particular needs. However, innovations often seem to occur by accident rather than by plan. The whole momentum for the establishment of the Peace Corps grew out of a campaign speech and public reaction thereto. From the time of the speech on November 2, 1960, until the inauguration of President Kennedy, the institutions of government in the foreign arena did not even take notice, let alone influence this innovation.

A more recent example, I believe, is to be found in the subject of Viet Nam. There is an inadequacy of systematic search for and organization of outstanding intellectual talent for the finding of new approaches—innovations—in this most difficult situation.

In the broader aspects of foreign assistance, the most damning criticism of the total foreign aid program and the manner in which it has been administered is the lack of creativity and innovation in the very process of approaching "the process" of how our rich society can effectively extend assistance to the great variety of developing countries.

What is required from our national government's point of view is the ability to involve directly an institutional group of people who have as their common characteristic a flair for producing new approaches and for being creative. Modern society cannot rely on individual creativeness and accidental individual imaginativeness to solve the kinds of problems which our country faces. On the other side of the coin, it cannot rely solely on the bureaucracies and planning staffs of the government departments to be innovative of new approaches which might, in fact, significantly modify major elements of these agencies. Thus a middle ground must be found—a middle ground of institutional and individual competence which in some sense can be innovative beyond the limited capacities of those institutions which have the present responsibility for the routine work of the federal government.

What is thus proposed is that the federal government is now of such character that it can no longer rely on the simple combination of individual Presidential Special Assistants and large-scale operating bureaus, departments, and agencies. The Bureau of the Budget, the Council of Economic Advisors, the policy planning office of State, the National Science Foundation, the National Security Council, special task forces, and a whole host of other organizations are, in a theoretical sense, designed to fill the void herein described, but they do not.

There follows a brief, typical, illustrative outline of potential areas for applied research on innovation:

C. Outline of Areas of Consideration for Emerging Theory of the Unfelt Need.
1. Creating the feeling of need for discovery of the unfelt need.
2. Assignment of priority within corporate business and public institutions—structural organization for talent allocated.
3. Techniques of search and discovery—analytical tools and processes:
   a. Use of analogy
      (1) "Accidental visual association"
      (2) Synectics type approach
      (3) Other . . .
   b. Use of "category extrapolation" approach
   c. Use of brainstorming/group interaction approach
   d. Use of "sequential analysis" approach
   e. Use of "projected development" method
   f. Other . . .
4. Techniques of diffusion following discovery.
5. Other . . .

Identification and Selection of Innovative Talent

Considerable theoretical work by psychologists has been done in this area and a great many managers of research and development programs are engaged in the practical business of selecting the innovator or the various varieties of innovators. However, experimentation and the scientific process itself have not been adequately applied to the selection process insofar as preliminary investigation has disclosed. This is particularly true if one refers to the laboratory approach of scientific experimentation. Although there is an interesting and long history concerned with the identification of creative talent, further theory with practical techniques of application needs to be elaborated, refined, and put into sufficiently concrete shape to enable better procedure.

Certainly our society does not have any nation-wide system to identify innovators at an early and incipient period—to identify the person with general creative talent or the person with a particular narrow creative talent. In our high schools and institutions of higher learning we have all kinds of identification programs, direct and indirect, for all kinds of purposes, but the potential *innovator per se* doesn't really become identified. We are not using, on a systematic nation-wide basis, that work that has already been accomplished in the field of identifying creative talent.

Selection ought to be a continuous process, not a one-time listing. It is here suggested that the process ought to start at the elementary level in the formal education system and continue throughout life. In much the same way as our society continually reexamines, by a variety of devices, other dimensions of ability, creative talents need to be continually sought out and measured.

The requirements for better identification of innovative talent range from the business corporations through the social and political organizations. Thus we need a dual program of further investigation of *how* to identify the innovator and potential innovator and a nation-wide action program to get it done.

Training of Innovators[3]

As the theory of innovation is expanded, we need to put it in a form and shape that will allow us to *explicitly* train the innovator. College courses are now being given in creativity, but we are far from professional preparation of the innovator. The appropriate preparation for the innovator may not be related to a "course," a "school," or an "institute." Training at preschool and primary levels may hold great potential. There needs to be a much wider organized search for knowledge and technique of training innovators so that our innovative talent can be used to the maximum. This is particularly true since some of our educational practices seem to stifle creativity rather than encourage it.

A field of particular importance is the additional training of those professional adults now engaged in the 30-billion dollar research and development programs

---

[3]This paper has not attempted to explore past achievement or present literature in the clearly related fields involved in the relation of creativity to the educational and learning processes.

in America, as well as those existing and potential programs throughout the world.

Probably the nature of the process of innovation is such that education of the participant or potential participant can best take place through integration of student and teacher as they both are engaged full-time in a realistic endeavor to solve problems or discover opportunities in a creative environment where goals and procedures are a part of the non-academic world.

Applied research on educational theory in the training of the human mind for the expansion of its creativity and inventiveness may well be a most productive endeavor. Certainly such applied research would both profit from and contribute to the development of an institutional setting where our society found its leadership for the innovational revolution. Such leadership must have as a major feature a teaching/learning—teacher/student aura.

Direction of Innovators

Most innovators are either highly institutionally directed or completely on their own. That is to say, in an employment relationship they are paid to examine a particular problem of how to get more horsepower from a gasoline engine, given certain limitations for weight of engine, size, fuel consumption, etc.—or else they are in the basement of their home trying to embody their novel idea in a working model without *any* direction from society. They may be in a university laboratory doing basic research—but basic research in a well-defined field in a well-defined department with a well-defined chairman within a well-defined budget and within a well-defined time period. They may be in their basement, during odd but infrequent hours, with inadequate facilities and without any real support from the rest of society.

Emerging theory on the relation of types and quality of direction and supervision of the innovator needs to be expanded through further analysis and experimentation. Such theory then needs to be applied throughout our society. However, this does not mean that support and direction ought to be centrally organized or that there should be a master plan. It means that we need to have further development of theory and understanding in this field of thought so that the innovative process can be more effective; so that improved plans of organization can be accomplished.

Environment for Innovators

Some theoretical postulates have been advanced by the psychologists and the sociologists about the environment of the innovator. Much work has been concerned with the environment of the learner which may be applicable to the environment of the innovator. However, by and large, it appears to be true that no large-scale, systematic, scientific experimentation has been done on the many many potential variations in the environment of the innovator.

By environment is meant all the planned and unplanned, recognized and unrecognized stimuli related to the innovator. Probably there are dozens of stimuli that have never been brought to bear on an innovator in the process of innovation. Clearly, we are only beginning to study the creativity of the innovator with the variables of his environment and the stimuli to which he is subjected. Further study needs to be made of the whole mental process (conscious and unconscious) of innovation vis-à-vis all the senses of the body and the variables of psychology and psychiatry. These variables in this context need to be analyzed in a dynamic framework over extended time.

For example, there is a vast unexplored field in the theory concerning the rewards for innovation. We have produced the patent and copyright systems which are available to a small segment of the innovative community and we have "studied" this institutional reward system at length. It doesn't reward the political innovator. It is only a narrow commercial reward of limited applicability in the broad innovative field. Nonetheless, in certain ways it is a dramatically successful reward/incentive technique.

The innovator who does not work in the commercial/patent/copyright field also needs to be involved in a stimulating incentive/reward system. Clearly much more theoretical work needs to be done on this consideration.

More important than the incentive reward system may be the innovational equivalent of the grubstake. A society so dependent on innovation needs to institutionally provide the equivalent of the scholarship, the sabbatical, the grubstake, etc., to free up the innovative talent that is now unstimulated or leashed because of economic considerations.

Exploration to date in the use of a variety of drugs, stimulants, relaxants, intoxicants, etc., in relation to creativity, gives encouraging suggestions for further research.

Institutional variability needs to be further related to creativity. Architectural innovation is one of the many environmental variables that needs to be explored to encourage creativity. Individual business corporations, for example, need a source of talent from which to draw that can relate the theory on the relation of environmental factors and innovation to their individual corporate opportunities.

Machines and Innovation

There has been some exploration of the relation of modern mechanical/electrical devices involving "memory," correlation, chance association, etc., to the innovative process. However, much remains to be done. We need to effectively explore on a grand scale the potential relationships of machines and minds to creativity.

Social Desire for Innovation

Much more understanding is needed about the social and institutional process involved in acceptance or rejection of an innovation. The study of the diffusion of innovation in developed and underdeveloped societies is a scattered and uneven development. Many many questions which probably can be answered by adequate research have only been asked. Other questions in this area have not been formulated.

A CENTER FOR NATIONAL LEADERSHIP

As indicated above, we have a national requirement to have a quantum jump in the amount of intellectual resources we devote to research in the process of innovation. Not only do we need to move in the direction of increasing the intellectual effort in this field by something like a thousandfold, but we need to bring the effort under some degree of focus and leadership. The job is at one and the same time to pioneer in the elaboration of a whole new field of thought, to stimulate large-scale effort in a new field of experimentation, and to lead a highly diversified effort throughout the United States. This in no sense indicates that we ought to "organize" or "structure" the national effort from a centralized headquarters or with an inclusive national plan. Diversity and decentralization may well be the key to success.

However, to provide for a new impetus and a minimum focus, it seems necessary to establish a center in which national leadership can emerge, in which the now divergent and scattered efforts of the various disciplines can be related, and in which the stage can be set to catch national attention for modification of the process of innovation. The center must be established in such a sufficiently dramatic fashion as to have a reasonable chance to become of national importance and to have the potential ability to lead, not direct, the country in the start of the innovational revolution.

It is doubtful if the present scattered efforts in research on creativity and innovation can evolve toward such a goal. The nature of the grand requirement is such that a difficult, dramatic, and quick institutional innovation on a large scale is required. The requirement is, simultaneously, in the course of a few years to produce new theory as well as demonstrated results and to disseminate that theory throughout the economy and the social and political structures, and to build an understanding in our country that the process of innovation can be improved.

It is believed that starting the innovational revolution poses a problem somewhat analogous to the creation of atomic and nuclear capability. In this latter case, theory was clearly necessary as well as a large-scale application of resources, over time, to produce the practical results.

In the case of the innovation revolution, we are not at the stage where theory clearly indicates that with the application of enough scientific resources the job can be done (the atom split). Instead, we have a recognition that there is a field of inquiry—namely, the process of innovation—which deserves large-scale and urgent consideration. The theory centers around the human mind and how to magnify one of its products—both quantitatively and qualitatively.

There is every reason to believe that the human mind's creativity and inventiveness can be significantly expanded or better deployed in a situation where a new order of result can be achieved. Even if the possibility is small—as long as it is a possibility—we need to turn a national effort to its exploration. Exploring how to make the human mind more creative and inventive ought, in a general value sense, to be equivalent to our efforts at space exploration (if for no other reason, that any significant advance in magnification or utilization of the creative potential of the human mind may well contribute more than *anything else* to the ultimate success of space exploration).

As one scans the United States to look for organizations or groupings of talent which might be developed into a national focus in this field, providing a new national leadership and experimentation on a new scale, none comes into view.

Research institutions, both public and private, have an amazing lack of interest in the *process* of innovation and creativity in which they put all their resources. In some senses, these organizations which might be the most "creative" intellectual groupings of our society are, in fact, among the most rigid and bureaucratic and structural when it comes to self-examination of the *way* in which they seek to be creative and innovative.

Universities also represent a highly structured approach to the innovational needs of our country. One of the tragedies of modern society is to be found in the overstructured institutions of higher learning that have failed to play a major leadership role (compared to government or commerce) in the designs for future society. In recent times, young students have played a more influential role *off campus* in redesigning our country. But more important than the universities' lack of leadership in new designs for society is the lack of intellectual inquiry into the nature of the human process of creating new designs.

Private foundations have come as close as any part of our country to examining the needs for change and providing an impetus for such change. Yet often foundations have sought to work in the clearly recognized areas of need, the "safe fringe" of need for change in the society. Dramatic quantum jumps, not yet recognized by the leaders of political, economic, and social life, have not been characteristic of their activities. Foundations, in general, in their expenditure of funds in innovative work, have not turned to the study of the process of innovation itself.

In such a field as innovation in the process of innovation, it seems rather clear that a major start needs to be made. (It is quite possible that research institutions, universities, and foundations would have a significant and possibly major role in the effect proposed, but it does seem doubtful that they can be expected to finance, run, or be "in charge" of the endeavor.) Instead, it appears that a center, a new corporation of national stature, is needed whose purpose is to lead the United States in the field of research in the process of innovation. A new constellation of intellectually creative talent is required to explore the theory and the procedure that will underlie the innovational revolution.

Leading our country in this field does not mean organizing a national effort or planning a national strategy. It is not proposed that the new corporation give direction or priority to any research group; it should not have any national budgetary responsibility. Competition, dispersion, diversity, and disparate centers of initiative ought to characterize the expansion of resources in process of innovation. The role of leadership of the proposed new corporation is that of an explorer seeking to open up new paths toward an unexplored horizon for others to follow.

The proposed new corporation should seek to be the consultant, the servant, the supporter of the efforts of others. Although it is designed to establish new theory, create new techniques, and establish new approaches, it should not seek to be "the agent" for implementation. Thus, even though it is here proposed that our country's use of talent and resources should be expanded in the measure of about one-billion dollars, the role of the proposed new corporation would be to influence and lead, not, in any sense, to administer such resources.

A NEW INNOVATIONAL FOCUS: A CORPORATION

This chapter suggests the possibility for an intellectual, operational, and research center—a corporation—to provide world-wide leadership for a full use of research in the process of innovation. Such a corporation would need to be financed entirely with non-governmental funds and managed entirely within the private sector. (Some "project" financing could, of course, come from the public sector, but all financing of institutional and administrative costs of the center should be private.) The corporation would develop close relations with and serve individuals, other corporations, foundations, universities, research institutions, and the local, state, and federal governments. Also, it should have important international relations. Perhaps the best way to establish the corporation would be to organize it as a constituent profit-making member of a major diversified corporate enterprise with world-wide interests.

It is particularly important that the corporation not be in the governmental sector. In a very real sense, there has been a "cold war" between government and business in the United States. In this war, the individual battles are fought in many forms and in the short run of the individual battle, business has, more or less, been able to hold its own. But in the longer run, this has not been true. Decade by decade, the federal government has been increasing its weight in the balance of power in this cold war between business and government. One of the principal reasons for this trend has been the federal government's dominance in the provision of resources for "research and development." It is estimated that less than half of the research scientists are now employed in private industry.

The private sector needs to redress this long-term balance and one of the great assets it has over time is to be found in its relative advantage in the innovative and creative fields. Central to the long-run success of the private sector in parlaying this superiority is the placing of more resources at the central opportunity: the improvement of the process of innovation itself.

Another central reason why the corporation should be in the private sector is that it must be free to fail in projects. Also, it must be free of any hint of any political control and be free of government restrictions in the hiring, remuneration, and dismissal of talent. It needs to be the epitome of the creative genius of the private sector at its best. It needs to secure its funds (until it becomes self-sufficient—see later discussion) without the sort of justification usually required by legislative bodies. Probably the corporation (at least with regard to some of its important functional sub-units) ought to be subject to the normal profit-making criteria of business success. The corporation should be controlled; reviewed, evaluated, and, of course, terminated if it does not succeed. It does need to be responsible to a parent corporation or an appropriate board of directors.

The corporation initially would attempt to become the international leader in the following two aspects:

1. The corporation would seek to become the intellectual, operational, and experimental center for the *development of the theory of the process of innovation* with particular reference to fundamental innovation in the theory of innovation itself. This function would be concerned with the elaboration of theory, the performing of experiments, and the launching of research projects in the fields of inquiry discussed earlier: the identification of need for innovation; the selection, training, direction, and environment of innovators; machines and innovation; and the social desire for innovation.

Historical analysis of the innovation process plus compilation of current thought throughout the world would be necessary for accomplishing these goals and the building and maintaining of a national library and data depot on the innovative process and related fields would be included.

2. Profit-making activity in the fields of the competence of the corporation would be a second and interrelated major objective. An "associated innovators" program would be established. This will be an *extensive program* to sell services of all divisions of the corporation to interested innovators. In the field of research, and in the field of research on the process of innovation, it will provide to corporations and governments on a world-wide basis:

(a)   Consultative services;
(b)   Experimentation and model-building for the "associated innovator," on a cost-plus fee basis;
(c)   Environment and facilities at the corporation for visiting innovators;
(d)   Facilities and staff for research projects to be sold to all organizations;
(e)   If the corporation is a subsidiary of a major diversified corporation, it would, of course, have a primary responsibility to serve the other corporate entities of the parent body in all of the service aspects for which the innovational corporation was created.

The corporation should take the lead in providing professional impetus to innovators concerned with the expansion of the theory of innovation (—a society? —a journal? —annual meetings? —exchange of ideas, problems, etc., etc.).

On a world-wide profit-making basis, it would seek to become a major connecting link between individuals and institutions on general and specific areas of operational and theoretical interest in research in innovation. Operational assistance in matching funds, matching disciplines, and matching personalities with planned or ongoing projects in the field of research in the process of innovation would be facilitated.

Additionally, "in-house" innovation, independent of, but related to all the other functions of the corporation, would be another goal of the corporation. This function would be heavily oriented to profit-making, patent-producing innovation. Work in this field would be undertaken as opportunities emerge from the corporate work in theories of innovation.

Thus the corporation would attempt to become the world-wide focal point of research in the process of innovation and commercial diffusion of emerging innovational theory.

CHAPTER 4

Travels in Search of New Latitudes for Innovation[1]

Frank Barron*

ALTHOUGH this may seem to be the vaguest chapter title in this book, I would prefer to think of it as accurate even if not immediately revealing. We at the Institute of Personality Assessment and Research sort of grope our way along and will continue to do so. It's only by looking both backward and forward that we realize we have come some distance and still have far to go. Exactly where we are going cannot be predicted very far in advance. To people who are better equipped with maps and plans this may seem too haphazard and directionless, but it is an appropriate strategy for exploration in an area where we are continually running off the edge of the map. As one of the poets who was to take part in our study of creative writers has written: "We learn by going/ Where we have to go."

Where I "had to go" last year was Ireland, and the IPAR research which grew out of my visit is one of the continuing studies reported here. The Social Science Research Council helped speed me on my journey with a Faculty Research Fellowship, by the way, and I would like to take this opportunity to acknowledge the Council's generosity.

INNOVATION IN IRELAND

My first visit to was to initiate research on the effect upon creativity of a variety of social and cultural value systems. The Irish weren't told what I was up to, because I wanted to go back again some other time, but actually what I did was to relate personal philosophy to creativity in two opposing groups, Catholics

---

*Frank Barron is Professor of Psychology at the University of California at Santa Cruz. He was formerly Research Psychologist, Institute of Personality Assessment and Research, University of California at Berkeley.

[1] Two of the three studies described here have subsequently been elaborated and presented in appropriate technical detail elsewhere. The interested reader is referred to the following publications:

Barron, F. Innovators in business management in Ireland. In *Creative Person and Creative Process*, New York: Holt, Rinehart and Winston, 1969.

Barron, F. and Egan, D. Leaders and innovators in Irish management. *Journal of Management Studies*, 1968, 5, (1), 41-61.

and Protestants in Irish universities. For this purpose I constructed a variant on the Guilford "Consequences Test." Called "Consequences for Ireland," it, of course, contains problems with a strong Irish flavor, most of them presenting some unlikely event in Ireland to stimulate the imagination of my respondents in guessing what the effect would be on Irish life.

It is not that study, however, but one that developed from it and that has special interest for those of you in the Richardson Foundation who have been studying biographies that I shall report at this time. It happened that my "Consequences for Ireland" test fell into the hands of the personnel specialist in the Irish Management Institute, Dermot Egan. Dermot thought the test would prove challenging to some of the more imaginative industrial and economic leaders in Ireland, and he proposed that we administer it to such a group. As most psychologists know, and some deplore, we at IPAR never give one test unless we can give a whole battery, and so one thing led to another until finally the Irish Management Institute agreed to conduct a full-scale living-in assessment study of 40 of the leading figures in Irish management. This, of course, necessitated the presence of the IPAR staff, and with the help of the Human Sciences Council of the Republic of Ireland we did succeed in bringing about an unlikely event indeed: the descent of a bunch of California psychologists upon the shores of Erin, which only a decade ago was entirely innocent of professional psychologists. What the consequences for Ireland may be is anybody's guess.

However, this will be restricted to a presentation of the results of an analysis of a biographical questionnaire based substantially on the one developed by Cal Taylor and his associates, with certain minor modifications to adapt it to the conditions of Irish education and upbringing. (See Barron, 1969; Barron and Egan, 1968.) First of all, these leading managers were very well-educated. Education was quite important in the life of the family. They described education as "imperative to the living of a successful life." The individual manager felt himself to have been considered by his teachers as a highly desirable student. He felt also that his teachers had done a very good job.

Up to age 14, as a group, these managers had rarely or never *read about science,* a fact which no doubt reflects educational emphases in Ireland when these men were growing up. They did not *play with chemistry sets* nor *collect biological specimens* nor *tinker with mechanical devices.* Also in the "rarely or never" category were such activities as *drawing, painting, modeling clay, playing a musical instrument,* and even *writing stories or poems.* The educational emphases were clearly on verbal comprehension and numerical abilities and on character development. This was shown in several ways. They described their homes as very stable and closely controlled. Typically, the individual lived at home with both parents until he was 17 or 18. Broken homes, whether by voluntary or involuntary separation of the parents, which in some of our comparable studies of American families runs as high as 25 percent, were rather rare. The family pattern was that of a rather strict mother to whom the boy felt very close and with whom he had little discord. The father was described as highly energetic, decisive, somewhat distant, and often preoccupied with business or professional matters rather than with family activities.

The most strongly tabooed activities in childhood and adolescence were staying up late, missing church on Sunday, and fighting with brothers and sisters. Social drinking was also strongly tabooed in the 13—18 age range, and none of the group admitted to having any problem or trouble arising from drinking. Most of them had been married ten or more years. Almost all of them said their marriages were very happy, and that wives had a primary interest in the husband and in the family which they considered important and desirable. They described their emotional state as being steady, with few ups and downs and rare depression. They rated themselves as having a very good sense of humor, and I think they were right, judging from the conversation during cocktails at the end of each day's work. Unlike some of our other assessments of creative individuals, these were almost entirely frictionless, pleasurable and good-humored, though not without salt.

The managers saw themselves as *open to new ideas,* yet they did not see themselves as *generating innovations.* In terms of the kind of persons they would like to be, they placed greatest value on *high character and dependability.* The thing they would most *not* like to be is "an original but controversial person." So, I think you can see the general picture here.

In analyzing the data, both from the biographical questionnaire and from tests, we took our own staff ratings of originality and the Irish Management Institute nominating board's ratings and looked especially at those persons who were rated as highly original. They were certainly atypical of this group, though they included some of the leading figures in Ireland. For this analysis, we selected the nine most highly rated men and compared them with the rest of the group. Listed here are some activities of the individuals who were rated as highly original.

The "original" subgroup rated "high" and as having given them pleasure those activities in which they engaged by themselves, such as *reading about science, building things that work, drawing things, carving, painting, modeling, reading ahead in school subjects, putting on shows,* and *playing with chemistry sets.*

There was much emphasis on achievement by their peers during adolescence. They have more friction with the mother and they have a less high opinion of their father's achievement. The father placed less emphasis on achievement. The father was more often permissive with regard to personal behavior. There was no taboo on not being nice to brothers or sisters or friends. Much more often they rate themselves as having an outstanding degree of self-determination of behavior as a manager, and superior ability to tolerate or to encourage change. They frequently have the desire to be alone to pursue their own thoughts and interests. More frequently they read materials in foreign journals or magazines. When they feel miserable or blue, they less frequently choose to try to sleep it off and they prefer to talk to someone or have a few drinks. They are much less sensitive to criticism, according to self-ratings. They say they greatly influence their associates in opinion, activities, and ideas. They more often find books more interesting than people. They have felt themselves to be well-liked by their associates. They have much more communication with regard to information about topics outside their field. When they need to think out problems, they often seek a new environment outside their normal place of business. They are less inclined to analyze the motives of others, and they much more often describe themselves as having an even self-confidence no matter who is around.

C: Don't these Irish businessmen see, from looking at other countries, that they aren't really innovative?

S: Such a feeling was expressed by some of the managers during our group discussions, where the topic was "Innovations Ireland Needs." The discussions yielded some 800 specific suggestions, but over and over again the statement was made, "We should adapt more of what we see in other countries like the United States." In fact, a good many of these managers felt that Ireland needed most of all to adopt American merchandizing and marketing ideas. However, the more original of these men had ideas of their own and were not slavishly copying American techniques.

C: Isn't religious orthodoxy and strict church control keeping Ireland out of the mainstream of development with other parts of the world? Do you have any data on the way religious conformity relates to creativity?

S: Yes, there is one interesting finding relevant to that. We used my own "Inventory of Personal Philosophy." It has four religious belief scales: Fundamentalist Religious Belief, Enlightened Belief, Enlightened Disbelief, and Fundamentalist Disbelief. As a group, these Irish managers scored higher on Fundamentalist Belief than any other group I have tested. On the Complexity of Outlook scale, however, they were about half a standard deviation above the general population mean, although normally these two scales are highly negatively correlated. Apparently one can be both complex and orthodox in Ireland.

C: Were their methods of *building* things more original than their *ideas* about things?

S: I would say that it was probably the opposite, though I have no evidence.

C: I anticipated as much.

S: We used also a "manager *Q* sort" deck of fifty items. We had the managers describe themselves and then describe the *ideal Irish manager.* They candidly describe themselves as not very innovative or original, but they rate both those traits as very high in their ideal.

C: In general, do they appear to have a large amount of patriotism for their country and patriotism for the Church? You have given a picture of them as being patriotic and having high hopes, but also very realistic about the profound power of the Church. To fight it would simply not be a feasible or practical thing to do. Everything you have said so far would be compatible either with people who are playing along with the Church instead of trying to fight it, or with people who secretly or privately felt there might be a head-on collision.

S: We did not explore this in direct fashion. I think that the ones who were more original tended to have their sentiments less engaged or identified with the Church itself, though realistically they recognized they were involved in it.

Let us turn now to some studies closer to home, after which we shall go again, this time to Italy. First of all, however, a report on some work I have been doing with elementary school teachers in Goleta, California (Barron, 1969, Chapter 13).

INNOVATION in CLASSROOM CLIMATES

One of the most provocative findings in recent research on creativity in children is that the school system itself has a damping effect on spontaneity and originality. Paul Torrance's work has documented this in convincing detail. This, of course, comes as no surprise to many observers of the run-of-the-mill elementary school. The cramping effect of early confinement to a narrow desk and a narrow view of what constitutes "good order" has long been noted, by children as well as by adults.

It is easy to err on the side of Rousseauian sentiment, of course, and there is no doubt at all that school can be made a most diverting, happy, and creative experience; indeed, the educational program discussed here is evidence enough that I believe ways can be found to *increase* the creativity of children in the classroom. But there is a wide need for intelligent attention to the question of whether the usual elementary school classroom climate is enhancing or reducing the creativity of the children in it.

This program is one of a set of interrelated activities being carried on in the Santa Barbara, California, school systems, with generous financial support from the Ford Foundation. This particular program was initiated by Professor George Brown of the School of Education, University of California, Santa Barbara. I was privileged to participate as a consultant and observer and to do some testing to provide the basis for an independent appraisal of the program's effectiveness.

The goal of the program was to enhance the creativity of children, but the strategy required that a beginning be made with the teachers rather than with the children. We reasoned that the classroom climate itself would be the crux of the matter. No amount of "technique" in teaching creative thinking would be effective without a general emotional climate favoring openness and experimentation. But the classroom climate reflects to a large extent the personality and the creativeness of the teacher. Ergo, begin with the teacher!

Brown presented his plan to the curriculum supervisor and the three principals of elementary schools in the Goleta Union School District (the University campus is located in Goleta). The plan itself was quite novel. He proposed that the principals and six teachers from each school should volunteer to take part in a year-long program of exploration *of their own creativity*. This was to be done through a series of weekend "retreats" in secluded spots some miles from Goleta, as well as in half-day meetings once a week in small groups. The Ford Foundation funds were used to purchase released time for the teachers, as well as to cover expenses of retreats and of testing to be conducted at the beginning and at the end of the program.

A basic premise in this strategy is that if the school system itself is to be an "open" one, the teacher too must be open rather than closed to new ideas and a new way of looking at education. To increase creativity, we must open things up at all levels: administration, classroom climate, teacher attitudes, and children's imagination. The educational establishment as a whole, like many social institutions, tends to develop into a closed system, to stick with established methods, to play it safe even in the face of evidence that new needs are coming into being and that old methods fail to meet those needs. Resistance to change within the institution generates violent pressure to change from without. Unfortunately, the closed institutional system tends to make the people within it into its own image so that they, too, become "closed people." To stimulate creative change, we must begin with *the psychodynamics of the individual.* Thus ran our line of reasoning in developing the program now described.

I might add that this approach to the teacher *as a person* has the advantage of engaging attention, interest, and commitment from the teacher. The teachers we worked with, almost without exception, became intensely involved in the process. This is very important, for the failure of many innovations in curriculum can be traced to the neglect of a strategy for introducing teachers to the innovation and keeping them committed to it, both intellectually and emotionally. Brown and I decided on a method of approach that would combine living-in assessment with a sort of semi-therapeutic personal relationship with the teachers. The living-assessment was defined not as "assessment," but as "a retreat."

The first "retreat" was held in a secluded spot in the hills east of Santa Barbara, an old country inn. A group of speakers representing rather diverse interests and professions were assembled for this weekend meeting with the teachers and principals. Each was asked to speak on the question of the importance of imagination and creativity in human affairs. One was a prominent California jurist, Judge Joseph Lodge, who startled the audience by proposing new and imaginative approaches to the problems of marijuana use, prostitution, and usury; in effect, he proposed making all three legal, though with various social controls. Another speaker, Dr. James T. Lester, Jr., was a member of the American expedition that had recently completed an ascent of Mount Everest. He showed photographs of the climb and developed the thesis that the resources of imagination had been as important as courage and mountaineering skills in making the expedition a success. He concluded by showing photographs of the

Sherpa guides in a journey by automobile across the United States (with him as chauffeur), using their delighted reactions to new experiences as an example of the joyousness of discovery. and exploration. These and other speakers were deliberately chosen to help set a tone of unconventionality, freedom from routine, and a certain amount of positively-toned daring as important to real efforts at change.

This first retreat was attended by teachers, principals, superintendents, and members of interested departments on the University of California campus. It was thought of as "the kick-off," to get the game started and to let people get acquainted with one another. Three smaller weekend meetings were then scheduled, one for each school. An important feature of these meetings was the participation of the principal, who took part in the "assessments" on an equal basis with the teachers. A battery of personality tests was administered, including the Minnesota Multiphasic, the California Psychological Inventory, the Gough Adjective Check List (ACL), and the Myers-Briggs Jungian Type Indicator. All participants were interviewed twice, once concerning their personal life history, and once on their experiences in their teaching career. Particular attention in the latter interview was given to their philosophy of teaching and to experiences that had been particularly rewarding or particularly distressing. They were asked especially about what kinds of students they liked or disliked and were asked to describe real students and to give concrete examples of behavior.

Five tests were selected for use in appraising the effectiveness of the year's program: the Barron-Welsh Art Scale, The Barron Complexity of Outlook Scale, and three tests from the Guilford battery: Alternate Uses, Consequences, and Plot Titles, scored for high quality responses. These were given at the first assessments in October and the last in June. Scores on these tests were not revealed to the participants until the year's work was completed.

As part of the strategy of engaging the personal interest of the participants, we decided to feed back the results of the personality tests at Retreat No. 3, held about one month after Retreat No. 2 for each school. This was done with each teacher or principal individually, of course, and with proper assurances concerning confidentiality of the transaction. They were given the actual scores on the personality tests in the form of test profiles, and the metric and rationale of the tests were explained. Then their own scores were discussed with them at length, without, however, any implication that the tests were "the truth" about them as persons. They were encouraged, in fact, to disagree with the test results if they felt the results were invalid.

This has been standard operating procedure at the Institute of Personality Assessment and Research since we began our work in 1950. Our invitation to take part in assessment research includes an invitation to go over one's own test results with an assessment staff member at some reasonable length of time after the assessment, usually one month or so. Many assessees have taken us up on this and have expressed themselves as pleased with the resulting conference. In the case of the Irish managers, we mailed them a packet of test results and arranged for interviews with the personnel specialist at the Irish Management Institute. Several of them, while on visits to California, took the opportunity to have individual conferences at IPAR. I have used the technique also with Peace Corps trainees and with students at the Rhode Island School of Design, and consider it to be an integral part of "assessment." It must not be forgotten that the assessment method is a "depth technique," and that those who take part in it are required by the tests and interviews to face up to themselves in a way that life usually doesn't require them to do. It is an intensely involving process.

A word now about the procedures that were used during the year, with a view to changing the teacher's approach to teaching and to stimulate imagination both in teacher and pupil. These "procedures" are exercises developed by the teachers themselves in their weekly meetings. They had two basic aims: (1) to increase emotional understanding and empathy, which would include reciprocal action or appropriate communication of feelings; and (2) to free the imagination through apt metaphorical thinking and feeling.

The "empathy" exercises were similar in some ways to the Stanislavski method of teaching actors. An effort was made to suspend ego-feelings and to feel exactly as some other person or animal, or even an inanimate object might feel in its essential being. A state of quiet meditation was thus the precursor of the effort at empathy. Sometimes particular persons were chosen for the imaginative act of empathy. For example, instructions were given to think of a person with whom one was at odds, or perhaps whom one hated or despised. The task now was to feel just as that person felt about himself and others. Or an abstract idea of a person might be chosen: for example, imagine yourself as a youthful soldier of the Viet Cong, or as a Ghanaian school teacher on his first visit to the United States, or as a young bride-to-be on her wedding morning. Impersonal, inanimate objects were also made the object of the empathy exercises: a seashell, e.g., or a pebble, or a microphone. One exercise that proved especially popular with both teachers and pupils was to imagine what it would feel like to be "a misspelled word."

By way of introduction to the "biological analogies" feature of the Synectics method, we developed an exercise in which step one of the instructions asked the participants to "think of all the gadgets or machines you can that are like parts or functions of the human body." Children are especially responsive to this exercise and manifest delight at realizing that so many mechanical things in their world are modeled on the human form. Then, in step two, the task is reversed and they are asked to think of things about people for which there is no mechanical equivalent. This is, incidentally, an intriguing way of inducing the fundamental questions in the mechanism-vitalism problem, and one soon realizes that children at age five or six have available to them all the necessary concepts for stating the classical problems of systematic philosophy.

To make a long story short, the program continued through approximately eight months of weekly meetings. Eventually another school was added, and a total of 29 teachers took part in this aspect of the research. Significant gains were registered on four of the measures of performance hypothesized to be related to creativity. For the Barron-Welsh Art Scale, pre- and postprogram test scores analyzed by the Wilcoxon Matched-pairs Signed-ranks Test showed a T score of 65.5, significant beyond the .005 level. A similar level of significance was demonstrated for differences in scores on the Complexity of Outlook Scale. The Guilford tests were analyzed for differences in mean scores before and after the program, and on both Alternate Uses and Consequences, scored both for low quality (Ideational Fluency) and high quality (Originality), statistically significant differences were found. (It should be added, however, that the average increment was relatively slight, ranging from 10 to 15 percent. In retrospect, we felt that tests such as these, with their characteristic emphasis on very close timing and rather brief work intervals for each problem, were not the instruments of choice, for the range of possible change for subjects who have been highly motivated to perform at first testing is rather limited.)

It is of some interest to look at the personality patterns associated with favorable or unfavorable response to this sort of program. Therefore, the personality test reports of the two teachers who showed the least change in terms of the measures of creativity we used as criteria are presented, and then the test reports of two who made the most conspicuous gains. These reports were written immediately after the initial testing and are "blind" interpretations of the test profiles, given without any other information about the person except age and sex. The MMPI and the CPI were considered together in formulating a psychodynamic diagnosis, and then the Adjective Checklist Scales scores were added to the picture.

"No Change" Case No. 1
MMPI-CPI: This 44-year-old woman is not without her problems. She appears quite constricted and somewhat compulsive and, in mood, is probably chronically depressed, although manageably so. The depression could get out of hand, however. The possibility of a serious involutional state in the next few years may have to be reckoned with. With good environmental support, however, she probably will go along much as she is now, somewhat down at the mouth and somewhat unsociable and retiring, but meeting her responsibilities well in a highly conforming yet not seriously rigid manner. She has a certain amount of flexibility and insight, as well as a reasonable amount of tolerance. She probably is plagued by a host of minor physical ailments and may feel tired a great deal of the time. In her quiet way she is feminine and probably rather nurturant in her relationship with the children in school.

ACL: "Need for order" stands out in this record. There is more indication here than in the CPI of a need to dominate, and some indication of a more aggressive manner, or perhaps more hostility, than her retiring demeanor had led us to expect. Her expressed needs make her look a lot "tougher" psychologically; she may even have a bit of the classroom tyrant in her though, as noted earlier, she is also nurturant.

"No Change" Case No. 2.

MMPI-CPI: This 45-year-old man is a highly responsible, stable, conventional, slightly rigid individual, perhaps a bit too "good" for his own good, yet withal, an effective model of probity for the young. He appears to be somewhat passive sexually and could, conceivably, have a real problem in sexual identity (with fantasies and near-action impulses coming into the picture occasionally). He is so conscientious, however, and also so suppressed that one would not expect any overt pathology. He is likely to be nurturant, perhaps even motherly in his attitude towards the boys he teaches. The psychic cost to him of the defenses he must maintain is fairly heavy. A chronic mild depression is likely. He can also swing towards paranoia easily, although this would be muted in its expression. He is quite self-critical (which may seem at times to be modesty, but isn't— rather, he is self-concerned and self-condemnatory). He is no dunce when it comes to appraising motives; he is probably underestimated in this respect. There is a fair amount of fortitude in this man.

ACL: The picture here is of a deferent, self-abasing, fearful individual, terribly lacking in self-assertiveness, who gets along by being orderly, obedient, cautious, openly dependent on others, supportive of the status quo, and the enemy of no one. This is probably true in practice almost all the time, but there may be another level of consciousness in this man in which a well-hidden narcissism has full play.

"Conspicuous Change" Case No. 1

MMPI-CPI: An energetic, active, rather self-possessed 25-year-old woman who is highly participative socially in a gay and sometimes superficial and frivolous manner. She is sensitive and insightful, able and indeed willing to think easily in terms of psychological motivation. She, herself, is psychodynamically complex, with much going on beneath a facade of carefree, almost irresponsible sociability. Insofar as there is a problem which might be manifested as a clinical symptom, it would center upon sexual identity; she is somewhat masculine in interest pattern, markedly so for this group of women, yet she is not a dominant or masterful person. She might manifest occasional social delinquency, although not of a harmful sort; she is somewhat impulsive, but not mean and, in fact, is quite accepting of others and very tolerant in her attitudes. Her ego-strength is excellent and she appears to be basically well-adjusted.

ACL: Here she appears somewhat overly independent—i.e., there is more than the ordinary healthy emphasis on autonomy. There is actual rejection of affiliative needs. She cares little for conventional patterns of achievement, and does not like to "show herself off" or win attention to her talents through planned display of them.

"Conspicuous Change" Case No. 2

MMPI-CPI: This 47-year-old man is a notably stable and effective individual, yet is markedly lacking in self-esteem. He is temperate and deliberate in manner, does not like to push himself and would easily be underrated at first meeting. He is quite astute in his psychological evaluations of others, and is notably flexible and independent and unobstrusively efficient. His responsibility and self-control make him someone to rely on over the long haul. He conforms easily, but he clearly values independence and a certain amount of criticism of social norms and he, himself, is basically an independent in spite of his manner and general style of representing himself. He has more sympathy for social deviance than one might expect. Why his self-esteem is low is the most important question one can ask about him. (Perhaps *events* of long ago?) This is holding him back. He needs assurance, but exactly what would be reassuring is not clear. He probably knows consciously that he's quite capable. The matter would probably be worth his exploring in depth.

ACL: Low need for dominance and achievement, high need to avoid trouble, publicity, upset of any kind. Self-abasing, deferent, friendly, unaggressive, etc.

Professor Brown is continuing to work along these same lines, although with even more emphasis on "depth" techniques, including dream analysis by the Gestalt Therapy method of Dr. Fritz Perls, and incorporating sensory awareness and encounter group training. This latter work is being carried on in collaboration with the Esalen Institute, which now provides the "away from home" setting for the weekend retreats. My own work with the Santa Barbara Project ended after one year, as I left that summer for the first step in the research in Ireland already described.

THE MIXED ROLES OF HEREDITY AND ENVIRONMENT IN INNOVATIVE POTENTIAL

We turn now to a very different sort of study which was carried out in Italy, a study of the role of heredity in creativity using the classical twin method. For this purpose, I applied a battery of tests to an unselected sample of Italian twins, ages 16 to 18. The research was supported financially by the Richardson Foundation, and it was made feasible through the generous cooperation of the Mendel Institute of the University of Rome, the Institute of Medical Genetics in Florence, and the Harvard Florence Research Project. I should like here to record my gratitude to Drs. Luigi Gedda and Paolo Parisi of the Mendel Institute in Rome and to Dr. H. B. Young in Florence. I was assisted in my work by several graduate students in Rome and in Florence, notably Mr. M. Noferi of the Institute for Applied Psychology in Florence. (See Barron, 1970.)

In the twin method, evidence for the inheritance of a given characteristic is obtained by comparing the intraclass correlation in monozygotic (identical) twins with the correlation in dizygotic (fraternal) twins. In the present study, the subjects consisted of 59 pairs of like-sexed twins: 30 monozygotic pairs, 15 male and 15 female, and 29 dizygotic pairs, 14 male and 15 female. One of the DZ female pairs had to be excluded from the sample after testing because of incomplete data. The average age of the sample was 17; all were in secondary school at the time.

Zygosity diagnoses were arrived at from medical data, including blood tests, and can be assumed to be highly accurate. All the twins had been studied since birth.

The tests selected for use were these: Plot Titles, Consequences, and Unusual Uses, scored both for total number of responses (Ideational Fluency) and cleverness, remoteness, and unusualness (Originality); the Gottschaldt Figures test, which in the earlier joint study by the present writer with Guilford and others was shown to have the highest loading of any test on the Adaptive Flexibility factor; the Barron-Welsh Art Scale, which in the same study had the highest loading on a factor called "Preference for Complex Display," or, more simply, "Preference for Complexity;" the Expressional Fluency test, which loads significantly on the Expressional Fluency factor; and the Barron Symbol Equivalence test, which was included because of correlations with Fluency and with Originality in earlier studies. The results, in the order of their clarity and importance, are as follows:

1. Adaptive Flexibility

The form of the Gottschaldt Figures employed as a measure of this factor is the Crutchfield Revision (MacKinnon *et al.,* 1961), which is well-adapted for group administration. The task is to discover in a complex figure, a simpler embedded one. Fifteen problems are presented. Scores ranged from zero to 15, with a mean of 7.16.

The correlation in the monozygotic group is *.86;* in the dizygotic group, *.35.* Both correlations are significantly different from zero and they are significantly different from one another as well *(t* of 4.79; *p* less than .01). A high degree of heritability for this factor is indicated ($h^2 = .78$).

2. Expressional Fluency

This is a test from the Guilford battery in which the subject is given the initial letters of four words in sequence and asked to complete the words in such a manner as to form a sentence. His score is the number of complete sentences he can form in a given time.

The correlation in the monozygotic is .91 in the dizygotic group it is .70. Again, both correlations are significantly different from zero and from one another. A substantial degree of inheritance of expressional fluency is indicated ($h^2 = .75$).

3. Preference for Complexity

The test for this factor is the Barron-Welsh Art Scale of the Welsh Figure Preference test. As you know, it consists of 62 line drawings, varied in terms of complexity. The subject is asked to respond "Like" or "Dislike" to each drawing. The scoring key is based on the agreement between the subject's preference and the preferences of artists as compared with people in general. There is a pronounced tendency for artists to prefer the more complex figures, but the key, nevertheless, is based on preferences of artists and was identified inferentially as a measure of preference for complex displays.

The correlation in the monozygotic group is .58; in the dizygotic group, .07. The MZ correlation is significantly different from zero, but the DZ is not; they are significantly different from one another (t of 3.05) and a high heritability component is indicated by the h^2 value of .55. Whether what is inherited is a preference for complexity or a greater ability to discriminate in the esthetic realm is not clear, however. For the entire sample of 118 subjects, the mean score on the Art Scale is 28 as compared with a mean of 14 for American high school groups, a highly significant difference. In view of the historical contribution of Italy to the arts, it seems possible that a higher than average level of esthetic discrimination may be carried in the Italian gene pool. Further studies to clarify these relationships are now in progress in a collaboration between the Institute of Personality Assessment and Research and the Harvard University Florence Project, in which groups of Italian and Sicilian adolescents are being compared with the American-born and bred offspring of Italian immigrants to the Boston area.

4. Ideational Fluency

The findings here are inconsistent and heritability is not indicated. Low quality score correlations for Plot Titles, Consequences, Unusual Uses, and Symbol Equivalence are:

	MZ	DZ
Plot Titles	.76	.66
Consequences	.38	.71
Unusual Uses	.72	.59
Symbol Equivalence	.42	.73

5. Originality

Results here are also inconsistent, but significant heritability is certainly not indicated. High quality score correlations are as follows:

	MZ	DZ
Plot Titles	.70	.65
Consequences	.72	.75
Unusual Uses	.59	.47
Symbol Equivalence	.15	.58

It is clear from inspection of the correlations that both MZ and DZ twins tend to be quite similar on most of the purported measures of Ideational Fluency and Originality. Could this finding reflect on environmental influence from the very fact of being twins? At this point, speculation is probably not in order; more samples are needed. We are going ahead with further twin studies, this time in the area of Berkeley.

CHAPTER 5

Creativity in Interpersonal Relations

J. P. Guilford*

AMONG all the concerns that have been expressed regarding creativity during the two recent decades, little has been said with respect to creative interpersonal behavior. Of the many steps that have been taken in attempts to understand the subject and to implement progress in development of more creative individuals, little has been done toward achieving those goals where interpersonal problems are concerned.

Most attention has been given to the creative performances of scientists, engineers, and technical personnel, in general, and to the creative aspects of the visual arts. Efforts have been made to develop educational procedures by which intellectual development along the lines of thinking skills in those same areas can be promoted. It may have been assumed that such training will automatically and adequately transfer to the domain of interpersonal affairs, and that nothing new or different needs to be done in that direction. For reasons that will be given and elaborated later, there is much doubt that this is so.

Let us consider first the many circumstances under which creativity is needed in interpersonal living, taking a fresh view of the scope and the importance of this problem. It is easy to make the general statement that interpersonal behavior occurs wherever two or more persons stimulate and respond to one another. But to give this generalization some substance, let us remember another generalization to the effect that creative behavior is needed wherever problems arise and that problems in the course of interpersonal situations arise on every hand.

Although all of us encounter such problems every day, they arise more commonly for those who have responsibility for others or who need to influence or manage others for one reason or another. The categories of people who are more likely to encounter interpersonal problems of some degree of seriousness are well-known to all of you. Business, industry, and government have their administrators, managers, and supervisors. Business has its sales personnel. Government has its politicians, its lawmakers, judges, and diplomats. Local government has its law-enforcement and probation officials; schools have their teachers, coaches,

*J.P. Guilford is Emeritus Professor of Psychology, University of So. California, Los Angeles.

and counselors; and all communities of sufficient size have their social workers and other professional individuals who deal directly with people and their problems—psychiatrists, clinical psychologists, and marriage counselors. Then, of course, there is the parent who, if he takes his responsibilities seriously, has his almost daily share of interpersonal problems with members of the younger generation and with the partner in marriage.

In mentioning all these categories of people, there is no intended implication that any of their members at any time shall be expected to invent a new social institution, design a new law affecting millions of people, or reach a novel court decision. It is time that we cease restricting creativity to the outstanding few whose creative productions have noteworthy social consequences—and recognize that John Doe has interpersonal problems to solve, and wherever problems are solved there must be at least a trace of creativity and that it is a precious commodity. In general, it might be better in many ways if we talked more about problem-solving and less about creativity.

INTERPERSONAL PROBLEM-SOLVING

Problem-solving in interpersonal situations has many similarities to problem-solving everywhere else, but also has many unique features. Let us consider the common features first.

General Pattern of Problem-Solving

The writer has elaborated a general model for problem-solving elsewhere (Guilford, 1965, 1966). In its general form, this model does not differ from others that have been proposed from time to time. It takes into account the fact that the problem-solver must first be aware that a problem exists and then he must develop an understanding of the nature of the problem in order to see what kind of a solution it is going to take and in what direction that solution lies. These steps are cognitive and involve cognitive operations and abilities. Having achieved some structuring or understanding of the nature of the problem, the solver searches for solutions or constructs solutions. The cognized problem structure serves as a search model, which supplies the cues needed for retrieving from memory storage any information that is possibly relevant and promising as a means of solving the problem. Lacking sufficient information in this store of remembered information, the problem-solver may actively direct his search to environmental sources. He rejects some of the potential solutions that suggest themselves or that he constructs, and he accepts one or more others. He may or may not actually try out his solution overtly, with the possibility of testing to see whether it works and whether it has any unfortunate side effects.

In this brief general account of the solving of a problem, five major kinds of intellectual operation are implied, corresponding to the five categories of operation represented in the writer's structure-of-intellect model (Guilford, 1959). Seeing that a problem exists and understanding its nature were identified as cognitive processes in the preceding discussion. Retrieving information from memory storage in the attempt to find possible solutions depends upon productive operations and productive abilities. In this connection, it has been found necessary to make a distinction between the case in which, with the generation of logical alternatives, a variety of ideas come forth, and the case in which, because enough information is available to determine one compelling answer, a single idea is produced. The former case is known as divergent production and the latter as convergent production. In an overwhelming proportion of our problems, there is no one right answer, so the production is divergent and the wealth of ideas generated provides the occasion for novelty, originality and, therefore, creativity.

Also involved in the general model of problem-solving operations, the choice of solutions and possible testing entail another major kind of operation—evaluation. Briefly, evaluation involves matching outcomes with expected or desired effects, and deciding whether ideas are suitable or adequate in terms of satisfying certain standards. Actually, evaluation is not reserved for the final step in problem-solving; there may be evaluative, self-checking regulation, all along the way. Even our cognitions may be scrutinized as a matter of telling us whether we are on the right track in understanding the problem.

The fifth operation is that of memory, or retention of information. The problem-solver notes and remembers earlier steps, a process that aids in later steps. The memory store containing residuals from earlier experience is helpful at all stages of problem-solving. It is necessary to distinguish between memory as an operation and the memory store.

Unique Features of Interpersonal Problem-Solving

If problem-solving everywhere conforms very much to the general pattern just described, why was the generalization stated earlier to the effect that training for creative skills in connection with one area of endeavor would not necessarily effect improvement with respect to creative behavior in interpersonal relations? The answer follows from structure-of-intellect (SI) theory, which is based upon considerable empirical evidence, some of it bearing upon abilities unique to interpersonal relations.

SI theory recognizes not only the five kinds of operations just mentioned but also four major categories of information. One kind of information is known as "figural," because it is either perceived or it maintains its perceptual characteristics when we think of it in the form of images. A second kind is known as "symbolic," because it is in the nature of conventional signs, such as letter or number combinations. Such signs are related and manipulated, as in mathematics. A third kind is called "semantic," and it is in the form of what we commonly call "ideas." Words are commonly the signs of ideas, but not all semantic information is necessarily verbalized. The fourth kind of information, which is of greatest concern in the interpersonal context, is known as "behavioral." Charles Spearman (1927) spoke of "psychological relations," which means about the same thing. E. L. Thorndike (1920) argued the case for a special area of ability he called "social intelligence," which is basically the same idea.

The most significant thing about the four kinds of information for us here is that the same individual is not equally capable of solving problems in all kinds of information. There are behavioral abilities that are distinct from abilities to perform in the same manner in the other three areas of information. The abilities are parallel in all four informational areas, according to SI theory and its supporting evidence. All five of the major operations apply in parallel ways within the four areas of information. But this does not make the abilities the same in dealing with all four kinds of information. This statement applies to the abilities that are most directly relevant for creativity as well as those of less significance.

In behavioral information, then, we find the secret of the unique aspects of creative problem-solving in interpersonal relationships. Let us take a closer look at behavioral information and see how it is different from the other kinds. This can be seen best in connection with the cognitive abilities, which have to do simply with knowing or understanding. Knowing the other person's behavior means being aware of what he is attending to, what he is perceiving, cognizing, thinking, feeling, desiring, and intending to do, and what his actions mean. Most of the sensory cues that come to us from him are what we can see or hear of his overt behavior. What we see or hear is figural information and, as such, is not behavioral information; it provides the cues from which behavioral information is developed. It is quite possible to interpret the other person's behavior in terms of semantic information, especially if we verbalize regarding it or reflect upon it. But there is a more direct, unverbalized mode of understanding. This is behavioral information as technically defined.

BEHAVIORAL COGNITION

In areas of information other than behavioral, it has been found that the abilities or functions most relevant for creative performance are in the operation category of divergent production. In that category, we find abilities coming under the sub-categories of fluency, flexibility, and elaboration. These abilities have to do with the retrieval of stored information for new uses and the revising of information to make it more adaptable. By analogy, we should expect that creative performance where behavioral information is concerned should also be found in the area of divergent production. In terms of SI theory, this should be true. But there are two important reasons for considering seriously the contributions of behavioral *cognition* to creative production in interpersonal relations. One is the role of cognition in problem-solving, as explained earlier. The other has to do with the relation of divergent production to cognition.

Cognition and Divergent Production

A number of studies have been made of the relation between the traditional IQ, as measured by ordinary intelligence scales, and abilities to perform in creative ways, usually represented by tests of divergent-production (DP) abilities in the semantic area of information. The typical result is a bivariate scatter plot that approaches triangular form. That is, individuals of high IQ vary widely over the range of DP scores, whether the latter are derived from a composite of DP tests or whether from single DP tests. Individuals of low IQ very rarely obtain moderate or high DP scores. There can be many high IQ but low DP cases, but there are no low IQ but high DP cases.

When we examine the orthodox IQ test scales from the point of view of SI theory, we find that they weight very heavily the semantic-cognition abilities, and even very few of that category. It is becoming clearer that because of the strong and direct dependence of cognition upon memory storage, cognition tests essentially measure the extent of our stored information. This does not make cognitive and memory abilities the same thing. Memory abilities are measured by assessing how much information is retained after all individuals have had equivalent degrees of exposure to the same information or, more precisely stated, exposure to the stimulating conditions for such information. Cognitive abilities reflect how much information is stored without regard to its sources, where opportunities for accumulating the information have varied, person to person.

The small degrees of correlation between IQ and DP scores and the unusual scatter plot are best accounted for in terms of the dependence of divergent production also upon the amount of stored information. Without stored information there can be no production of information; if the information needed is not in storage, it obviously cannot be retrieved for use in problem-solving. This may be why individuals with low IQ have little chance in production tests. But the possession of great quantities of information in storage is no assurance of divergent production. The information needed may well be in storage but the individual cannot readily retrieve it for use. This would explain the low DP scores among many who possess high IQs or high cognition-test scores. High status in cognition is a necessary condition for high status in divergent production, but it is not a sufficient condition.

Incidentally, this suggests that those of high IQ but low DP abilities are creative underachievers. They have at least the cognitive potential for becoming effective problem-solvers. We should determine whether educational procedures could bring them up to creative levels on a par with their cognitive levels. This does not mean that those of low IQ should be ignored in broad educational efforts to train problem-solvers. Some of them, also, may be creative under-achievers, and there is also the possibility of increasing their chances of problem-solving by building up their stores of information.

Behavioral-Cognition Abilities

The preceding discussion has given us reason to give attention to the cognitive abilities in the area of behavioral information, for they are crucial to the derivation of information that is basic to creativity in that area. In areas of information other than behavioral, it has been amply demonstrated that there is more than one cognitive ability in each case, and that the cognitive abilities differ with respect to the kind of product of information that is involved. Six basic kinds of products have been recognized in each area of information—units, classes, relations, systems, transformations, and implications. We should, therefore, expect to find six distinct abilities of behavioral cognition. A study that was aimed to test this hypothesis was quite successful (O'Sullivan et al., 1965). A brief review of some of the more pertinent aspects of that investigation follows.

Behavioral Units. In the development of tests for the cognition of behavioral units, it was assumed that a unit of such information would be a single state of mind for a single person, as indicated by his facial expression, his posture, the positions and dispositions of his limbs, hands, and feet. A test called "Faces" presents a single face and four other faces, representing alternative answers, with the examinee *(E)* to say which of the four portrays the same state of mind as the single face. The alternatives are from a person of different sex than that of the single face, as a step toward controlling similarities of figural properties.

Another units test, "Expressions," is composed of line drawings of faces or other parts of the body, alone or in various combinations. It is also a multiple-choice test, with *E* to select one of four expressions indicating the same mental state as the given expression. An "Inflections" test presents tape-recorded sounds in the form of words or short phrases, such as "No" or "I did it," with different inflections. *E* is to choose from a set of four line drawings of faces the one that should go with the sound stimulus. A fourth units test, called "Questions," presents the expressive face of the actor Fernandel in each item, with four alternative statements, each of which might have been said to him just before he looks the way he does.

It will be noted that with the exception of the last mentioned test there was avoidance of the use of verbal items and verbal responses, lest there be some contamination with semantic abilities. Asking E to name expressions or explain situations was studiously avoided. Among 23 tests designed for behavioral-cognition abilities, only one had a minor loading for a semantic-ability factor.

The heavy use of visual-figural items suggested a danger of contamination with visual-figural factors. An effort was made to avoid presenting figural cues that would give an item away, an effort that was apparently quite successful. Thus, we have consistent evidence that behavioral information stands by itself, distinct from both figural and semantic information. There should be no doubt on logical grounds of its distinction from symbolic information.

Behavioral Classes. Like other kinds of information, behavioral items of information can be classified and class concepts can be known. Of four tests designed for factor CBC (cognition of behavioral classes), two were successful. "Expression Grouping" presents in each item a set of three line drawings of expressions, differing somewhat in terms of body part and in variations from the same identical unit but having the possibility of representing a class of mental states, such as actions indicating approval. There is a variety of ways in which approval can be expressed and there are subtle variations in the nature of approval or approbation. A multiple-choice format gives four alternative expressions, one of which belongs to the class.

A "Picture Exclusion" test presents in each item four expressions, three of which belong to a class, but not the fourth, with E to mark the latter alternative. The expressions in each item include two photographs of faces, one photograph of hands only, and one of a whole body in a certain posture with face blocked out. The photographs are of amateur actors who posed for them.

Behavioral Relations. Most of the tests designed for behavioral relations involve two individuals who are reacting to one another with some definitive relation involved, such as animosity, admiration, or domination, but one test is restricted to independently acting individuals in the form of stick figures.

"Social Relations" presents in each item two simple outline faces in near profile positions, with different expressions of forehead, eyes, and mouth. With the faces turned toward one another, the speaker is indicated by an arrow. Four alternative statements are given, one of which the speaker is saying to the other, in view of their relationship, In this instance, the verbal statements are carriers of behavioral information. No variance due to semantic information is involved, for there can be no doubt about the semantic meanings of the statements.

"Silhouette Relations" is similar in that it presents two silhouettes of head and shoulders facing one another: one obviously male, the other obviously female. Different relations between the pairs can be indicated by raising or lowering one of the pair or by tilting either or both forward or backward. In this test, unlike

"Social Relations," the alternative answers are four photographed facial expressions, with E to say which one goes with the male or the female silhouette, considering the relationship portrayed.

The stick figures test, "Stick Figure Opposites," gives a stick figure in one posture, for example, a relaxed body, and three alternative stick figures as alternative answers, with E to select the one that expresses the opposite behavioral condition. In spite of the fact that the same relation of opposition is used in all items, this test was modestly successful for measuring individual differences in seeing behavioral relations in general.

Behavioral Systems. A behavioral system may be expected to involve two or more individuals in some kind of interaction, but the possibility of a system pertaining to one person should not be excluded. The most obvious case of cognition of a behavioral system is that in which a person grasps the nature of the network of inter-relations existing among interacting individuals. Some examples of tests that were designed successfully for factor CBS will show what is meant.

In the test "Missing Pictures," each item is in the form of two or three persons photographed in a sequence of four stages during a single episode. The four pictures shown in the proper sequence represent a little story. In developing the test, the scenes were staged using amateur actors—university students. Dr. Richard de Mille was in charge of direction and photography, so we may call the "Missing Pictures" test a "de Mille production." In each item of the test, one of the four pictures is missing. Three alternative candidates are provided, with E to say which one is best for completing the set of four. Solving each item requires sizing up each situation, each of which is a system in itself, and tying the pictures together to make a reasonable story, a story being a system of larger scope. A "Missing Cartoons" test is very similar to "Missing Pictures," the four parts of an episode being represented by cartoon drawings from the syndicated comic strip *Ferd'nand,* in which the stories emphasize psychological events in pantomime.

If these two tests alone had determined the finding of a CBS factor, we should have been left with doubt as to its generality; a factor with only two very similar tests on it could be a specific factor. But two other dissimilar tests helped to identify the factor. One of them was "Facial Situations," in each item of which faces of a man and a woman in separate pictures are shown, each face with its own expression. There may be implication of one or more other persons, not shown. In one item, for example, he looks pleased and she looks annoyed. E is to select one of three statements, each of which might be taken as a reasonable explanation of the situation. The keyed answer to the item mentioned is, "They are watching a beauty contest."

In an item of the fourth systems test, two people are shown in one scene from a *Ferd'nand* cartoon, with four alternative statements that possibly explain the situation, one of which is most reasonable, everything relevant in the situation considered. In one picture in a store, Ferd'nand has torn his coat on a protruding object and a man is rushing up, hands in air. The keyed answer is, "The man will say how sorry he is."

Behavioral Transformations. A transformation in information is some kind of revision or change. We are concerned here with a change of meaning or interpretation and how good an individual is in seeing such changes. In "Picture Exchange," another de Mille production, as in "Missing Pictures," four photographed scenes from a short sequence of events are involved, except that instead of choosing the missing picture, E is to replace one of the pictures with one of four alternative pictures that would mean a radical change in the whole story; the others would change it very little. A parallel test composed of *Ferd'nand* cartoons, "Cartoon Exchange," calls for the replacement of a designated scene with one of four alternative scenes that changes the story.

Tests of different kinds help to determine the factor, along with the two similar tests just mentioned. "Social Translations" is of entirely verbal content. Given first in an item is a short statement like "I don't think so," which the examinee is told has been said by a parent to a child. E is then given three other pairs of people, such as "teacher to student," "student to teacher," and "student to student," and is asked to say between which pair the same statement, if made, would have a quite different meaning.

"Expression Exchange" presents first a head and a body separately, each with its own expression, but if put together, a single impression of mental state would be fairly obvious. Alternative heads are then given, each with a different expression, with E to say which head, if placed on the body, would yield the greatest change from the first head-body combination. The body's expression is somewhat ambiguous when taken alone and takes on more definitive meaning from the head that is placed upon it.

Behavioral Implications. In the product of implication, something is expected to follow from given information, as when we make a prediction. In tests of behavioral implications, given a certain item of behavioral information, E is to say what is likely to happen next. The best test, "Cartoon Predictions", shows a cartoon character in a certain situation, perhaps stranded on a roof with his little son watching. What will the little boy do? Alternative scenes involving the little boy and his mother show possible outcomes. From knowledge of the situation and of human nature, what would be the most reasonable prediction?

Another CBI test uses in each item a statement such as is often made by a person who is in the presence of his counselor. E is expected to decide what the counselee is really saying. The counselee's statement is also presented from a tape recorder with appropriate inflections. Alternative statements that might describe the real meaning are given. This was the only behavioral test in the

O'Sullivan analysis that had some significant relation to a semantic ability, the factor for cognition of semantic relations. Some of the examinees must have utilized some semantic interpretations to advantage in this test. Some changes in the task might direct the test more in its intended direction.

Implications of the Behavioral-Cognition Abilities

The demonstration of six behavior-cognition abilities, distinct from one another and from abilities in figural and semantic areas of information, yet parallel to the latter two categories of abilities, is the first important step in accounting for some of the aspects of social intelligence. First of all, it demonstrates the uniqueness of kinds of abilities involved in understanding other people. Further, it lends some degree of reasonableness to the hypothesis, generated from the SI theory, that there should be a set of six parallel divergent-production abilities dealing with the generation of items of behavioral information in response to various needs.

TESTS OF BEHAVIORAL DIVERGENT-PRODUCTION

Efforts have already been directed by the Aptitudes Research Project at the University of Southern California toward the development of tests for the hypothesized abilities of divergent production of behavioral information. Having already found nearly all (16 out of 18) the divergent-production abilities in the areas of figural, symbolic, and semantic information, it is much easier to generate ideas for tests and test items by analogy for the behavioral area.

Some new difficulties have been encountered, however, which present problems to be solved. It is rather easy to find or to produce the visual-figural and even the auditory-figural material to use in behavioral-cognition tests. But in divergent-production tests, we cannot ask examinees, as we should like to, to produce responses in the form of drawings or vocal expressions. They are very unequally skilled in such performances. It is simplest procedure to call for written, verbal responses, but then the danger of getting the production over into the semantic area is of some concern. It is necessary somehow to make examinees aware of the difference between verbal statements that pertain to behavioral information as distinct from statements that pertain to semantic information. It is possible to train scorers to make the same kind of distinction. It may be possible to have examinees act out their responses or to produce them in the form of paper dolls on a stage, but this gets into individual testing where group testing is almost a necessity for efficient factor-analytic studies.

Some Examples of Divergent-Production Behavioral Tests

These few examples will show the kinds of printed group tests with which some progress has already been made. They are all in early experimental stages.

A test called "Expression Meaning" asks E to make a list of all the meanings he can think of for some described expression, such as a person narrowing his eyes to make slits. In "Picture Meanings," the same kind of task is involved, but the expression is presented in a line drawing, such as that of a man holding his eyes closed with thumb and forefinger with head bowed. Both are designed for the ability for divergent production of units.

For the divergent production of relations, relations between two people are utilized as in most of the successful parallel cognition tests. In "Social Problems," E is asked to list things that may happen in the relations a designated kind of person would have vis-à-vis others, for example, a teacher, where the others may be of varied types with opportunities for varied relations.

For divergent production of systems, social situations and story plots offer kinds of systems that might be used. In "Story Plots," three characters are briefly described, such as sisters A and B, both romantically interested in the same young man C. One day C arrives suddenly. How many different story plots can the examinee generate, emphasizing the stated personal characteristics and feelings? In "Character Combinations," three people are briefly characterized with respect to their present states, for example, a man in pain, a woman who is sympathetic, and an excited man. Again, different stories are to be generated.

In the case of *cognition* of implications, it may be remembered that a test calling for E to make predictions showing that he sees the implications of a given situation is successful. For a hypothesized factor of DBI, E is to make a variety of predictions, given the same starting information. "Cartoon Completions" gives two beginning scenes of a cartoon sequence, with E to list a number of scenes that might reasonably follow next. "Predictions" presents some condition, such as a boy or a girl discovering a spot on his (her) clothing, with E to give a list of consequences in terms of his (her) behavior and the behavior of others who see the spot.

These examples should be sufficient to show the kinds of tests that are possible in this area. For a factor analysis, of course, additional tests of varied nature will be needed. Preliminary testing with small groups of examinees is being done in order to obtain advance information regarding how well the tests seem to be performing and to try out different scoring procedures.

SUMMARY

In this chapter it has been pointed out that creativity in interpersonal relations involves an area of information that is quite distinct from three other areas in

which intellectual functions also operate. The uniqueness of the area of behavioral information, has been demonstrated by the finding of six behavioral-
cognition abilities or functions that are parallel to cognition abilities in the areas
of figural, symbolic, and semantic information, but relatively independent of
them.

By the time of this conference, a number of tests had already been constructed
for the six hypothesized abilities in the area of divergent production with
behavioral information, with some early indications that such tests are not only
feasible, but also somewhat promising for the differentiation of those abilities.

C: What happens to a very original person who takes one of your multiple-
response tests in the area of cognition?

S: In this area they must give conventional responses to make good scores—
the keyed responses. Some people may possibly make low scores because they
are creative. They may indulge in some projections or make unusual interpretations of the items. We can sometimes see evidence of this.

C: That's what I mean.

S: I should add that this probably does not happen very often.

C: I am always intrigued with the variety and ingenuity of the new tests
produced in Guilford's laboratory. If anyone wants to do a study on a good
climate for creativity, they should do a study of his laboratory, for I am always
amazed at what comes out of his lab, including this report he has just given.

C: Another way of saying this is that his lab reminds me of Thurstone's
laboratory.

CHAPTER 6

Group Dynamics and Creative Functioning

E. Paul Torrance*

BEFORE discussing my more recent studies of group dynamics and creative functioning, I will summarize briefly what we have accomplished in our program at the University of Minnesota since our last conference.

Listed below are the things that I think represent our most significant progress since the 1964 conference:

1. IMAGI/CRAFT Materials: Recorded dramatizations and exercises: Great Moments of Scientific Discovery, Great Moments in Invention, Great Moments in Geographical Discovery, and Fantasies.
2. Ideabooks: Exercises for developing intellectual skills involved in creative thinking.
3. *Rewarding Creative Behavior: Experiments in Classroom Creativity.*
4. *Constructive Behavior: Personality, Stress, and Mental Health.*
5. *Gifted Children in the Classroom.*
6. *Torrance Tests of Creative Thinking.*
7. Monograph for USOE on "Assessing and Motivating Creative Behavior."

The first item is a set of instructional materials, involving recorded planned sequences of creative thinking activities. We (Cunnington and Torrance, 1965a) have used the trade name, IMAGI/CRAFT; and these are finally available commercially after about four years of developmental work. You will note that there are four series: "Great Moments of Discovery," "Great Moments in Invention," "Great Moments in Geographical Discovery," and "Fantasies." These materials consist of dramatized recordings of the highlights of some discoverer such as Alexander Graham Bell ("Messages for the Millions"), recorded exercises to engage the children in thinking activities similar to those of the great discoverer, and an instructors' guide containing a great variety of additional exercises and suggestions for creative thinking activities.

All of the dramatizations attempt to familiarize children with the nature and value of creative achievement, the problems of the creative person, and creative ways of thinking and finding out things. The dramatizations are first used as the basis for various kinds of exploration. Then the recorded exercise is used to involve the children in kinds of thinking similar to those displayed by the great

---

* E. Paul Torrance is Chairman, Department of Educational Psychology, College of Education, University of Georgia, Athens. He was formerly Professor, Bureau of Educational Research at the University of Minnesota.

discoverer. The teachers' guides suggest individual and group activities related to the dramatization and ways of relating these activities to various subject matter areas of the curriculum. In other words, one of the recorded dramatizations might begin as a social studies lesson and end in a lesson in language arts, music, visual art, dramatics, or history.

The fourth series consists of fantasies. Some of these are adaptations of classical fantasies and some are original. In all of them, we start with the fantasy and let it lead to practical, creative problem-solving. The one based on the famous Italian legend of Giovanni and the Giant is a good example of the classical fantasies. Giovanni was a cowardly fellow who became an imaginative and courageous man. In one suggested exercise, the story is used as an analogy. Children are asked to think of the "giants" in their lives that make them cowardly. After discussing the ways they now use to cope with these "giants," they are urged to think more imaginatively and boldly about them. In another suggested exercise, use is made of the fact that Giovanni used deceit to overcome the giant. Practice is given in detecting possible deceit in newspaper and magazine advertising, door-to-door selling, and similar experiences. It is also suggested that use be made of some of the great hoaxes and swindles in history. These can be related to the curriculum in history and geography, because almost every period in history and every geographical area has its famous hoaxes. There are even collections of them (Klein, 1955).

The ideabooks give us another format for presenting planned sequences of creative thinking experiences. We studiously avoid the term, "workbook," and we hope that they are not used in the ways that workbooks are frequently used—as instruments of busy work. They bear such titles as: *Can You Imagine?* (Myers and Torrance, 1965a); *For Those Who Wonder* (1966a); *Invitations to Thinking and Doing* (1964); *Invitation to Speaking and Writing Creatively;* and *Plots, Puzzles, and Ploys* (1965b).

An essential feature of these materials is having children produce something and then do something with what they produce. The rather lengthy teachers' guides give suggestions for letting one thing lead to another and encouraging this process. Throughout the creation of the exercises in the children's booklets and in the guides for teachers we deliberately tried to apply the findings that emerged from our program of basic research and the best in theory and research that others have produced. Almost all of these materials have been field-tested rather thoroughly and their use in the hands of reasonably capable and imaginative teachers seems to result in general creative growth, at least as measured by the *Torrance Tests of Creative Thinking* (1966a).

We got into the creation of instructional materials because we found that it was extremely difficult to train teachers to apply research findings concerning creative development and functioning. Our first attempts at in-service education were rather unsuccessful (Torrance, 1965a). We decided that we might possibly make more impact on what actually happens in classrooms by creating materials that have built into them many of the research findings. I have studied the history of attempts to develop a more creative kind of education, going back to antiquity (Torrance, 1967). From this study, it has seemed to me that the ideas that have lasted longest and have had the most impact on classroom practice have been those that have been spelled out and transformed into instructional materials. They may be rejected or even forgotten for a while, but they have a way of coming back. An example of this is the Montessori materials.

The third item on my list is the publication of *Rewarding Creative Behavior: Experiments in Classroom Creativity* (Torrance, 1965a), which is a report of a series of over 20 experiments in creativity. I consider this in itself an achievement—for a commercial publisher of college textbooks to publish a book reporting research studies. Royalties from this book are now supporting almost all of the small amount of research that I am doing.

Our experience with the ideabooks illustrates quite well some of the problems involved in innovation in education. Myers had developed a number of exercises and he and I had used them experimentally and had evaluated the results. To do this, we had had to mimeograph copies. Somehow copies of these traveled from one person to another through some kind of grapevine and the demand for them became overwhelming. We were financially unable to supply interested persons even with sample copies that they could ditto or otherwise reproduce. Publication seemed to be the answer. Initially, a dozen or so publishers expressed interest. When the publishers went to their advisors, they all backed out. The material, they discovered, did not fit into the buying patterns of school systems, since it could not be classified as specific subject matter such as social studies, language arts, or the like. Unanimously, the concluded, "Nobody will buy it. It is interesting material but we do not want anything to do with it."

Myers and I discovered that we had created a monster. In self-defense, we scraped together enough cash to have a local printer produce 2000 copies. Very quickly, with no advertising, these were sold. Then we had another 2000 copies printed and then another 2000 copies. Finally, a publisher became sufficiently interested to agree to publish them. Thus far, the publisher has not shown a great deal of interest in marketing them. Educators continually complain to the authors that their orders are cancelled because the materials are out of print. I still feel, however, that the mere creation of materials can be a powerful force. Once ideas have been translated into concrete instructional materials, they are there to bother people and something constructive may result.

C: The publisher of these materials did not even send a set of your materials to display at a national meeting that I attended. Now I am beginning to understand.

S: Well, I think the publisher has displayed them at several meetings, but thus far there has been no advertising in educational journals.

C: This reminds me of the experiences of Brewster Ghiselin (1955) with his book, *The Creative Process.* It took him six years to find a publisher, though numerous publishers agreed that it was good material. He finally went to the University of California Press which printed a couple of thousand copies. Once it was published, it was reprinted as a Mentor paperback and it has sold over a half-million copies. As one publisher told me, it was just another case where the editors missed.

S: This again illustrates the point that once something tangible was produced, the demand for it set up a tension within the whole system and eventually this tension produced action. I think that even though a new but important idea is rejected and may even be forgotten for a while, its very existence creates a tension that will eventually cause it to be reevaluated.

C: Are you saying that publishers are not trying to be creative?

C: They cannot spot a good new idea.

S: This problem has existed throughout the history of educational publishing. It is illustrated in one of our unpublished dramatized recordings "Eyes at Their Fingertips" (Cunnington & Torrance, 1963). It is the story of Louis Braille, a twelve-year-old blind boy who was bothered by the fact that the books then available for blind children were so huge. Furthermore, reading from them was very inaccurate. By the age of fourteen he had virtually perfected what is now known as Braille writing. For the next five years, this type of writing was tested in the training institute where Braille was located. He demonstrated conclusively that the method could be taught easily and that it resulted in more accurate reading. Nevertheless, it was not until 43 years after Braille's death that his innovation was accepted, even in France.

There were two great forces that worked against the acceptance of Braille and those same two forces still work against sound educational innovations. One of these forces was the training institutes. If the innovation were accepted, teachers would have to learn something new. It would make obsolete much of their prior training and practice. Secondly, it would make obsolete the materials of the publishers. Doubtless, publishers had huge investments in the embossed books then in use.

Although teacher education institutions and publishers have continued to be major deterrents to innovation in education, we can be somewhat encouraged by the willingness of certain publishers to take risks. For example, the publisher of the Imagi/Craft materials and the ideabooks was willing to take a considerable risk to complete the Imagi/Craft materials and produce them commercially.

In any kind of innovation, there is struggle. Perhaps one of the toughest struggles will be in the area of college textbooks. My own ventures at innovation in this area have been quite unsuccessful. I am hoping that my next textbook publisher will be willing to permit me to go ahead with some of the innovations I believe will prove productive.

C: This reminds me of an informal conference of a group of my friends in California. We were talking about a climate for creativity. The greatest bottleneck we could think of and the greatest resistance to the enhancement of creativity was commercial publication. We decided that the best way of breaking through this particular bottleneck would be the formation of a publishing house of our own. These people talked among themselves about promising all of their future publications in advance to this publishing house, so it would have enough money to market the things that it wanted. So maybe we just have to hold on.

S: Inevitably, this will probably always be a problem in a society such as ours where textbooks are not controlled by the government, where it is a free enterprise and a matter of willingness to risk. I am encouraged by small concessions to innovation in publishing. Prentice-Hall permitted me to write both *Guiding Creative Talent* (1962) and *Rewarding Creative Behavior* in the first person. Of course, every other publisher with whom I have dealt has been unwilling to make such a concession.

C: I have been having a very interesting experience with the International Textbook Company. From dealing with art people, they are apparently more flexible than they would have been from dealing solely with educational people. They also have a pretty good analysis system. They have begun to learn that some things that do not start well persist over a long period of time and have longevity. Things that do not persist over time are not worth much. This company seems to be more open by publishing a certain percentage of genuine risk books, and they take these risks. I also think they are aesthetically oriented. That is, they like to do a book well.

C: Did this group who were talking about the formation of a publishing house also decide that the conventional journals are at a loss for innovation? One thing that has been done with such a proliferation of journals in psychology, and in other fields too, is to break out of the bind. In a big outfit, the editors tend to become good organization men and follow "safe" past patterns.

C: Thurstone likewise had problems with editors of journals, so he resorted to multilithing his own reports, in full, hoping later to get them into the "established" journals. I see that Guilford has done the same with his factor studies and we mimeograph all of ours. We have found a farsighted editor, Gordon Ierardi, at John Wiley, who saw the value of the books emerging from these creativity conferences and said he would publish whatever I would give him on creativity.

S: Another phenomenon operating in college textbook publishing amounts to a kind of coalition between the publishers and the training institutions. When I wanted to use a self-involving technique in a textbook, the editor made a quick survey of college and university instructors who were teaching this kind of course. He asked these college and university teachers if they would adopt a book that used this technique and they said "No." This indicated to the publisher that the use of this technique would be a bad risk.

C: We have been doing a lot of night work in the last six weeks on just this problem. The thing is that a publishing company will have what they want. Education defaults some control of them. There is real introspection among publishers right now on the whole matter of orientation and format. Second, there is still a lot of resistance to innovation. Where we have been heartened is in the response of companies such as Xerox, Raytheon, IBM, CBS, and IT & T. These are companies that are beginning educational programs that go beyond the textbook materials and lead into inner dialogue and audio-visual kinds of communication. More interesting, there is a feeling that textbook materials may be a phase-out aspect of the total educational package in the next 15 or 20 years. There is a lot more creativity going on in American industry, especially in that segment which is interested in education and is now using different materials.

C: Sure, the publishers are going to have a great deal of copyright trouble. Just last week, for example, I had two requests to reproduce an article of mine in a book of readings that was to be sold only to a particular class. This is increasing enormously. Every professor is putting out his own book of readings.

C: Large companies are buying publishing houses that need the money. The most recent example is when Xerox bought American Press. In many cases, American industry is taking over for the private sector.

C: Obviously, with a whole area of new ways of teaching, such as educational TV, every publisher will be doing it. Publishers are beginning to see that they are not infallible and that they do not move rapidly enough. As you point out, there is a merger of the computer people and the education people, of the TV people and the book people. This is a period when everyone is going in and trying to grasp this thing. It is a question of how fast you move. There is also the question, "Are you too far ahead of the times?"

S: To get back to the problem of innovation in college textbooks, I should mention that I was able to achieve a small degree of innovation through the instructors' manual for the text. For each chapter, I gave at least one tested idea for teaching that chapter in a creative way. Of course, it is virtually required that such a manual give examination items. Instead of giving just the usual multiple-choice items, I gave some memory items, some convergent thinking items, some divergent thinking ones, and some evaluation ones. Through this, I hoped to help college teachers do something about assessing a variety of kinds of achievement.

C: This discussion has narrowed down to the thought that maybe what is wrong with commercial publishers as innovators is the advising system. Even though some in a publishing house may be eager for innovation, the professional adviser type is not necessarily the most innovative or most eager to change. A thought at this point is that a research group such as this could offer themselves as advisers to commercial publishing houses. This might be a possibility.

C: There are problems with that. We are not all available and we do not all stay on one thing.

C: Let me tell what happened to a suggested book of mine. I wanted to put together some new kinds of materials and it was suggested that I do so. I tried two or three publishers and in each instance the editors said, "Yes, fine!" but the trade department took a look around to see how many they could sell and said, "Nothing doing." So it isn't just the advisers.

S: I can relate at least one successful experience through which I have been able to contribute to change by serving as adviser to a publisher. Some three or four years ago, I was asked to review a manuscript on creative teaching in the elementary school. I was impressed by the possibilities of the book but it was far too long for a single book. I suggested that it be made into a series of books and made other suggestions regarding its development. There will be a single theory book on setting the conditions for creativity in the elementary school and several smaller books, each on a different area such as reading and literature, language arts, mathematics, social studies, and science. The series is due off the press soon and has in it many of the things that I wanted to put into my own book but was not permitted to do so. I am very happy about this and I believe that the series will make a tremendous contribution to a more creative kind of education in elementary schools. Provocative questions and problems appear at the beginning of chapters instead of at the end of each chapter. It represents a tremendous investment on the part of the publisher. As the reviewer, I also found out that it was a tremendous job. The author is very imaginative and has tremendously rich experiences and has integrated them in an excellent manner.

The publication of *Gifted Children in the Classroom* (1965c) represents an attempt to put into an undergraduate education series an enlarged concept of giftedness and information about the creative development and teaching of gifted children. Another achievement has been the publication of alternate forms of the basic batteries of creative thinking tests that I have been developing. The verbal forms are called *Thinking Creatively with Words* and the figural forms, *Thinking Creatively with Pictures.* The *Technical-Norms Manual* is lagging but it should be available shortly (Torrance, 1966a).

C: Before you go on, I would like to intrude just a moment. As I reported earlier, most of the college professors who conduct summer institutes for elementary and secondary teachers know practically nothing about this whole area of creativity. We have been conducting a little study recently and found this to be a fact. Yet when you assemble these materials (and we get some of your materials there), they are intensely interested in them. There is a growing interest and I think we are going to have to work out ways of reaching these summer institutes to be sure that the materials are available because of this demand. This summer there will be about 600 of these institutes reaching some 25,000 elementary and secondary teachers. These institutes are supposed to be innovative, by and large. In effect, we can help them be innovative.

S: Yes, I think there are a great many important and encouraging things happening in education. Such a scheme as the one just proposed might provide an excellent opportunity to conduct some of the research on research that was discussed earlier. We need to know more about the process by which new ideas are disseminated and accepted. I have been intrigued by the possibility of making one small analysis of the problem as it is reflected in the five or six thousand letters I have been receiving each year about my research. Thus far, I have been unable to do anything on this.

The following is a brief listing of still unfinished projects:

1. Cross-Cultural Studies of Creative Development.
2. Longitudinal Studies of Creative Development.
3. Seven-Year Follow-Up Studies of High School Seniors and Elementary Education Majors.
4. Characteristics and Problems of Originators and Elaborators.
5. Cross-Cultural Studies of "What Is an Ideal Child?"
6. Cross-Cultural Studies of Concepts of Divergency.
7. Creative Functioning of Disadvantaged Children.
8. Teaching Children How to Do Research.

I have placed at the head of my list our cross-cultural studies of creative development, now already five years overdue. Our experience here exemplifies the problem of becoming bogged down by getting into a fascinating new and productive problem area with an inadequate budget to carry out the work undertaken. Since I had never done any research in this area, I grossly underestimated the amount of time and money required. Our funds were exhausted long ago but much work remains to be done.

The longitudinal studies are actually a part of the same project as the cross-cultural ones. They also turned out to be more time-consuming, complex, and expensive than anticipated.

Right now, we are in the midst of our first long-range studies of predictive validity. We are now obtaining follow-up data seven years after the administration of the tests of creative thinking abilities to University High School seniors and University of Minnesota juniors in elementary education.

In another study, we are investigating differences in the life experiences, personalities, and other characteristics of originators and elaborators.

I am also anxious to complete our cross-cultural studies of the ideal child and cross-cultural studies of concepts of divergency. In each of these studies we have data from a dozen or so different cultures and subcultures. We are using both the imaginative stories of children and the children's literature of the culture to study concepts of divergency.

During the past year, I became involved in some studies involving the creative functioning of disadvantaged children. As a result, I have become greatly concerned about the need to understand the creative development and functioning of disadvantaged children and to identify high levels of creative talent among them.

Of all of my unfinished projects, I am most enthusiastic about a book for children on how to do research. This has grown out of my developmental work during the past six years in teaching sixth-grade pupils some of the concepts and skills of doing educational research.

C: What do you do with your spare time?
S: I dream.

GROUP DYNAMIC FACTORS IN CREATIVITY

Now I shall try to give a glimpse of some of the new directions I have taken since leaving the University of Minnesota Bureau of Educational Research two years ago. In my course in group dynamics, we devote a two-hour laboratory period each week to conducting small group experiments to study group dynamic factors affecting creative behavior. After the first quarter the course was offered, we have had the maximum enrollment of 55 each quarter. Thus, for any session, we can usually count upon having about 10 five-person groups, 12 or 13 four-person groups, 16 or 17 three-person groups, or 25 to 27 two-person groups.

A typical pattern has been to present a set of what I call "Great Ideas in Group Dynamics" in a lecture-discussion session and then to extend or challenge one of these ideas through an experimental test at the next session. In all of these experiment, we have been trying to get at what forces in groups enable a person to behave more creatively or less creatively than he ordinarily would. Listed below are the sets of "great ideas" in group dynamics chosen for this purpose:
1.   Field Theory of Groups.
2.   T Group Theory.
3.   Psychoanalytic Theory of Groups.
4.   Sociodrama as a Group Creative Problem-Solving Process.
5.   Group Creative Problem-Solving Process (Parnes and Osborne).
6.   Synectics Group Theory.
Some of our little experiments may appear to be rather obvious and commonplace but each has been designed to fill some gap in the experimental literature on the creative functioning of groups. I shall try to summarize some of them without giving the details concerning the underlying theory, procedures, instruments, statistical analyses, and the like.

In one of the experiments illustrating field theory, we manipulated the acquaintance variable. A random half of the entire group were given an opportunity to become acquainted with one another. The others were given no opportunity to become acquainted with one another. In groups of five, both the acquainted and unacquainted subjects were given a group creative thinking task. First, they responded as individuals to *Sounds and Images* (Cunnington and Torrance, 1965b), a recorded device for obtaining images in response to sound effects of varying complexity and strangeness. Then the five-person groups were asked to function as groups and to produce a set of the most original images they could from their stockpile of individual responses, by building onto their individual responses or by producing completely new images. We were able to determine whether or not they ended up with a collection of responses produced

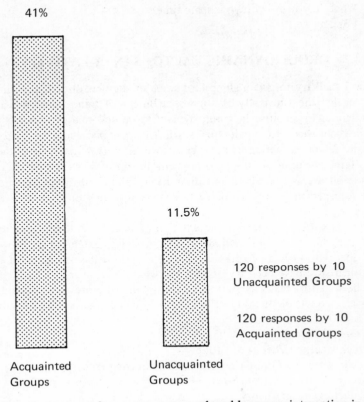

Fig. 1. Percentage of new responses produced by group interaction in Acquainted and Unacquainted Groups.

by individual group members or produced new responses out of their group interaction. The combined results for two classes are shown in Figure 1.

From the data presented in Figure 1, it will be noted that 41 percent of the responses submitted by the acquainted groups arose from group interaction compared with 11.5 percent for the unacquainted groups. This difference is statistically significant at the .01 level of confidence.

Since many of the studies involve the manipulation of personality variables in group composition, I feel the need for giving some information concerning the personalities of the participants and of the changes that occurred during the process of participating in this educational experience. The personality data used for purposes of manipulation included the *Runner Studies of Attitude Patterns* (Runner and Runner, 1965). Near the beginning of the course, the predictions made on the basis of the scores derived from this instrument seemed to be

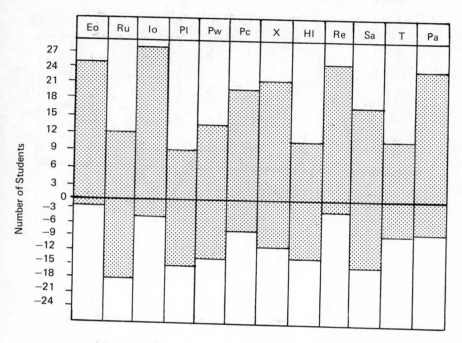

Eo: Experimental Orientation.
Io: Intuitive Orientation.
Ru: Emphasis on Rules and Tradition.
Pl: Practical Planfulness.
Pw: Desire for Power and Authority.
Pc: Passive Compliance.

X: Extroversiveness
HI: Hostility and Blamefulness.
Re: Resistance to Social Pressure.
Sa: Social Anxiety.
T: Pleasure in Tool-Implemented Hand Skills.
Pa: Performance Anxiety.

Fig. 2. **Number of students showing increases or decreases of two or more points on each of the Runner Scales during ten-week period of Group Dynamics Course.**

surprisingly accurate. As the course approached a conclusion, however, the accuracy of my predictions diminished. We began wondering if one reason for this might be that the subjects had changed in the process. Thus the *Runner Studies of Attitude Patterns* was readministered after about ten weeks. Figure 2 depicts the upward and downward movement on the Runner scales. The bars above the zero line indicate the number whose scores on the particular scale rose two or more points and the bar below the line represents the number whose scores fell two or more points. The total number of subjects supplying complete data was 45.

From Figure 2, it will be noted that there was a big movement upward on experimental orientation, downward movement on rules orientation, upward movement on intuitive orientation, downward trend on need for structure, and a big movement upward in resistance to social pressure.

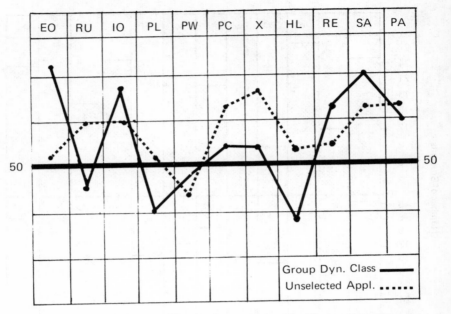

EO	RU	IO	PL	PW	PC	X	HL	RE	SA	PA

50

50

Group Dyn. Class ▬▬▬
Unselected Appl. ▪▪▪▪▪▪

Fig. 3. Mean runner profiles of Group Dynamics Class and unselected sample of summer job applicants of college age.

These changes take on greater significance when it is recognized that the class as a whole tended initially to be high on experimental orientation, intuitive orientation, and resistance to social pressure and low on rules orientation and need for structure. Figure 3 compares the mean Runner profile of the group dynamics class with an unselected group of unselected job applicants of college age.

The orientation of both the Group Dynamics students and the directions of their measured changes in orientation are in line with the patterns we are obtaining for creative individuals as identified by the Torrance Tests of Creative Thinking. Figure 4 presents the mean Runner profiles of highly creative high school senior boys and girls, representing the upper 20 percent of the senior class of a metropolitan high school.

In teaching one class, I became interested in understanding the process by which students in this kind of educational environment develop new ideas. In one experiment, we conducted an investigation which involved considerable interaction in three-person groups. The experiment was conducted on Thursday morning and the next session was held on Tuesday morning. At the beginning of the Tuesday session, I administered a brief questionnaire in which students were asked to list the new insights that had occurred to them about group behavior

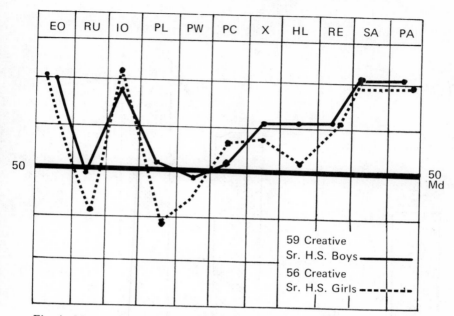

Fig. 4. Mean runner profiles of 59 senior high school boys and 56 senior high school girls scoring in upper 20 percent on *Torrance Tests of Creative Thinking.*

and creative functioning as a result of the previous session. They were then asked to describe how these ideas occurred to them. The results of the analysis of these data are summarized in Figure 5.

From these data, it will be noted that 32 percent of them said that a new idea was set in motion by the session itself. Four percent reported that a new idea occurred during the feedback conducted at the end of the small group session. Forty-four percent reported that their ideas "popped" soon after the end of the session. In many cases, it occurred in extended group discussions in the cafeteria near the building where the class met. Fifty-six percent of them reported having developed a new insight later in the day or at some other time prior to the Tuesday meeting of the class. In 14 percent of the cases, an idea occurred only when I confronted them with the questionnaire. Fifty-four percent reported that their new ideas occurred through some kind of group interaction.

Several of our studies have involved experimentation with different kinds of group composition. One such set of data was developed from experiences in using a modified group creative problem-solving process (Osborne, 1963; Parnes, 1967). The group experience was preceded by three hours of training in the creative problem-solving process. The group experience itself extended over two sessions of two hours each. Five-person groups were formed on the basis of the

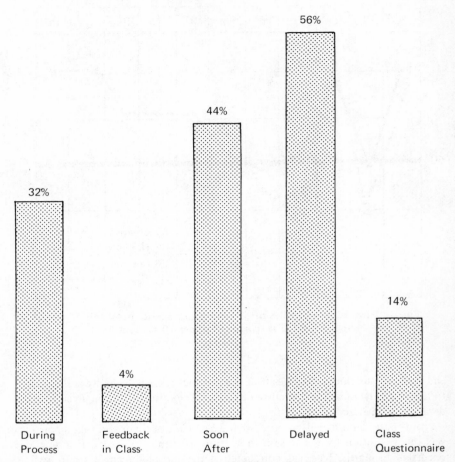

Fig. 5. When new ideas emerge: Summary of reports of 50 students
describing when new ideas concerning group factors affecting
creativity occurred following a group experiment.

freedom orientation and control orientation as derived from scores on the
Runner instrument (Runner and Runner, 1965). In the group experience, all
stages of the creative problem-solving process were followed. Following the
group experience, each student was required to prepare a detailed description
and analysis of their group's experience. One analysis of the resulting data was
concerned with expressions of need for more structure from the instructor. The
results of this analysis are shown in Figure 6 for each of the 10 groups, ranging
from high freedom orientation to high control orientation. It will be noted that
the groups composed of freedom-oriented individuals expressed little need for

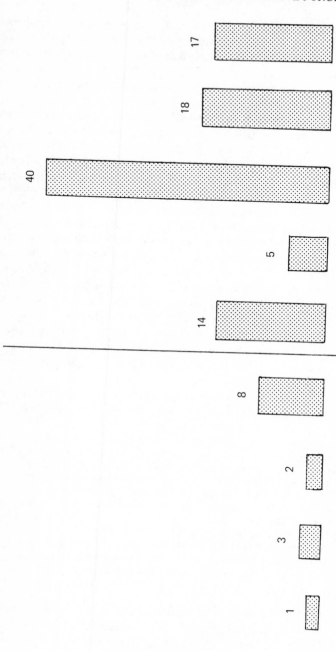

Fig. 6. Number of expressions of need for more structure by instructor in high freedom-oriented groups and high control-oriented groups.

additional structure or clarification from the instructor. Considerable expression of such needs came from the more control-oriented groups. Twenty-six percent of the members of the five most freedom-oriented groups expressed some need for more structure, while 83 percent of those in the most control-oriented groups expressed such needs. This difference is statistically significant at less than the one percent level of confidence.

Several other experiments have also involved the freedom-control-orientation variable in group composition. One, of special interest, involved manipulation of the kind of feedback given following a practice session on a creative thinking task. In the lecture-discussion session, the class had examined Lewin's (1947) generalization concerning the necessity for evaluative feedback in improving group performance. Since there is evidence that evaluation may impede the flow of creative thinking, this generalization was challenged, insofar as it applies to the stockpiling of original ideas. Since there is also evidence that some people require more structure than others in order to think creatively, we also wondered if the generalization would apply to groups composed of freedom-oriented persons.

The experiment was performed first in a class with 10 five-person groups and then replicated in a class with 11 five-person groups. The division of the classes into five-person groups was again based on the freedom-orientation and control-orientation scores derived from the *Runner Studies of Attitude Patterns* (Runner and Runner, 1965). The five persons having the highest freedom-orientation were placed in Group A; the five persons having the next highest scores were placed in Group B, and so on.

The creative task chosen for this laboratory experience was the Dot-Squares Test, adapted from Simpson's (1922) measure of Creative Imagination. The instructions for this task are as follows:

> Upon this and the following sheets of paper there are groups of dots in the form of squares. When I say 'Go' you are to add two more dots to the four that are in the printed square, and see how many different drawings of objects, or of designs, you can make in ten minutes. You may place the two extra dots anywhere you like. You must use every one of the six dots. You can make as many straight or crooked lines as you like. Do not be too careful with your drawings. The objects must be intelligible and the designs or patterns must use the two 'extra dots' in important places in them. We know that some of you can draw better than others. That makes no difference. Originality counts for most. Strive to make as many different things as possible. You are searching for 'new' ideas. Try to make every one of the drawings different.

The task was administered first as an individual one for warm-up purposes, then as a group task when the ten groups had been assembled, and finally as a group task following the differential experimental manipulation. In both group administrations, instructions were given to avoid repeating responses that had been given by individual group members and that no credit would be given for duplications of response within a group. Following the first group performance of 15 minutes, a 20-minute period was allowed for the experimental manipulations. In Class I, Groups A, C, E, G, and I were assigned to the Evaluative Feedback Condition and Groups B, D, F, H, and J were assigned to the Creative Feedback Condition. In Class II, the assignment of the first ten groups was reversed and the eleventh group was assigned to the Evaluative Feedback Condition.

In the Evaluative Feedback training session, groups were instructed to evaluate their practice performance and plan how to improve their performance as a group in the test task that was to follow. To give them some criteria for their evaluations, the visual aids shown in Figures 7 and 8 were shown as samples of scored responses. Groups in the Creative Feedback Condition were instructed to look at one another's responses, noting them so that they could avoid duplicating them and could hitchhike upon them for more original responses. They were further instructed to avoid evaluating one another's responses of the performance of the group as a group, but to continue the freewheeling, hitchhiking, idea production that they had started. In all cases, the test period was 15 minutes. All responses were evaluated for originality according to a scoring guide (Torrance, 1965d).

The measure derived from the final group session was improvement in originality score (posttest score minus pretest score). Using the results obtained from all 21 groups, the findings shown in Figure 9 were obtained. There was a tendency for the freedom-oriented groups to obtain higher scores than the control-oriented groups on both the pre- and posttest but, as Figure 9 shows the control-oriented groups made greater gains under Evaluative Feedback Conditions than did the freedom-oriented groups. Under Creative Feedback, the opposite results were obtained. The interaction effect is statistically significant at about the two percent level ($F = 8.22$). The results were essentially the same in both the original experiment and in the replication. Freedom-oriented groups appeared to profit most by Creative Feedback and control-oriented groups appeared to profit most from Evaluative Feedback. Thus the orientations of group members should probably be considered in determining what kind of feedback is likely to result in improved performance.

C: In your group dynamics experiment, did you develop ways of scoring individuals in respect to their occupations?

S: Certainly one's occupation influences the kinds of responses he will make on the task such as this, but it did not seem necessary to consider this factor in evaluating the outcome of this group dynamics experiment. All of the subjects were educators, nurses, public health workers, and the like.

From experiment to experiment, the design varied somewhat and in most of the other experiments the nature of the feedback was not varied. For example, one of the others that I had planned to discuss involved triads. We were interested in studying the effects of coalitions in three-person groups on both

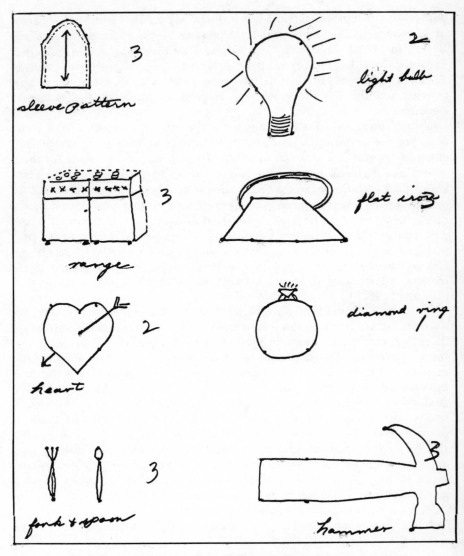

Fig. 7. Sample scored record used in evaluative feedback condition.

creative and evaluative thinking. In this case, the hypotheses being investigated were derived from psychoanalytic theory of groups. In preparation for this experiment, subjects were asked to write in advance imaginative stories about three interacting persons, animals, objects, or the like. Groups were assembled in various sex combinations and varying combinations of creative orientation, as

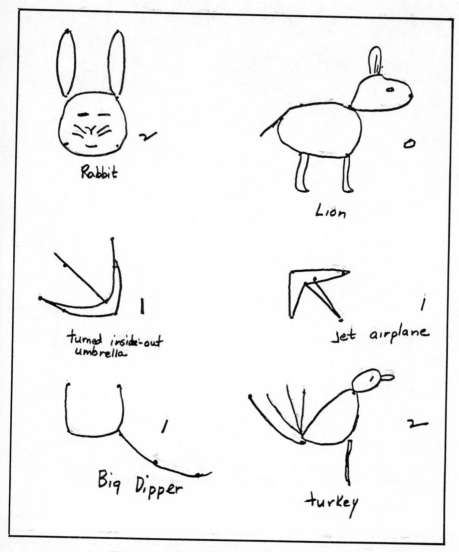

Rabbit

Lion

turned inside-out
umbrella

Jet airplane

Big Dipper

turkey

Fig. 8. Second scored record used in sample evaluative feedback
condition.

assessed by my "What Kind of a Person Are You?" instrument (Torrance,
1966b).

In the triads, the subjects read and discussed the imaginative stories prepared
in advance by each group member. After a member had read his story, the other
two members attempted to interpret the story in terms of what it tells about the

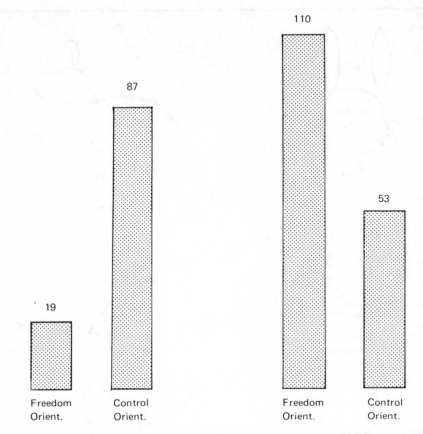

Fig. 9. Mean gains on originality scores of freedom- and control-
oriented groups under evaluative and creative feedback conditions.

writer's orientation to group functioning. Subjects were asked to rate the
interestingness and originality of each member's story, the accuracy of each
member's interpretations of his story, and his own accuracy in interpreting the
stories offered by the other two group members.

In terms of the coalition problem, it was found that there is a tendency for the
two less creative group members to form a coalition against the most creative
member. A considerable amount of interesting data regarding confidence in the
value of one's own ideas also emerged in these experiments conducted in two
classes with an N of 90. As might be expected, the most creative members

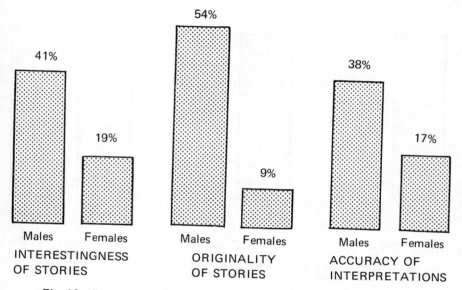

Fig. 10. Comparison of males and females on percentages rating own stories as most interesting and as most original and own interpretations most accurate in triads.

expressed greater confidence in the originality and interestingness of their stories. The sex differences in confidence in one's own ideas were also interesting. As shown in Figure 10, the men expressed greater confidence in the interest and originality of their stories and of the accuracy of their interpretations of the stories of other group members. All differences are statistically significant at the .05 level or better.

Both the men and women evaluated the interpretations of the men as being more accurate than those of the women. The trends regarding the hedonic ratings of the experience, derived from a semantic differential, are also of interest. These results are shown in Figure 11. It will be noted that more creative women enjoyed the experience more than the more creative men, but the less creative men, tended to enjoy it more than the less creative women.

Time does not permit the presentation of results from any of the other studies. In summary, it seems clear that the composition of groups, the kinds of feedback they are given, the procedures they use, and the like are powerful enough to make differences in the creative functioning of the group, as a group and as individual members of groups.

C: How did you get the high and low creatives? Was it your test of creative thinking?

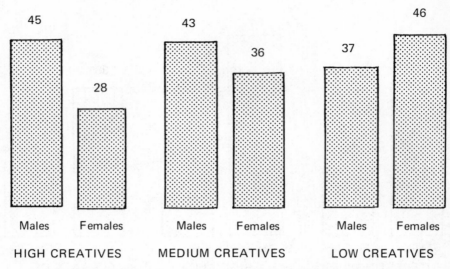

NOTE: On the hedonic ratings, a low score indicates a high degree of pleasure and high scores indicate low degree of pleasure. Total number of subjects is 90.

Fig. 11. Mean hedonic ratings of males and females of triad experience according to top, middle, and low one-thirds.

S: No, I used a personality type instrument I developed, called "What Kind of Person Are You?" (Torrance, 1966b). It makes use of a forced-choice technique, composed largely of the same adjectives used in the Ideal Child Checklist. The subject has to make choices of self-descriptive words, such as "liking to work in groups" versus "liking to work alone" or "curious" versus "energetic." Scores on this instrument correlated .73 with the originality scores derived from the scoring of the imaginative stories, according to a scoring guide developed some years ago (Torrance, 1965a). It correlated .75 with originality scores on the *Sounds and Images* device (Cunnington and Torrance, 1965b).

CHAPTER 7

Assessing the Relationships Between the Industrial Climate and the Creative Process

J. H. McPherson*

THE "CREATIVITY DOMAIN" includes several concerns that must be considered simultaneously if the persons in an industry choose to increase their creativity. Some of these major concerns are:
1. The selection of persons with high creativity potential.
2. The teaching of the many variations of the creative process.
3. The provision of an "industrial climate" that enhances the creative process.

This particular chapter presents a review of several efforts to assess and improve industrial climate.

THE SETTING

The Dow Chemical Company (annual sales of over a billion dollars) with more than 35,000 employees is world-wide in its efforts. The headquarters of the corporation are located in Midland, Michigan. At their headquarters there is an active Corporate Education Department and there are active consulting and staff psychologists. Usually the psychologists are concerned with individuals and the training departments with groups. The overlap in their work is obvious and many of the goals sought require a collaborative effort. The data reported here represent a result of this collaboration.

The training departments of the Dow Chemical Company have been offering managers an opportunity to participate in a training experience called "Management Training II" or "sensitivity training." This training is similar to the kind of training sponsored by the National Training Laboratories (NTL). Each training group is composed of approximately fourteen managers from different parts of the organization. Approximately two-thirds of the one week's training time is spent in unstructured group situations and one-third of the time in discussing theories of group growth and development, leadership styles, membership roles, and similar topics. Approximately 100 such groups have experienced this training at Dow. There are 19 Dow "trainers" trained to work with these groups. It has been common practice for each manager, prior to entering this training, to

---

*J. H. McPherson is Senior Behavioral Scientist, Stanford Research Institute,.Menlo Park. He was formerly Manager, Personnel Research & Development at Dow Chemical Corporation, Michigan.

ask his subordinates to complete an Adjective Check List describing the "Personal Characteristics" of the manager, and another instrument, "My Work Group," describing the group that the manager supervises. In some instances, the members of the training group will *also* describe each member using the Personal Characteristics instrument. In many instances, the manager has asked his subordinates to repeat the description of him and the group using the same devices six months after the manager has had the MS II (sensitivity) training experience in order to assess the changes that have occurred.

The same instruments—the Personal Characteristics instrument and the My Work Group description have been used in many other situations. Research group leaders (from various research laboratories) have participated in a three-phase program. The first step of this program is the self-appraisal step which involves the collection of Personal Characteristics data about self from subordinates, a variety of psychological tests, and integrating these data with the help of a staff psychologist. The second step in the group leader program is an appraisal of each subordinate using a special appraisal device, the history of the subordinate's training and performance, and the data from psychological tests. The third phase of the group leader program is the collection of data from the subordinates about the nature of their work group using the My Work Group instrument. Many managers of top rank in the corporation have been using the "self-appraisal" step of this program. The two basic instruments have been modified for use in the many other studies of groups in the Dow Chemical Company.

Although the Personal Characteristics instrument was developed by L. C. Repucci and the My Work Group instrument was designed by the author of this chapter, F. C. Taylor has been the person who has developed the program for processing the data in Dow's Computations Research Laboratory, collecting the normative data, studying the internal relationships between the items, and assessing the pre- and posttraining data.

THE RESULTS

The results are presented according to the following classifications:
1. The "normative" data using the two basic instruments.
2. The data differences between the four functions (Research, Development, Marketing, and Production) that are classic to industry.
3. The measurement of "change" using these instruments and the use of the results.

The Normative Data

Table I provides the normative data (before training) in the Adjective Check List for 615 trainees (Dow managers from all over the corporation and from all

TABLE I

Personal Characteristics of MS II Trainees
as Seen by Themselves and Their Work Group Members*

	Before Training during 1963, 1964, and 1965		
	Approximately 615 Trainees—3680 Total Observations		
(9)	Mean	s.d.	(1)
1. Responsible	7.70	1.16	Undependable
2. Intelligent	7.60	1.12	Unintelligent
3. Cooperative	7.50	1.18	Uncooperative
4. Keep trying	7.48	1.39	Quit easily
5. Friendly	7.45	1.09	Unfriendly
6. Energetic	7.36	1.38	Tired
7. Mature	7.20	1.45	Immature
8. Efficient	7.18	1.32	Inefficient
9. Confident	7.15	1.53	Unsure
10. Careful	7.10	1.36	Careless
11. Practical	7.10	1.42	Impractical
12. Cheerful	7.02	1.34	Gloomy
13. Grateful	7.00	1.36	Ungrateful
14. Thoughtful	6.92	1.49	Thoughtless
15. Frank	6.74	1.71	Secretive
16. Calm	6.62	1.70	Upset
17. Bold	6.35	1.56	Timid
18. Easygoing	6.10	1.74	Quick-tempered
19. Modest	6.00	1.78	Boastful
20. Patient	5.90	2.10	Impatient
Average	6.97	1.46	

*Tables I-IV are from Taylor, F. C. Normative data for personal characteristics of supervisors and work group descriptions for Dow Midland locations January 20, 1966.

functions) who attended Management Skills II (sensitivity training) during 1963, 1964, and 1965. These data were provided by 3680 subordinates to the 615 managers.

Table II provides the normative data using the Work Group Appraisal instrument for 600 trainees (managers) attending MS II during 1963, 1964, 1965, gathered from 3300 subordinates.

These two tables are samples of the normative data being gathered. Such data have been gathered for a variety of subgroups in the corporation. In many

TABLE II

Work Group Descriptions for MS II Trainees
as Seen by Themselves and Their Work Group Members

Before Training during 1963, 1964, and 1965
Approximately 600 6-Man Work Groups—3300 Observations

		Mean	s.d.
1.	Have a lot of pride in their achievements	7.81	1.49
2.	Extend themselves to meet the goals of the group	7.18	1.56
3.	Set high standards for their work	7.18	1.36
4.	Are open in making suggestions to the leaders	7.08	1.71
5.	Group achieves a high level of work output	7.08	1.44
6.	Want to find out what is going on at other places	7.06	1.44
7.	Help each other out with daily work	7.04	1.47
8.	Loyal to the leaders	7.02	1.67
9.	Like the challenge of different jobs	7.02	1.48
10.	Talk freely with one another about their work	7.02	1.66
11.	Loyal to each other	6.98	1.39
12.	Will fight for what they want to do	6.92	1.35
13.	See how their efforts "fit in" with company goals	6.90	1.64
14.	Accept differences of opinion and work through them	6.85	1.41
15.	Confident of each other	6.83	1.48
16.	Like to tackle difficult jobs	6.80	1.70
17.	Feel their work will be used by the company	6.80	1.70
18.	Feel they know how to evaluate their work	6.78	1.55
19.	See their work as exciting and rewarding	6.73	1.56
20.	Members listen to one another	6.45	1.60
21.	The group believes they have a good future	6.40	1.94
22.	Are able to receive stimulation from each other	6.40	1.64
23.	Help each other develop	6.01	1.84
24.	Like to socialize with each other	5.20	2.00
25.	Too many (9)—Too few (1) idea men	4.71	1.34
	Average	6.74	1.57

instances, additional items have been included to meet the demands of certain circumstances.

Table III and Table IV present a comparison of the manager's opinion of himself and his group with his subordinates' opinion of him and their group.

TABLE III

Difference in Perception of MS II Trainees by Themselves and by Their Work Group Members

May 1965 through December 1965—185 Work Groups

		Trainee	Member	Difference	
1.	Frank	7.00	6.77	+0.23	Secretive
2.	Practical	7.38	7.19	+0.19	Impractical
3.	Grateful	7.23	7.09	+0.14	Ungrateful
4.	Keep trying	7.54	7.52	+0.02	Quit easily
5.	Responsible	7.76	7.81	-0.05	Undependable
6.	Mature	7.19	7.30	-0.11	Immature
7.	Thoughtful	6.86	6.99	-0.13	Thoughtless
8.	Easygoing	6.02	6.18	-0.16	Quick-tempered
9.	Cooperative	7.45	7.64	-0.19	Uncooperative
10.	Calm	6.54	6.74	-0.20	Upset
11.	Cheerful	6.90	7.12	-0.22	Gloomy
12.	Confident	6.96	7.21	-0.25	Unsure
13.	Bold	6.11	6.36	-0.25	Timid
14.	Modest	5.83	6.10	-0.27	Boastful
15.	Energetic	7.20	7.49	-0.29	Tired
16.	Careful	6.85	7.16	-0.31	Careless
17.	Friendly	7.22	7.63	-0.41	Unfriendly
18.	Efficient	6.84	7.33	-0.49	Inefficient
19.	Patient	5.37	6.04	-0.67	Impatient
20.	Intelligent	7.03	7.75	-0.72	Unintelligent
	Average	6.86	7.07	-0.21	

Taylor has also done some factor analytic studies of these two instruments. At the "work group level," it appears that three factors seem to account for most of the variance. We have chosen to call the first factor the "vigor" variable, the second factor the "tribal loyalty" variable, and the third one the "faith" variable.

The use of these normative data indicate that:

1. A number of the departmental groups are significantly different from the mean for all groups to permit meaningful conversations as a prelude to change.

TABLE IV

Difference in Perception of the Work Group by MS II Trainees and by the Work Group Members

	May 1965 through December 1965—185 Work Groups	Trainee	Member	Differences
1.	The group believes they have a good future	6.93	6.37	+0.56
2.	Talk freely with one another about their work	7.44	6.92	+0.52
3.	Feel their work will be used by the Company	7.21	6.77	+0.44
4.	Loyal to the leaders	7.30	6.88	+0.42
5.	See how their efforts fit in with company goals	7.23	6.89	+0.34
6.	Are open in making suggestions to the leaders	7.28	6.96	+0.32
7.	See their work as exciting and rewarding	7.08	6.78	+0.30
8.	Extend themselves to meet the goals of the group	7.40	7.11	+0.29
9.	Help each other out with daily work	7.28	7.01	+0.27
10.	Have a lot of pride in their achievements	7.41	7.15	+0.26
11.	Confident of each other	7.03	6.82	+0.21
12.	Help each other develop	6.21	6.01	+0.20
13.	Group achieves a high level of work output	7.20	7.01	+0.19
14.	Loyal to each other	7.22	7.04	+0.18
15.	Accept differences of opinion and work through them	7.01	6.88	+0.13
16.	Like to socialize with each other	5.44	5.33	+0.11
17.	Like to tackle difficult jobs	6.91	6.83	+0.08
18.	Like the challenge of different jobs	7.08	7.05	+0.03
19.	Want to find out what is going on at other places	7.15	7.12	+0.03
20.	Too many (9)—Too few (1) idea men	4.83	4.80	+0.03
21.	Will fight for what they want to do	7.03	7.05	-0.02
22.	Are able to receive stimulation from each other	6.48	6.50	-0.02
23.	Members listen to one another	6.38	6.46	-0.08
24.	Feel they know how to evaluate their work	6.65	6.73	-0.08
25.	Set high standards for their work	7.10	7.20	-0.10
	Average	6.89	6.71	+0.18

2. The group descriptions provided by these instruments seem to have validity when compared with the subjective observations of these groups by its members and others.

Some of the next steps we are taking:

1. The development of samples that will permit greater generalization about the corporation.

TABLE V*

Frequency of Industrial Functional Data

	F Manager Data	F Subordinate Data
Production	32	184
Research	43	239
Development	13	81
Marketing	16	95

*Taylor, F. C., Personal and group self-descriptions of four functions: Research, production, development and sales. Dow Psychology Department, Midland, Michigan, May, 1965.

2. Assessing the relationships between responses to these two instruments and the composition of the groups according to:
   a. rated performance of the members,
   b. the distribution of certain personality orientations in the group, and external measures of the group's effectiveness.
3. Additional research is required to understand:
   a. the range of changes for each of the variables from the two instruments over time,
   b. how these changes are related to significant small group changes and organizational changes.
4. Our factor analytic research on these variables has just begun and will continue.

The Measurement of Functional Differences

A person or a group's concept of their "domain," "territory," or "field of specialization" often prevents an idea from someone outside this domain from having an adequate hearing. The literature about the creative process indicates that it is most logical that the best ideas, the ones that will bring about the greatest changes, *will come* from outside the domain. Because of these two conditions, it is necessary to attempt to understand the nature of the boundaries between disciplines and functions and consider ways and means to makes these boundaries more permeable.

Taylor reports the results of a study designed to assess the relationships among the four classical "functions" of industry: Research, Development, Production, and Marketing. Using the same two instruments, The Adjective Check List and The Work Group Appraisal Form, data were collected according to the four industrial functions.

TABLE VI*

Number of Items Significantly Different
Among Four Functions

	Research	Development	Production	Marketing	Total
Research	–	1	2	20	23
Development	1	–	6	9	16
Production	2	6	–	18	26
Marketing	20	9	18	–	47

*See footnote Table V.

Table VI indicates the number of items that were significantly different among the four functions.

For the purposes of this report, only the information about how marketing men see themselves when comapred with research will be given for illustrative purposes.

Compared with the research men, the marketing men
> are bolder,
> fight more for what they want to do,
> like to socialize with each other more,
> have more pride in their achievements,
> help each other develop more,
> are more confident,
> receive more stimulation from each other,
> listen to one another more,
> see their work as more exciting and rewarding,
> see the relationship more between their efforts and company goals,
> feel they know how to evaluate their work more,
> keep trying more,
> are more mature,
> believe they have a better future,
> extend themselves more,
> accept differences of opinion more,
> are more impatient,
> are more quick-tempered,
> are more efficient,
> are more cooperative.

The significance of such findings for the "fate of ideas" in a large corporation can be expressed in these terms. To get an idea through the various "screens" necessary to get the money, the power, the attention that is necessary, requires considerable "push." Research personnel are least inclined to "politic" on the behalf of their ideas. Many of them need to learn how to influence others. Sales personnel, on the other hand, who have ideas from the field, must learn that their very dominance and enthusiasm may drive the research man underground.

Many large corporations are pushing the decision-making processes down into teams made up of functional representatives. These teams must recognize the differences that stereotypically separate them if they are to do their best work.

The Measurement of "Change"

The measurement of the changes that occur as a result of a training program has always plagued the educator. The response of the personnel to the internal organizational changes and to the changes in direction of a large corporation are of vital interest to all the people who have a stake in the corporation. So far, the data about the changes in individuals' managers and the attitudes of their subordinates to them provide us with more than "testimonial" evidence about the values of "sensitivity" training.[1] The changes over time in normative data for a large sample of the corporation for a six-month period indicate the effect of corporate changes and provides significant clues for Corporate Industrial Relations to use as a basis for action steps.

When an organization expands in its activities, when significant internal organizational changes occur to accommodate this expansion, when managers are required to integrate substantially more data in their decision-making processes than before, the efforts of these events upon the creativity of their subordinates can be detrimental. It takes managerial time to evaluate ideas and to fight for them. Knowing how the work on ideas fits in with general corporate goals, knowing about the wisdom of corporate planning, knowing the nature of the "changed" corporation, are all factors affecting the individual's attitudes and output. The use of the two instruments on a wide enough sample over time to provide management with temperature-taking information is important to the maintenance and improvement of organizational health.[2]

At this point, the data gathered from the administration of the devices mentioned have been used primarily to assist managers to achieve insight into how they are perceived by their coworkers and how their perceived behavior relates to perceptions gained from the results of psychological tests and from appraisals by psychologists and psychiatrists.

[1] Taylor, F.C., Effects of M.S. II as Determined by Open-Ended Questionnaire to Trainees. The Dow Chemical Company, Midland, Michigan, December, 1965.

[2] Taylor, F.C., Change in Dow Environment as Measured by Information about M.S. II Trainees and Their Work Groups. The Dow Chemical Company, Midland, Michigan, January, 1966.

OTHER ISSUES IN THE MEASUREMENT OF THE CLIMATE

Other Instruments

Although the data have been provided from the use of the two instruments, The Adjective Check List and the Work Group Appraisal instrument, other instruments of a sentence completion type have been used. The time available for use in attending to new ideas is always in competition with the time required to attend to quality of and quantity of production, safety, and other significant managerial concerns. These sentence completion devices permitted an expression of attitude toward the adequacy and relative perceived importance of quality of work, quantity of work, safety, ideas for improvement, and other central issues.

Relationship Between Internal and External Assessments of the Climate

From time to time, behavioral research groups from outside the corporation are invited to assess the overall health of a certain segment of the corporation or look at specific issues. Learning how to integrate their findings with internal assessments is an important task. Learning how to manage the two-fold task of continuity and feedback to the people as these multiple measures are obtained is a constant task. At the moment, behavioral scientists from Harvard Business School, Case Western Reserve, and the Institute for Social Research in Ann Arbor are at work in different parts of the corporation.

The Search for New Variables

The use of the instruments described so far has resulted in progress, but the question "Are we sampling the most significant variables?" is always a plaguing one. One technique that can be used to obtain some answers to this question is to go out and live with involved groups. Recent experiences with Dow development groups who are struggling with how to be more "successful" has led to the underlining of certain important variables:

1. How to influence others:
    a. How to manage sufficient commitment to build up the force needed to influence.
    b. How to have the courage and faith required to influence.
    c. How to, once commitment and courage are present, influence the system.
2. How to deal with personal issues that reduce creative effort:
    a. How to have sufficient ideas to prevent the overprotection of a few.
    b. How to avoid describing self or permitting others to describe self in

narrow terms. (A technologist is not "just a pair of hands," a chemist is not "just a chemist." A technologist is not just a Ph.D. in waiting—he's supposed to be an influence now.)

c. How to avoid placing either exploratory research or applied research higher in the "pecking order" and how to manage the realization that creativity emerges from a synergistic relationship between the two.

d. How to deal with experience. Experience and time are not positively correlated. How can time/experience be integrated with depth experience?

e. How can the emotional and intellectual loneliness that derives from a high degree of specialization be reduced? How can complex issues be simplified so adequate social feedback can be achieved?

f. How can time, priority, and routine pressures be managed to contribute to the creative process?

g. How can the feeling (intuitions and enthusiasms) be expressed for the sake of one's own and other's ideas?

h. How to deal with the need to be a single hero or to find a single hero as it affects creativity.

3. How to be a partner to others.

a. How to understand enough of what he is doing to be a valid partner.

b. How to see mutuality of goals sufficient to make the partnership a valid one.

c. How to deal with the ambiguities of ownership of ideas that originate from vital interaction.

d. How to influence on behalf of the other person.

We are in the process of building from these concerns new variables for inclusion in our measuring devices.

4. The Detroit Edison data.

For some time, Paul Chapman, a change catalyst for the Detroit Edison Company in Detroit, has been gathering opinions from managers about the factors that block their creativity. Twenty blocks are given for the manager to use in his assessment. So far, Chapman has accumulated data from 721 managers from different levels within Detroit Edison and from other companies. The results of this data gathering indicate that of these twenty blocks the ones that receive a high level of significance are:

a. Judging too quickly.

b. Inability to sell ideas.

c. Tendency to get too involved in extra-job activities.

d. Failure to acquire sufficient information.

e. Desire to conform to an accepted pattern.

f. Fear of being too aggressive.

Chapman is working toward a systematic presentation of these results. These results underline again the need to point up the need for commitment to one's ideas, and the need to learn how to be more influential in the social systems if the best ideas are to thrive.

5. The relationship of individual variables and climate variables. We are continuing to find significant relationships between such individual variables as ego strength, confidence, dominance, independence, and success at the Dow Chemical Company and are simultaneously rediscovering the ambivalence that the social system maintains toward such people.

I predict that some of the most significant breakthroughs in the individual areas will arise from research on the relationship between certain physiological characteristics and individual behavior, on the one hand, and on the reciprocal social relationships between the strong and the weak in the social context.

As an example of the breakthroughs that can be expected in the physiological realm, a summary quote from Brooks and Mueller's article, "Serum Urate Concentrations Among University Professors" (1966), should suffice:

> The purpose of this study was to test the hypothesis that personal characteristics of drive, achievement, and leadership are positively associated with the level of uric acid in the serum. Among seven behavior scales which were developed, drive, achievement, and leadership correlated most highly with serum urate levels. The correlation coefficient between the total of all behavior scales and serum urate in 51 University of Michigan professors was $r = 0.66$, a very high order of relationship for such studies between behavior variables and physiological ones. The results of this study lend substantial support to the hypotheses that a tendency to gout is a tendency to the executive suite, and that serum uric acid is related to behavioral characteristics that lead to outstanding performance. There is now a need for pharmacological experiments to see if the concept of serum urate as an endogenous cortical stimulant can also be supported.

One summary statement: As we all work diligently to provide ourselves and others with the insights necessary to having and sponsoring good ideas, we must simultaneously attend to the nature of man as an individual organism and as a part of a complex social system.

CHAPTER 8

The Identification and Use of Creative Abilities in Scientific Organizations

Gerald Gordon*

IN THE EARLY stages of science, the lone scientist could and did make contributions of a highly creative nature. Like the artist, he relied on his own knowledge, skill, and a few simple tools. Today, however, scientific experimentation is highly complicated, involving such equipment as multimillion-dollar accelerators as well as highly trained technicians to run them. Not only has it become increasingly difficult for the scientist to work alone, but all available evidence indicates that it will become increasingly difficult for the lone scientist to make creative contributions to science. The individual artist, on the other hand, can still make an important contribution working alone using only very simple materials. To understand the difference between scientific creativity and artistic creativity, one need only examine the goals and methods of the two fields.

The goal of scientific work has been defined as increased systematic prediction or increased control of the universe. Using either definition, the scientist has an external framework upon which to judge whether or not a given scientific accomplishment aids in our understanding of the universe. The existence of external criteria has led to increasing and more precise knowledge about how the environment behaves. Each new understanding provides the groundwork for the next insight or leads to the abandonment of a current misconception.

This is in sharp contrast to what occurs in the arts. Because of the amorphous nature of artistic goals (inner truth, meaning, etc.), external criteria viable for all cultures and times have not and probably cannot be developed. The result is, for the most part, a cyclic and non-cumulative form of creativity. In art, both a sophisticated Parisian and an untutored African native can make socially valuable contributions. The cumulative characteristic of scientific creativity, on the other hand, makes a creative contribution from an African primitive all but impossible. Not only does it require a high degree of training to contribute to modern science but, increasingly, advances are dependent upon the cooperation of men possessing different types of training. Another characteristic which differentiates scientific creativity from artistic creativity is the reliance of the scientist on the inductive method. In essence, the inductive method is an extension of our five senses. For most of man's existence, his understanding of the

---

* Gerald Gordon is Professor of Industrial & Labor Relations and Sociology, Cornell University.

environment has been limited or distorted by his sensory organs. Where the artist, by reinterpretation, seeks to maximize sensuous experiences, the scientist, through artificial reconstruction and the use of instruments, seeks to overcome the limitations imposed by his senses. In the first stages of science, the extensions beyond our senses were simple and cheap. But, as these initial extensions were exploited, further extensions became increasingly complex and costly. In comparison to accelerators, radio telescopes, and computers, the tools of Galileo, Hershel, and Maxwell appear childishly simple. To use modern research tools effectively, organizations must be established and teams of researchers and technicians must be employed. Tools for extending our senses have become so complex and costly that, where once tools were purchased to enable men to work, men are now hired as adjuncts to machines—Argonne and Brookhaven being cases in point.

The accumulation of knowledge and the complexity of research tools used in any advanced science result in interpersonal rather than personal contributions. Science is a social product in which even the most individualistic of theorists is dependent upon a multitude of researchers to provide him with the data necessary to build a theory. This is not to deny that the breakthroughs which are essential to scientific advancement appear to be highly personal. Quite the contrary, we have been working on the assumption that the relating of apparently diverse pieces of data into a new conceptual product, in the final instance, is the result of individual processes. But these individual processes take place within and are directly affected by an organizational and social milieu. Within the context of modern science, we must distinguish between personal potential which we subsume under the term "creativity," and unique social contribution which we will refer to as "innovation." By our definition, creativity is a psychological input or potential and innovation is a social end-product or output. Despite widespread speculation, little of a factual nature is known about the relationship of the social milieu and creativity to scientific accomplishment. This chapter will report on our investigation of some aspects of these relationships.

The data being reported were obtained from studies of three groups of scientists: (1) researchers in a defense-oriented research and development firm, (2) chemists, and (3) medical sociologists. These studies resulted in a number of interrelated findings which, when viewed in juxtaposition, provide a framework for understanding some of the dynamics of scientific innovation.

For the purpose of measuring creativity, the Remote Associates Test (RAT), recently developed by Sarnoff Mednick, appeared promising. The subject is given a series of three words such as "cheese," "blood," and "water" and is asked to find a fourth word which is common to all three words. The correct answer in this case is "blue." The test was derived from Mednick's theory that creativity is:

> the forming of associative elements into new combinations which either meet specified requirements or are in some way useful. The more mutually remote the elements of the new combination, the more creative the process or solution. (p. 221)

Mednick cited several studies which indicate that the Remote Associates Test provides a valid measure of creative ability. The question remained, however, as to its accuracy in measuring scientific creativity. In an attempt to arrive at an answer, studies employing the Remote Associates Test were undertaken in both the research and development and chemical firms.

Working on the assumption that creative people made more responses to stimuli and that, in a competitive non-structured situation, their solutions would be superior to those of less creative people, we compared the Remote Associates Test scores with contract proposals written and research contracts won in an industrial research and development company. Half of the scientists in this firm had Remote Associates Test scores of 19 or more, out of 30. As can be seen from Figure 1, this group wrote about three times as many proposals as did the low Remote Associates Test scores (18 or less) and won almost 81 percent of all contracts. We controlled for age, seniority, times project engineer, and found little effect on the results.

In the chemical firm, we compared the Remote Associates Test to the Harris Simberg AC Test for Creative Ability and the Rokeach Dogmatism Scale. Both of these tests have been employed extensively to measure creativity. In the chemical company, an intraorganizational "disclosure" is the initial step in obtaining a patent. From it, the research division administrator decides whether or not to seek a patent. Patents are sought only when they are perceived to be of explicit value to the company. In a sense, disclosures are analogous to contract proposals and patents are analogous to contracts obtained. As can be seen from Figure 2, the Remote Associates Test was a much more accurate predictor than either the AC or Dogmatism test for both criteria. In terms of final criteria—patents obtained—the top Remote Associates Test scorers won 93 percent of the patents, whereas on the other two tests there was no appreciable difference in the number of patents obtained between high and low scores.

We also attempted to see if the Remote Associates Test would reflect job grade classification. "Job grade classification" indicates how the company classifies a scientist in comparison with other persons holding similar positions. Here again, the Remote Associates Test was a much more efficient predictor than the other tests, having a Kendell Q of .86. In sum, while the other two tests failed to predict, the Remote Associates Test proved to be a very effective predictor in two different companies and on three related but different sets of criteria. In one company, the top Remote Associates Test scorers were responsible for 81 percent of the research contracts obtained and, in the other, for 93 percent of the patents obtained. In both companies, the power of the tests increased as we moved from the preliminary stages (proposal or disclosure) to the final stages (contract or patent).

Concurrent with the validation studies, we engaged in a study of 245 projects dealing with the social aspects of disease. In the past, investigators measuring research performance have usually counted a scientist's patents or papers or have

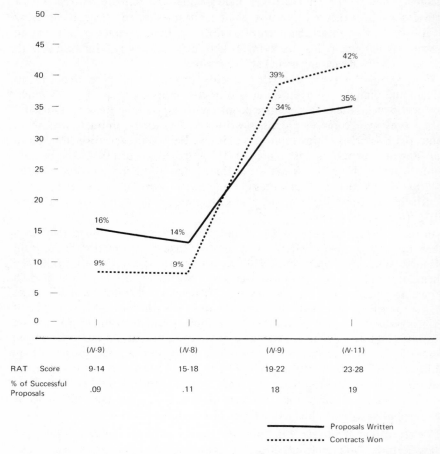

Fig. 1. RAT Score, authorship and success in writing contract proposals (R&D).

obtained evaluations of the scientist by his peers and superiors (Folger and Gordon, 1962). While both methods provide some indication of the *quantity* of a scientist's output, neither permits fine distinctions with respect to quality. In order to obtain qualitative assessments of the projects in our universe, we adopted a suggestion of the Criterion Committee of the 1955 Research Conference on the Identification of Creative Scientific Talent. A panel consisting of persons chosen as leaders in medical sociology by the members of the American Sociological Association was asked to evaluate standardized and anonymous summaries of the projects on the basis of the following definitions:

Innovation—the degree to which the research represents additions to our

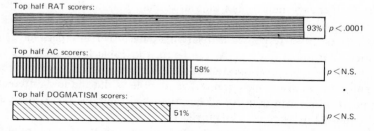

Fig. 2. Percent of disclosures, applications, and patents won by high RAT, AC, and Dogmatism Test Scores.

knowledge through new lines of research or the development of new theoretical statements or findings which were not explicit in the previous theory.

Productivity—the degree to which the research represents an addition to knowledge along established lines of research or an extension of previous theory.

Each evaluator was given 25 randomly selected and ordered summaries to evaluate, and the average number of panel members evaluating a project was 4.5.

According to these ratings, the projects were divided into fifths—quintile 5 indicating highest ratings.[1]

Employing these ratings as our dependent variable, we investigated the relationship of a variety of organizational and interpersonal factors to research accomplishment. Information on these variables was obtained by mail questionnaires sent to the project directors. Over 90 percent of these questionnaires were completed and returned. One of the variables we were particularly interested in was the quality of professional relationships within a project. Each project director was requested to list the professionals working with him. He was then asked to indicate on a 10-point scale (poor—1 to excellent—10) the nature of his professional relationship with each associate. Initially, our results showed little relationships between the quality of intragroup relationships and innovation. It was noticed, however, that some project directors confined their assessments to a narrow portion of the relationship scale, while other project directors had wide variance in their ratings. In other words, some project directors rated their relationships with associates all alike on the 10-point scales (e.g., 5,5,5,5 or 10,10,10,10). Other project directors utilized the total scale (e.g., one relationship was rated 2, another 10, another 5 and so on). When we controlled for this factor, our results were surprising. The scales were collapsed into three categories: "poor" (5 and below), "moderate" (6 to 9), and "excellent" (10) professional relationships. When all the responses of a project director fell into one of the above categories, he was considered a low differentiator. When his responses fell into more than one of the above categories, he was considered a high differentiator. As can be seen in Figure 3, at all times, projects led by high differentiators were much more innovative than projects led by low differentiators; at no point do the two lines of the figure intersect.

Analysis of these responses in relation to the other interpersonal questions confirmed our initial findings. As can be seen in Table I, for each of a series of responses to interpersonal questions, high differentiators had two to three times as many projects in the most innovative quintile as did the low differentiators. (Ten-point scales were used for all questions and the same breakpoints as those for the conflict measure were employed.)

Continuing this line of investigation we returned to the R&D firm and asked the *leaders* of the six research groups there to rate each member of their groups on creativity, productivity, and sociability. Again, 10-point scales were used. The difference between the high differentiating and the low differentiating group leaders in terms of the performance of their groups was impressive. As can be

---

[1]As the interpretation of the intervals on the rating scale was found to differ from evaluator to evaluator, the 25 ratings for each evaluator were converted to t scores, and the mean t score for each project was determined. According to the ranking of the mean t scores, the projects were divided into quintiles. Nine of the projects, which had no findings at the time of the evaluation, during the follow-up two years later were found to have publications then available. Feeling that the evaluations of the projects were, therefore, inaccurate, we removed them from all analysis using the dependent variable.

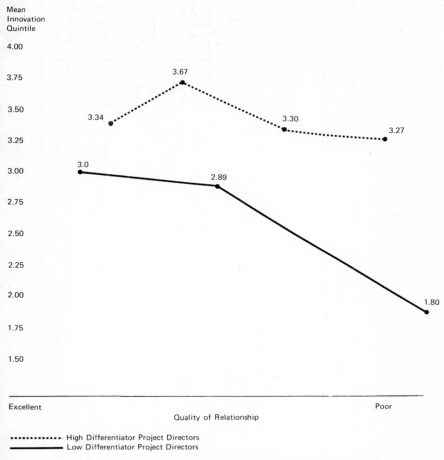

Mean
Innovation
Quintile

Fig. 3. Average innovation of high differentiator and low differentiator project
directors related to conflict (medical sociologists).

seen in Table II, there was a .66 correlation between the differentiation (variance) score of the group leader and the company rating of the group's significance to the company, and a .86 correlation between contracts won by a group and the leader's variance.[2] Analysis of the leaders' accuracy in assessing the creativity of the researchers under them revealed another major difference. The high differentiators were more accurate in their prediction of an individual's

---

[2]In this and later investigations, the actual variance in an individual's ratings of his fellow workers, rather than the 1-5, 6-9, and 10 breakpoints, was used to determine differentation.

TABLE I

Differentiation and Innovation (Medical Sociologists)

TYPE OF QUESTION	Total N	% studies in most innovative quintile Dif.	Non-Dif.	X^2 Test p
a. Relationship with professional associates (Personal)				
b. Relationship with professional associates (Professional)				
c. Relationship with professional associates (Communication)				
d. Relationship with professional associates (Understanding)				
e. Relationship with administrative superior (9 questions—number of different responses)				
f. Relationship with administrative superior (9 questions—variance)				
DIFFERENCE BETWEEN HIGH DIFFERENTIATORS AND LOW DIFFERENTIATORS				
g. Measure based on differences between "a" and "b" (For same staff members)	171	28.4	14.4	p .05
h. Combined measure of "e" and "f" (High on both vs. all others)	155	29.0	16.1	p .10
i. Combined measure of "a", "b", "c" and "d" (High on one or more vs. high on none)	128	27.7	3.7	p .01
j. Combined measure of "a" and "e" (High on both vs. all others)	92	40.6	11.7	p .005

TABLE II

Differentiation Correlations (Chemists)

PREDICTED DIFFERENTIATION (VARIANCE) RELATIONSHIPS

Variable	r	P
Group Leader's Average Variance* and Group's Significance to Company	+ .656	p .10
Group Leader's Average Variance and Group Contracts Won	+ .862	p .025
Group Leader's Average Variance and Group Contracts Won per Man	+ .544	p .20
Group Leader's Average Variance and Group Growth	+ .839	p .025
RAT Scores and Creativity Ratings	+ .772	p .05

TENDENCY TO MAXIMIZE OR MINIMIZE DIFFERENCES

Variable	r	P
Creativity Variance minus RAT Variance–Group Leader's Variance	+ .933	p .005
Creativity Variance minus RAT Variance–Correlation between RAT and Creativity	+ .554	p .20

DIFFERENTIATION (VARIANCE) CORRELATIONS PREDICTED NOT SIGNIFICANT

Variable	r	P
Group Growth–RAT Variance	+ .180	NS
Variance–Average RAT Score	- .180	NS
Variance–RAT Variance	- .329	NS
Av. RAT Score–Contract Awards Per Man	- .394	NS
Av. RAT Score–Group Growth	+ .170	NS

*Average variance in his ratings of men in his group for creativity, productivity, and sociability.

creative ability than were the low differentiators (correlation of .77). Surprisingly, the lack of accuracy on the part of the low differentiating leaders was not random; the low differentiators tended with some consistency to rate non-creative researchers as highly creative and creative researchers as non-creative. In addition, differentiating group leaders perceived more variation in the ability of

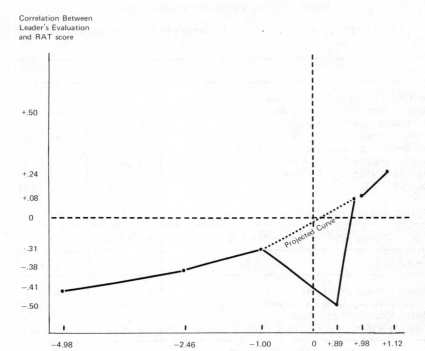

Correlation Between
Leader's Evaluation
and RAT score

Tendency to Exaggerate or Minimize Differences. (Variance in leader's ratings of group members' creativity minus variance among his group members' scores on the Remote Associates Test.)

Fig. 4. Group leader's tendency to exaggerate or minimize differences in creativity and the ability to predict creative ability among group members—(R&D).

the men in their groups than was indicated by the Remote Associates Test scores (comparison of intragroup Remote Associates Test score variance with group leader variance in rating the creativity of the members of the group) while the low differentiating leaders were suppressing or ignoring differences. They were tending to see the universe as more uniform than it really was (see Fig. 4).

This last finding provides a clue to understanding the relationship between measures of response variance and group innovation. Project directors who stress differences (high differentiators), we hypothesize, increase the availability of different types of data enabling themselves and the members of their group to make remote associations. On the other hand, low differentiators seem to suppress such differences which reduce the opportunity to make these associations. The tendency for scientists to perceptually reject differences and anomalies has been well-documented. Kuhn (1962), for example, reports numerous instances where perceptual biases on the part of the investigators led either to a misperception or neglect of findings contrary to their theoretical preconceptions. As one example, he notes that prior to Hershel's discovery of the planet Uranus in 1781:

> On at least seventeen different occasions between 1690 and 1781, a number of astronomers including several of Europe's most eminent observers, had seen a star in positions that we now suppose must have been occupied at the time by Uranus. One of the best observers in this group had actually seen the star on four successive nights in 1769 without noting the motion that could have suggested another identification. (p. 114)

It would, therefore, appear likely that the differences suppressed by low differentiators tend to be data which contradict their particular scientific preconceptions. This rejection inhibits speculative discussion, cerebral experimentation, etc. Under these conditions the research team concentrates instead on "state of the art" solutions rather than the more innovative solutions.

In terms of the criteria employed in our study, this research, characterized by tried and true approaches and by perceptual denial of anomalies and contradictions, would be defined as productive—*the extension of knowledge via traditional theory and methodology.* Since we had obtained separate assessments of productivity and innovation for the bio-social research projects, we were able to test this hypothesis.

We hypothesized that projects led by low differentiators would be rated higher on productivity than innovation, while projects led by high differentiators would be rated higher on innovation than productivity. In order to minimize the possibility that minor differences between productivity and innovation would affect the results, quintile position rather than the actual rating scores was used in the analysis. Ratings of productivity and innovation were not mutually exclusive and it was possible for the ratings on productivity and innovation to fall in the same quintile. In this case, we defined a project as being equally productive and innovative. The projects were therefore divided into three analytic groups:

1. Similar productivity and innovation quintile.
2. Productivity quintile rating higher than innovation quintile rating (productive projects).
3. Innovation rating quintile higher than productivity quintile rating (innovative projects).

As predicted, Figure 5 shows that groups led by low differentiators were twice as often more productive than innovative, and projects led by high differentiators were twice as often more innovative than productive. With these findings in mind, we asked *all* the researchers in the chemical firm to rate their fellow researchers on creativity, productivity, and sociability. Using the ratings as sensitivity measures, we found that, compared to low differentiators, high differentiators wrote 96 percent of the disclosures and obtained 90 percent of the patents. The correlation between disclosures and differentiation scores was .38, and for aggregated data along seven points, .91.

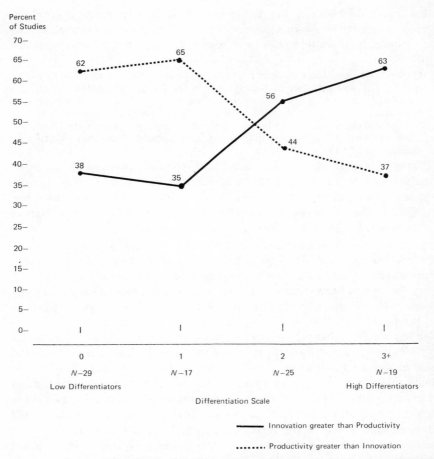

Fig. 5. The relationship between medical sociology project director's ability to perceive differences in his relationships with subordinates to innovation and productivity.

The similarity in the predictive abilities of the Remote Associates Test and the differentiation scales and their substantiation of one another during our study might lead to the conclusion that the two instruments are measuring the same factor. For a number of reasons, however, this conclusion appeared untenable. The relationship between the Remote Associates Test and accomplishment appeared non-continuous, while for the differentiation scales the relationship appeared continuous. The Remote Associates Test increased in power from preliminary stages (proposals and disclosures) to the final stages (contracts and patents), while the differentiation scales decreased in power from disclosures to patents (Table III). Finally, the correlation between the Remote Associates Test

TABLE III

Comparison of
Remote Associates Test and Differentiation (Chemists)

| | RAT $>$ 18 | Differentiation | | |
		$<3/>7$ $=$ $=$	$<3/>6$ $=$ $=$	$<4/>5$ $=$ $=$
% Disclosures 1961 - 1965	80*	92*	89*	74*
% Patent Applications 1961 - 1965	87*	79*	79*	72*
% Total Patents	93*	90*	84*	63

* significant at $p < .05$.

and the differentiation scales was low, .24. The evidence supports the contention that the tests, to some degree, are measuring two separate factors.

Before identifying what we believe these two factors to be, let us reexamine the composition of the Remote Associates Test. The subject, as mentioned earlier, is given three words, such as cheese, blood, and water, and is told to find a fourth word that is common to all three words. In essence, we feel that the Remote Associates Test is measuring the ability to solve a predetermined problem which requires an innovative solution. But the Remote Associates Test is not measuring the individual's ability to recognize anomalies and problems. Quite the contrary, the design of the test precludes such measurement. On the other hand, we feel the differentiation scales are tapping an ability to perceive anomalies or problems. It is our contention that both of these abilities play a role in the creative act.

From these assumptions we would expect that persons who were both able to recognize anomalies and to find solutions to them would be most innovative. Persons who lack the facility to locate problems would be innovative if external agents (e.g., administrators) presented them with anomalies requiring solutions. Persons who could recognize anomalies but not solve them would be much less innovative than either of the two preceding groups. Finally, persons who could neither recognize nor solve anomalies would be least innovative. To test these predictions we divided the chemical scientists into four analytic groups on the basis of the Remote Associates Test and the differentiation scales, and then we compared them in terms of disclosures and patents.

Analytic Groups
1.   Integrators—High Differentiators-High RAT.
2.   Problem-Solvers—Low Differentiators-High RAT.
3.   Problem-Recognizers (Focusers)—High Differentiators-Low RAT.
4.   Technicians—Low Differentiators-Low RAT.

As can be seen in Figure 6, with one minor exception, the predictions held both in terms of magnitude and direction. Further supporting our assumption, we found that the differences between Groups 1 and 2 in the patent applications are due to differences in their disclosure rates. Both groups converted approximately 30 percent of their disclosures into patent applications, but Group 1 produced many more disclosures. On the other hand, only 10 percent of the disclosures of Group 3 (problem-recognizers) resulted in applications.[3]

Let us now speculate on the relationship of these findings to the administration of science. Clearly, if the creative act involves both the location and solution of problems, then in constructing research teams the administrator should design such teams to include both problem-solvers and problem-recognizers. Persons scoring high on both measures appear to require minimal external direction. Indeed, the ability to recognize problems suggests administrative competence. On the other hand, persons in Group 2 (problem-solvers) appear to require direction or orientation in regard to problem selection. We have all heard anecdotes of good scientists failing in administrative tasks. It is our suspicion that these administrative failures, in large measure, are persons who have a facility for solving problems but have difficulty recognizing new problem areas. When they bear little responsibility for the selection of problems, their performance is good. But when they are given administrative responsibility, not only does their performance suffer, but the performance of persons relying on their direction also suffers. Another group of anecdotes concerns persons who while relatively poor scientists become excellent research administrators. These are administrators whose perceptions and suggestions contribute directly to the successes of those below them and, we feel, are in large measure persons having low Remote Associates Test scores, but scoring high on the differentiation scales. Persons lacking both abilities, we suspect, do well in highly technical and non-innovative areas.

---

[3]The question of reliability of the social differentiation measure was something we could not respond to at the time of the conference since our work on differentiation occurred just prior to the meeting. However, Edward Morse has recently reported in "Re-examination of Social Differentiation" (mimeo), that in a readministration of the measure in the chemical company, although a major change in staff had occurred, of the 28 scientists that remained, there was a .59 correlation between differentiation scores obtained in 1965 and those obtained in 1968.

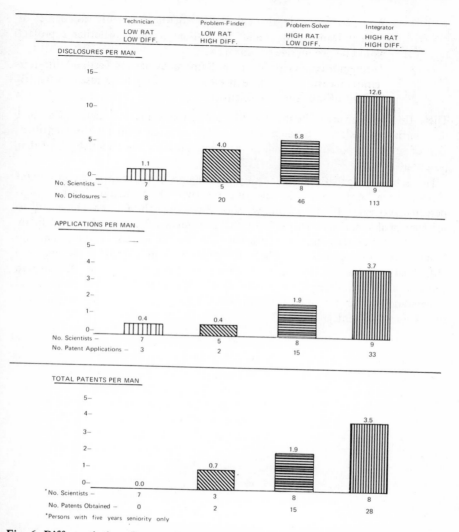

Fig. 6. Differentiation, Remote Associates Test and output measures for industrial scientists (chemists).

Admittedly, the above is speculative, but it is speculation consistent with empirical evidence.

1. We have found the Remote Associates Test to be an effective predictor in two different types of research organizations and the differentiation scales to predict accomplishment among medical sociologists, research and development scientists, and chemists.

2.   We have been able, through the use of the differentiation scores of project leaders, to predict with some accuracy whether a project would be productive or innovative.
3.   Through a combination of the Remote Associates Test and differentiation measures, we have been able to predict the research contributions of four types of scientists.

These findings lead us to believe that the use of the Remote Associates Test and differentiation scales, in tandem, may provide valuable tools for the identification of scientific potential as well as providing cues for the effective use of that potential.

The relationship between leadership assessments and group accomplishment supports the contention that scientific creativity is mediated through interpersonal processes. If this is true, we should examine the factors which lead to interpersonal creativity, particularly the attributes of persons involved in research groups as they inhibit or promote the creative output of the group. My basic contention is that the whole is different from its parts, and that the individual members of the research group are parts of a system designed to produce change. Identifying the individual propensities is but the first step in understanding the creative processes within the group and increasing innovative accomplishment.

CHAPTER 9

The Interest of the U.S. Civil Service Commission in Creativity

Nicholas J. Oganovic*

IN ORDER to place the Civil Service Commission's interest in creativity in proper perspective, let me sketch for you some of the factors involved— especially as they relate to the variety and scope of Commission responsibilities.

The Commission has a very direct and vital interest in creativity and great leadership. As the President's staff for personnel administration, we must do everything possible to see that the needed talents are provided for the many new public programs. Creativity is, of course, one of the talents in critical need for effective public administration. So we are deeply interested in defining, finding, and developing creativity. Within the Commission itself, there must be a high level of innovation to carry out the wide range of our responsibilities.

Even a brief review of the variety of our programs may startle those of you who are not acquainted with the many ramifications of the merit system. There are in the United States some 12,500,000 government employees, including both state and federal job holders in that total. Of the two groups, the federal government is the smaller, with nearly three million employees.

The Civil Service Commission is the central personnel agency of the federal government. We are basically responsible for staffing the government. We must recruit and place fully qualified applicants in virtually every government agency. Thus there is a great interest in identifying creative leadership in college, since we hire thousands of graduates a year for federal service.

In fiscal 1967, we received 2,872,789 applications from people who were interested in government jobs. We have 25 psychologists and support psychometricians who are engaged in full-time research in development of selection devices. We have a turnover in the government of roughly 300,000 people. Just to replace the people who are leaving for one reason or another, we have to have a program at all levels: all the way from the blue-collar worker up to the highest executive.

In response to these requirements, we are in the large-scale business of constructing, validating, and administering written examinations. But we also have other appraisals, which we call "examinations," but which are not based on a

---

* Nicholas J. Oganovic is Executive Director, Civil Service Commission, Washington, D.C.

written test. Instead, the examination consists of a careful evaluation of the applicant's experience and education. For about one-half of all our examinations we use non-test methods to appraise human ability and *potential*. We conduct continuing research into improving the effectiveness of appraisal systems—for appointment, promotion, and better utilization of employees.

Among other methods of evaluating people, we conduct background investigations of various types, for a variety of different purposes. We are charged by law, for example, with the conduct of security investigations of contractor employees requiring access to exclusion zones and security areas of the Atomic Energy Commission.

We are likewise designated by law to investigate candidates for the Peace Corps. We have worked very closely with Dr. Henry and many other people from the Peace Corps, and I think we have come to the conclusion that this background investigation is one of the most important techniques in the selection of Peace Corpsmen—both in the initial selection process, and as a part of the broad mosaic of tests and appraisals on which judgment is based when people are eliminated during the training period—people who would be poor risks for successful performance overseas.

The Civil Service Commission also makes full-field investigations of prospective astronauts—both those in civilian occupations and those actively in military service. As with investigations of Peace Corps volunteers, our investigators emphasize development of information about personality traits, mannerisms, and attitudes of the candidates, plus examples of their past behavior under stress, to make possible a more perceptive selection.

The Commission also makes full-field investigations of all applicants for positions designated "critical sensitive" for agencies which do not have their own security investigative facilities. We also make less extensive investigations, through mail inquiries and record checks, of all appointees to non-sensitive positions.

In connection with its investigative responsibilities, the Commission makes a continuing study of the government-wide security program, to determine whether agency security programs indeed fulfill the interests of national security. At the same time, we are concerned that these programs respect employee rights under the Constitution, and that they provide fair, impartial, and equitable treatment to applicants and employees.

It is not only in our security appraisal function that the Commission has a responsibility for equitable treatment; we administer the total equal employment opportunity program for the entire federal service—a very difficult and complex undertaking.

We operate what might be called "miniature State Department" within the commission. Roughly a thousand people a year come to us from many different countries around the world. They spend days and months in our offices, studying the federal civil service system.

We administer the whole range of salaries and wage systems that are found in the federal government, and we were given the special assignment of working out the wage scales for similar blue-collar work in different government agencies, and to set up machinery to set those pay rates to correspond with local rates. We also administer the retirement system for all federal employees except those in TVA, State Department, and some of the organizations affiliated with State Department. We administer and operate the largest life insurance program in the world, covering three million people. We administer and operate the largest health insurance program in the world, covering 12 million people, federal employees and their families.

Another function assigned to us as a responsibility under the law is to furnish staff in certain areas to carry out civil rights laws. When the federal government required the services of federal examiners to list certain American citizens as being eligible to vote, Congress and the President turned to the Civil Service Commission and it was from the ranks of our investigators that the first voter examiners were drawn. These same Commission employees were assigned the delicate task of monitoring the actual elections to make sure that the persons listed as eligible would, in fact, be able to vote and that their votes would be counted.

The Commission provides technical advice and information regarding merit system administration to state, local, and county governments.

In the continuing nationwide program to hire the handicapped, the Commission has a leadership role. Our most recent emphasis has been on employment of the mentally restored and mentally retarded. This latter program has been highly successful when mentally retarded persons have been properly placed in jobs suited to their skills. We have a medical staff actively engaged in research on the physical, mental, and emotional demands of jobs, to determine the critical medical standards on a realistic basis. In these two areas, the mentally restored and mentally retarded, where I thought we would have serious difficulty identifying people who could be trained and then put to work, the successes have been far beyond expectations.

Speaking of training, the Commission is very deeply involved in that field—and not merely for people who are handicapped in some way. Our central office and each of our ten regional offices serve as coordinating centers for training of federal employees, all the way from young people fresh out of college up to the top level, including the political levels.

Training courses coordinated by the Commission are offered by various agencies of the government in fields where they have particular expertise, and these courses are made available to personnel of other agencies when appropriate. The Civil Service Commission training centers offer interagency courses when a need exists which is not adequately met by training already developed in an individual agency.

We have two Executive Seminar Centers: one at King's Point, Long Island, and the other at Berkeley, California. Recently the Commission, in cooperation with the University of Virginia, opened its Federal Executive Center at Charlottes-ville. This is the capstone of the government training program—the long dreamed of "staff college" for top level civil servants.

Throughout these training programs, at every level, wherever appropriate, we are trying to utilize the theme and theory of creativity. Indeed, creativity is a much-needed commodity throughout the government. You can gather from the short review I have given of the tremendous variety and scope of the Commission's activities, that ours is a changing, challenging role. Rigid attitudes and slow reactions are distinctly out of place. These responsibilities put a premium on the creative abilities of all career employees, but especially on those who are the leaders of government agencies. It is for this reason that the Civil Service Commission has such a keen interest in creative executive leadership.

Creativity means different things to all of us. And creative leadership involves many characteristics, some known and some unknown. I think enough research has been conducted to establish at least some identifying traits of creative leadership. They can be classified in a variety of ways. Since I am not a creative individual, my classification of the creative leader's principal traits is going to be very simple. They are grouped into two broad areas: intellectual characteristics, and personal characteristics.

My basic assumption is that the best predictor of a creative executive is an evaluation of an individual's past creative performance. In government, each person does many things, but all executives have to communicate—either orally or in writing. The *intellectual characteristics* which I believe creative executives must have are as follows:

1. Verbal comprehension or the ability to define words. Verbal comprehension is an important component of most IQ tests. Some will agree, however, that there is not necessarily a high correlation between a high IQ on an aptitude test and a high level of creativeness.
2. Conceptual ability: a facility for organizing ideas and relating them to each other.
3. Mental imagery: the ability to get a clear mental picture of an abstraction and to translate it into words and specifics.
4. Rational reasoning: this is self-explanatory.
5. Rapid thinking: the ability to think of new ideas which relate to the problems to be solved. Here we must consider the total context of the problem and its interrelationship with the environment in which the problem is being studied.
6. Logical and sequential fluency: the ability to place words in meaningful relationships. A person may have the ability to express himself well, but he may be bárren in ideas and associations.
7. Intellectual flexibility of an adaptive nature. A person has to be flexible in order to solve problems creatively. If he imposes rigidities upon himself,

which may be the result of previous ways of doing things, in all probability he will fail.

8. Imagination; and to me that is almost synonymous with creativity.

9. Convergent thinking: the ability to summarize, or produce a needed result, such as solving an urgent problem by rearranging data already at hand.

10. Unorthodox thinking—most important, the crucial characteristic of a creative executive: the ability to move and travel in areas where others fear to tread. This is a rare trait and its costs are high to an executive who displays it.

11. Awareness: the creative person is more active and knows what is going on about him. This awareness may be quite special and selective at times, depending upon interests and circumstances in which he is involved.

These are the intellectual characteristics that I associate with the creative executive.

Now let me summarize the personality traits of a creative executive. None of us will fully agree on any kind of a listing, for each person has his own ideas and his own list of characteristics. Here is an area where *thoughtful research is needed*. The following are not complete, but they are indicative of some areas and some ideas. I would label the *personal characteristics* of a creative person as follows:

1. He desires recognition.

2. He desires a variety of experiences and if he doesn't get them he gets bored. He needs new challenges and new problems. And he should be over his head in work.

3. He desires to work with a minimum of supervision. But emphatically underscore that he *needs supervision* and here is where the scientific fraternity and I may part company.

4. He doesn't want to fail.

5. He has high energy and tremendous output and usually good health.

6. He has the desire and willingness to take risks over the short and long hauls.

7. He demonstrates a high degree of *loyalty* and a moral commitment to work.

8. He displays independence, resourcefulness, self-sufficiency, and impatience with others who don't meet his high standards of performance.

Now from the point of view of the executive, creativity has two further aspects. One is intrapersonal and one is interpersonal. First, the creative executive must develop his own creativity. There are a number of ways of going about this, including academic courses in creative thinking. Research seems to indicate and substantiate the view that creativity can be developed by various educational and training endeavors. Moreover, it is likely that anything that forces a person out of accepted and traditional ways of thinking and analyzing problems, any type of "mind stretching" activity, tends to induce some measure of creativity. I am not prepared to accept this without further research and valid evidence.

Second, and perhaps of greater significance to an organization is the role of the executive in creating and fostering an atmosphere in which other persons' creativity is encouraged. The results of this creativity can then be harnessed in many ways for the benefit of the organization. If subordinates can be made to feel that creative thinking is not frowned upon, not feared, but is encouraged, supported, and rewarded, they will allow their creative impulses to function instead of limiting or suppressing them. The federal government has an Incentive Awards Program and, during the past ten years, thousands of awards have been made under this Program. Federal employees all the way up and down the line have received awards for their ideas, and these have resulted in savings to the government in the neighborhood of 100 million dollars a year, at a minimum.

Impeding the natural creative characteristics of an individual can result in significant costs to the government, most of them measurable in dollars and cents. First, if the organization contains a large number of natural creative persons who are hampered in expressing themselves, there will be a high rate of turnover. This turnover obviously creates costs in hiring and training. Second, many of the creative persons who stay in the organization will become unhappy and frustrated. This will lead to increased cost and reduced efficiency. Finally, and perhaps most significant, the flow of ideas from creative members of the organization, ideas which in the long run are likely to produce values of much benefit for the organization, will be greatly impaired. Though the least tangible in dollar amount, this last cost is likely to prove, in the long run, to be the most ruinous of all.

In closing, the Commission is performing research in this whole area of creativity at all levels. We are trying to develop techniques which will identify the creative individual. We are trying to learn how we can further develop creativeness in one who already has it, especially in people who are at college levels. How do we develop creativeness in others? And finally, and very important no matter how valid the technique from a clinical point of view: does it have *face validity,* and can it successfully be merchandized to our many publics? The most important of these is Congress. The law says that our tests in the government service must be practical and related to the job. I have not gone into these various areas of exploration as to what we are doing in the techniques and policy on testing. But this gives you an outline of what we are interested in from the Commission's point of view and why we think that creativity is a very important part of the executive organization.

From what I have told you of the Commission's varied and changing responsibilities, I am sure it is quite clear why we regard creativity as so essential—without it we could not survive.

CHAPTER 10

Making Organizational Changes Toward Creativity

Andrew Kay*

I WILL describe my organization first, before telling of my attempts to re-organize it for innovation and creativity. Our company started in 1952. By 1953 we had developed a digital voltmeter which was the first of its kind to be sold as a single product. We have revenues of about five or six million dollars a year and have about 200 people in our organization. We have a stereo receiver that was built in the same way the aerospace instrumentation was built. We are trying to find out if there is a market for such a thing. I am now also interested in teaching machines for English vocabulary building.

In 1958 I went to Bethel, Maine, with Mrs. Kay and our four children. We all went through sensitivity groups on the lake there for three weeks and came through all right. Jack Gibb was there, too. The next time I met him was when I was invited to join the board of trustees of the Western Behavioral Sciences Institute in La Jolla, California. In the fall of 1958, Richard Farson and Frances Torbert of that Institute put on a management seminar and, by the fall of 1959, there was a second seminar which I attended also. Richard Farson talked about innovation. I accepted the idea and I said, "You don't have to sell me on innovation; I am already sold."

One person there looked at me in a very direct kind of way, saying, "But there must be *real* innovation." I replied, "What do you mean by real innovation?" At that point, she described the experiment of Dr. Bavelas in rearranging people and solving problems. That was when I decided I had certainly been committed to the *idea* of innovation, but in top management areas where I had the power to innovate, I really was not doing enough.

In the summer of 1960, I arranged different ways of reforming the organization, and introduced these new ways to my company. We shifted the viewpoints of functional managers and executive council, moving toward no day-to-day focus for these people. The idea was to have them perform as general management for all departments. The idea was that they would have to enlarge and to grow, and, similarly, they should enlarge the tasks of the people working for them. We arranged to have four organizational levels. Up to that time the workers on the assembly line performed simple tasks. We changed so that each

---

* Andrew Kay is President, Non-Linear Systems, Inc., Del Mar, California.

individual learned more of the task until he achieved and produced an entire instrument by himself. This was the ultimate climate as we saw it.

We changed the purchasing department's relationship to the vendors and how information came in from the field. As a group, we sat around rearranging various relationships in the company. I had a ball doing this—I thought the other fellows were having a ball, too. After two years I noticed things were not going as well as they should have gone. I certainly was not feeling well about it either.

Meanwhile, other influences came into my life. At the same time I attended those seminars I was given a book list. I bought the books and put them on the shelf. By the middle of the second seminar in 1959, I started to read some of the books. One was *The Practice of Management* by Peter Drucker; another was *Motivation and Personality* by Maslow.

By the summer of 1961, Farson suggested that Maslow come to work in the Western Behavioral Sciences Institute for eight months, which he did. I had some time then to get acquainted with him. During the following summer Maslow came out again, this time for four months, and he had an office with quite a luxurious atmosphere. He had two secretaries to whom he could dictate, plus a dictating machine. He had the material continually typed up by about two or three days later so he could read it and keep on going. I believe that material was distributed to about 500 people in the country and later was published in a paperback book called *Eupsychian Management*.

When he was about to leave in the summer of 1962, I asked him for the one single most important thing he could tell me. He made quite a statement to me. He said that the fellows didn't match me, the fellows in my top management group. He suggested that I contact Professor James Clark at the Graduate School of Business Administration at UCLA, so I did. By the summer of 1963, I had convinced Clark to come down and do some work with us. The first thing he suggested was sensitivity training with the vice-presidents. That is what I felt I had been doing all along, but it wasn't accomplishing anything. I thought that he came highly recommended, that he looked smart and interested, and also that I was paying him. I was motivated to accept his advice. We spent eight months, instead of the suggested four months, in the sensitivity training group run by Clark and Frances Torbert. During that time, I became aware of some things that I did not realize, but that my vice-presidents knew and felt. They were quite aware of it. I could not believe that anyone could be that fearful of me, personally. Since then, I've learned differently. My position, to put it mildly, sometimes is frightening to others. It sometimes frightens me, too. In about November, 1963, because of the publicity of a newspaper article where I challenged everyone to grow, I did a five-minute taped television program on a local station. I later obtained a copy of that tape because I did not see myself the night that it was shown on TV. The host on the program was supposed to be doing the interviewing, but it looked like I was really after him. All I needed was two guns and I would have been right in tune with some of the westerns on television.

Up to that time, the creativity in the company with various people, especially myself, consisted more in improving my own psychological health, my emotional health, and knowing myself better. The other aspect was to do something about that knowledge. Was I able to do something in orienting the company, my life, and the situation totally? I felt that if I could do something about this knowledge and feel good about it, I could then do more work. In the meantime, our sales fell off in 1963. I also felt that we fell behind in innovation—the progress in the product area. I turned to the product area about a year and a half later.

In the meantime, I arranged to free myself from several other things so that I had much more time to spend on these challenges. Some people seem to eat up operational meetings, day by day, and will live with the habit of meeting the same people daily, talking about the same thing, i.e., what to do, how, and things like that. They have such a job and seem to thrive on it.

C: As I listen to your descriptions, I received an interesting impression that change is important, but you are not convinced about any, or at least not all of the changes.

S: I am not convinced that all changes are 100 percent for the better. I make changes which are changes on change.

Taylor: Three of us had the chance to visit this organization and we experienced at least three surprises. He was showing us through his plant. One of us asked him what one of the workers was doing and how he was doing it. As president of the organization he replied, "I don't know exactly and I'm not sure I should try to find out." (We learned later that they had been making their own changes so that he wasn't really sure that he knew exactly what they were doing and he really was uncertain as to whether it would be wise for him to intrude to find out for himself.)

Before we had finished the tour, he was called away to a phone call. As he left us, he told us to finish the tour of his buildings on our own. "Just go into any of the buildings and talk to any one you want." We certainly thought that was most unusual.

On our own we walked up to a worker who happened to be developing a new product. We asked him how he liked to work in this organization. He said, "Well—well—it's heaven." His description was that he had all the equipment he wanted and that he was doing everything that he wanted to do. We wondered, both then and many times later, how many workers in this world would give such an answer. A couple of weeks later he appeared in a featured full-page newspaper story about his new product. These were our main experiences.

C: Instead of the straight assembly line process, were you able to build all the way down the lowest levels of the assembly line in the development of a product? How widespread were you able to do this?

S: Our goal is building the pattern instruments. Sometimes we are running four or five different models, so it is quite flexible. We are, of course, able to avoid too much commitment to any one particular product. We eliminated the usual assembly line procedure in October, 1960.

Taylor: Do you have a flat organization? Do you consider it to be flat?

S: A good part of it is right now, but vertical, too. In some cases it has become flatter than it was—but in other areas, more vertical.

Taylor: After we visited your organization, you had provoked us to talk at length about how ready people in other parts of the world are for democracy. We remembered your discussions about how much our own people differed in their ability or readiness to handle the freedoms you were ready to give them inside of your company in America. Tell us some of your experiences in giving greater freedoms to your people.

S: In almost all areas of the company, we found it was worse for some than for others to be given greater freedom. The closer people get to the top, the worse it seemed to get. With too much freedom and almost no structure at the top, talented people became quite passive. In the middle management areas, they weren't so passive. Many of them made lots of progress, but then they reached a plateau. On the work level, a good half of the assembly workers were able to put at least one instrument together by themselves, essentially from memory. They had few drawings upon which to draw. Twenty percent of them could put more than one instrument together. Others still are learning. There is a dramatic learning which takes place in women who are 45 to 50 years old, who had been housewives all their lives. It almost goes without saying. Some of them had never had a very high self-rating of self-worth. But after looking at their accomplishment in putting a complex thing together by themselves, it all seemed worthwhile; in fact, they were thankful for the opportunity to discover greater worth in themselves.

C: What happens to expenses, overall, when you give people this increased freedom?

S: Many things. It went up during the time when one supervisor with a group of five people experimented a little too fast. He went from roughly 100 hours for one instrument to 140 hours for the next instrument. He thought the people were ready to put an entire instrument together and integrate all their knowledge. Each one had been through the work of learning each and every part of every instrument. The next batch came along and they put it together. They averaged 140 hours each, even trying as hard as they could. So they went back to each one producing a piece of it. Larger and larger pieces were then integrated more slowly. They couldn't make the integration in one set time. They didn't know how to organize the whole instrument in one process.

I keep recalling the one thing that I still remember from the sensitivity group, namely, that one vice-president kept telling me that I had been making 98 percent of the decisions of the company and I was down to 90 percent. I found that startling. I wondered what to do about that. He talked about a number of not very important decisions. It wasn't until a year or two later that I was able to think about that. It turns out that if I make the decision, it's important—as seen by others. I'm the fellow who runs the company, so it must be an important decision. If I don't pay attention to innovation in the company in a new product area, that isn't important—and that's unfortunate. Wherever I turn my attention in the company, it seems like that's the important area for everybody. You see I don't have to tell them this is important; all I have to do is to be interested in it. So I force myself to be interested in profit mostly.

It's the hardest thing for me in that I don't see that profits reflect the operation's assumptions. I know too many other things besides what the accountants know and they won't ever tell me these things. I find that they have all sorts of ways of being ambiguous in exactness—all those things which to them seem so frightening when it comes from an engineer or production manager on what he is going to ship, or from a sales manager on what he is going to sell. They can't stand ambiguity from others, if it shows.

But, in turn, they have never thought what ambiguous bookkeepers they are. What I have are impressions from inquiring about entries in the books. They make statements like $14,000 for something. I ask, "What is that for?" They answer, "Well, that is to balance the books."

I have a case I don't think the fellow in the Harvard Business School gets. I once went to one of these schools, so I could learn how to run my own business. Fortunately, I went to a management seminar and I found that the people who were in business felt they were flying absolutely blind. So profits as shown by accountants do not accurately reflect the operation's assumptions.

C: One of my worries concerns one fine manager who has done a great many things and who has been through sensitivity training. He is now trying to conduct his group according to theory "Y", and I pray for him. Another one was brought in who used the most classic authoritarian procedures. The profit from his side of the picture is what he got. You see it so often. They say theory "Y"; it didn't work.

S: One thing I learned from Maslow is the difference between the words "authoritative" and "authoritarian:" a matter of being more authoritative than authoritarian.

C: But one thing that persists in the lives of most people is the clear discovery that a creative climate, at least a climate of freedom and opportunity, is devastating to a large proportion of the population. So this business of a creative climate is a way of "killing" people if they are in the wrong field. Clearly, we have to tie in the complexities. The question is, "Who can profit from the creative climate and who can not?"

S: To me, the creative climate you are talking about is one that was created for the most creative people. It turns out that some people require a lot more structure than others so that they can be free within that structure to do something. That doesn't mean everything is structured just because they need a lot of structure. They can still be creative within such structure, at least to a degree.

But to us, as idealists, such a structure can contain many restricting features that may limit the creativeness possible within it.

C: I carry that a little further, to seeking several somewhat different ideal climates for creativity. I sense that there is a discrimination about human people, human psychopathology, such as the recognition that an atmosphere of trust is wrong for a paranoid character. It won't work. It is our job, as those who are attempting to formulate a particular creative climate, to be very, very aware of the people for whom this will not be ideal.

C: It has occurred to me that we should mistrust one atmosphere. The other thing that is important is the self-knowledge that takes place in that atmosphere. In teacher training programs, teachers have to learn not to be good, happy, and cheerful to some people in the classroom. They go through a process of guidance, in terms of themselves, to come to a very calm, quiet, ordered disposition and allow other people to be free. It is something like a broad system which allows people to introduce a diverse set of systems within it and not just one system.

C: At this early stage of research, I believe in multiple climates and in trying to learn how to match people and climates. One of the things I was very curious about in your particular organization was whether your problem was one of internal versus external creativeness. I mean internal creativeness in terms of what is functioning inside the organization, and external creativeness in terms of how your organization is doing in terms of the creativeness of the world at large. You can see these two sets of problems and are they different?

S: It's a job to get them working together, not just one of them. I did a very good job of avoiding commitments to a particular theory or a particular kind of product by committing myself to processes. I'm committed to the idea of innovation, innovating all over the place, but not innovating in the business that the company was in. That results in half a dozen engineer teams, since they have a creative climate, with no directions from the top essentially, just some rough requirements, such as being told to innovate. We tried it and they did it. We combined them into a formidable team, taking the best of all these people, and put them together about a year ago, giving them all a few months. As an outcome, we were able to exhibit an instrument that by the end of this year will make obsolete everything we can manufacture today. As foreseen today, we won't make anything next year that we are making this year.

C: We are obviously going to get eventually to the point of matching people in their environment. I would add a modification to that. We are going to find the mismatching of people in their environment up to a tolerable level.

S: And continue further so that, if we let people go and grow, they can stand a new situation and that's what we're trying to do. As people get used to a new situation, they can run up to a plateau. It appears that we have to keep changing, and every time we change away from that which now seems good, people ask if we are going back. I don't even know what "back" is any more.

C: Can you set up any hierarchy of contributions to this, so that you can say this is the one most important contribution? I am looking for cause and effect, some sequence relations. Would you say that any particular thing came from any organizational decision? Apparently something important happened. Can you trace any lines into this thing?

S: The man whom I put in charge of the team made the greatest contribution, both in the electronic and the mechanical areas.

C: The main thing you can pin it on is on one man and that man is there because you made a decision.

S: He had been there for several years and made his contributions, also, but not really until he got going.

C: What got him going? Did you say, "Make a machine like this?" Did you say to make something new, or did you tell him, "You have freedom?"

S: The whole team became enthusiastic because I was interested in that.

C: Were you equally enthusiastic about three or four other possible developments or did you really pick this one as the one most likely to become the most important one?

S: There weren't a lot of developments. We started from scratch with requirements for what was needed.

C: I extract two things. You picked a man or picked a product somehow and exhibited strong interest, which is not like commanding your workers to "do this." It seems to me it is subtle, but it carries the same information. The other thing, lying behind this somewhere, was a need, possibly expressed or otherwise exhibited, for new products. This can be coming from a variety of sources, and I have been trying to get some sense of input and output because it's perfectly obvious something had happened which was significant in terms of the health of the company. And nothing resembling any causal relationships or any decisions came out of the discussion. That's why I asked the questions.

S: I don't understand what you mean about products. I keep saying they are requirements, which to me doesn't mean a product. Besides it is a pretty general statement of what kind of a product might be needed.

C: What requirements a product should meet. Yes, an idea of what would meet a market. Did you tell the chap, "See if you can cook up something to meet this market," while they're waiting?

S: No. I discussed this with some middle and top management people for several months. The team was formed. We dropped everything we were doing and cancelled all the projects in which we had some money, stopped them dead, scrapped the whole works, and put the best team together.

C: Was somebody leading the team—this fellow you mentioned?

S: That man didn't lead the team until several months later. In fact, he's the one that came to me and said, "We need a leader."

C: In the general meetings, did this fellow emerge as the one who had the most ideas? Is that why you picked him?

S: No.

C: Did they vote for him?

S: No.

C: Then you picked him? The original requirements came from the marketing people and various judgments of the market. Then somehow comes a key decision for this fellow to be in charge.

S: I had to make a decision among three people. One was, I would say, not as innovative as this man. I hated to put one man over the other. Another man hadn't been with the company long. He was very good, but I wasn't sure how innovative he was. It turned out that I picked the man from these three who seemed the most involved and dedicated.

Shockley: It was certain that not all decisions were equal to that in importance.

C: May I ask what's behind your question?

Shockley: My notion is that a series of decisions are made that are not all of the same importance. There must be some a lot more important than others. I want to single those out.

C: It may be the pattern that was important.

Shockley: Then what was important about the pattern?

S: He focused on something that was present and said that could be important; we'll put a maximum effort on it. Then he seemed to find people who matched that focus.

Shockley: Do you intend to appoint that same man for another development of the requirements you need?

S: I like the way he operates very much. I probably will.

Shockley: What function did he perform in the fragmentation of this?

S: He did the fundamental design work and came up with a fundamental idea.

C: This is my first and only comment. If anyone believes that the company represented by this man is anything but a one-man show, he should avow that belief. I do think however, that it is a very enlightened kind of leadership and, therefore, should probably be largely a one-man effort.

S: Initially, I, for one, felt strongly that it was not a one-man company, but I found out differently. Upon realizing the fact that it is, I'm acting like it is now, and now it is going ahead again—with more innovating.

CHAPTER 11

Major Weapon System Advances Through Multiple Innovations

Chalmers Sherwin*

THE PROGRAM in the Defense Department is very very pragmatic. It is not guided by subtle principles of psychology or sociology, but by the conviction that great experiments have been done in the past and somebody ought to look at what is being done with them. We have an enormous history of real events which could be examined. True, many things are tangled up. On the other hand, the real world and the lessons learned from it could probably be very significant. Astronomers have played with this for a long time. There has been essentially no laboratory astronomy. They spend their time looking at the past and the world as it used to be and have figured out a tremendous amount. I think the same thing can be true in things like creativity. This approach may be a valuable one especially for the criterion problem in creativity and also for the study of creative processes within individuals and within organizations.

We started out with a project a few years ago, which we now call "Project Hindsight" (Sherwin and Isensen), whose objective was to look at what happened to the last ten-billion dollars that the Defense Department had spent in research and technology. If you ask most scientists or even engineers what the output is of what they are doing, they will point with enthusiasm to the future and will say that two years from now or five years from now or, if they are more realistic, ten years from now, this will have to be a great device; it will have some application in the world. You ask them, "What happened to the last efforts; what happened to the efforts in the past; what happened to the last billion dollars?" They tend to say, "Don't bother me." So you ask, "Are you sure you're managing it efficiently?" They reply, "Yes, I am. The seat of my pants tells me I am managing this in the most efficient possible way." They show almost no interest in the past, plus almost no interest in the payoff of what they have been doing. They wave their arms and point to the future.

So we said, "Let's use enough self-discipline to look at the past and see what has happened." Consequently, Project Hindsight was aimed at determining the payoff of technology and research through the Defense Department as a result

---

*Chalmers Sherwin is Vice President, Special Products Division, Gulf General Atomics Corp., San Diego. He was formerly Deputy Director, Dept. of Defense Research & Engineering, Washington, D.C.

of the investment that had been made since 1945 to that time, which added up to about ten-billion dollars. It is a little hard to tell exactly how much is involved because it is funded in so many different ways. But this is an order magnitude estimate of funding. This is only a very small fraction of the total money spent in research and development. It is probably 20 percent or so of the total money, but it is that money spent in the research and the applied research and technology end of the total spectrum.

We were interested in finding out what the payoff was but, just as important, we were interested in finding out whether there is any typical pattern in the organizations which have a high productivity of useful applied results as compared to those that have low productivity.

So we started a systematic study—a first cut at it. We initially analyzed about ten weapons systems that have become a part of our official military system. We analyzed them by the following means. A group of engineers and scientists, mostly engineers, dissected a weapon system into the critical components (new information, concepts, and components) that make it distinctive from its predecessor and clearly contribute to its utility. This is not actually as hard as it sounds. It is a strictly technical operation that involves a great deal of technical judgment as to which components really are unimportant and do not affect cost or effectiveness very much, versus those which are important and significantly contribute to the performance of the system or to the reduction of its costs. There is another category in the Defense Department, in addition to research, which is called "Exploratory Development:" mostly technology and applied research. These two funding categories, Research and Exploratory Development, are expected to be a prime source of useful innovations, or "events," as we called them.

As we suspected, the event was a fairly well-defined state where a new concept has been identified and recognized, or a new gadget has been built, or some partial part of a system has been demonstrated as useful or functional. From the first ten systems, we found about 400 events that have been carefully recorded and we expect to have close to a thousand events in the file when we are through this stage of analyzing about 16 weapon systems of very different properties.[1]

We obtained a lot of information about each event, such as where the event occurred and who participated. We collected personal resumes of the people who participated in these events and determined why they did it by asking them. We tried to find what motivated them to make this invention or to extend this concept or whatever the event may be. How did they get financed? Where did the initial money come from to get them going? Where did the solution of the problem come from—was it something that was handed down or created by them? Was it found in the performing level or was it found in the management level of the organization? We sought answers to a great number of factual

---

[1] By the end of the study, there were 710 events in 20 weapon systems. (For a summary of this study, see Sherwin and Isensen, 1967.)

questions. It turned out that people could remember these pretty well. Often we had to talk to two or three people before getting a consistent story, but we did get it.

It seems that going backwards in time to trace the way in which ideas progress is actually much easier than tracing ideas forward. People who make an invention very seldom really know how it gets used. They often have no concept of its applications. But the people who *apply* it can almost invariably recall where they got the idea. Thus, in a step-by-step process, you can go back to the origin. There is a lack of symmetry which makes it easier to trace backward in time than forward. It is in the basic nature of scientific and technical communication that there is a connected chain backwards in time. Since most inventions end up not being useful, people who produce them get sort of tired of worrying about how or even whether each one is used. Thus, if you start from a set of inventions in the past and trace *forward* in time, you end up running down many blind alleys or lost trails. Most of the inventions or concepts are still on the shelf and have not found any significant application; whereas if you start with inventions proven to be useful and work backwards, you have a positive connection with the past.

What were the lessons learned from this very brief summary? Probably the most important one is that the sequential systems that are developed in very rapidly changing technological situations, such as are now characteristic of military technology and of military weapons systems, have very great differences of performance compared to their cost. Typically, there are very few systems that are not twice as good as their predecessors a decade ago, and many are 10 to 20 times as effective per dollar input.

Taylor: I wish we could say that in our behavioral science fields.

S: That's right, I think it is perhaps unusual. But it just happens to be true in this area. It is also a characteristic of the "growth industry" in this country. The computer industry has been like this. With the computer, you can multiply two six-digit numbers together today for less than one ten-billionth of what it cost to multiply those two numbers in 1946. Anyway, military technology and systems in computers, information processing, and many other equally important areas are also extremely sensitive to high performance and logical advance and the payoff from these advances is very big. The engineers who dissected the systems found that about a third of the time there wasn't even a predecessor system— that is, there was no machine or system that did this particular job before. But in the cases when there was a predecessor, these engineers felt that, at the time the predecessor was designed, there was no way to make it significantly better than it was then. This was demonstrated by the fact that the innovations used by the successor to improve its performance were almost all created *after* the design date of the predecessor.

Engineers have many faults, and one of them is that they are often overly optimistic. They invariably attempt system performance *higher* than the technology really permits. So if you go back, with one or two possible exceptions, the performance of most systems is right up against the stops as far as technology is concerned. If you try to imagine redesigning a system with the technology *they* had available, it is almost impossible to imagine building it much better than it actually was built. In other words, engineers really push out to the edges. They develop performance limited only to the materials, the components, and the information they have at the time. This leads us to very important conclusions which I will soon mention.

Taylor: I wish we had large numbers of "behavioral engineers" available who were functioning as you describe by pushing to develop practical performances and implementations in our fields out at the edge of our current insights and potential capabilities.

S: Another important item is that typically 50 to 100 distinct technological or scientific advances (events) are needed to make this great difference in performance. In the progress from the C130 to the C141 airplane, an example of our analyses, 85 distinct events were initially found and further careful analysis shows that there are at least 50 more, so there are well over 100 technological advances. Any one of these events, by itself, would never have made a very big difference in improving the performance of the predecessor system. They all have to work together in a very unique and synergistic way. The sum of their effects is very non-linear and very large. It is as if each event makes a one or two or ten percent difference. Some of them are more important than others, obviously, but none of them by themselves would make very much difference. Thus it is rarely worthwhile to build a more advanced system based upon only one or two new events. It is only when you put the 100 events together that major advances are made in the total system. The problem many innovators have is that they have one idea: their pet idea. To make it really useful, someone has to create the other 99 ideas and put them all together. Almost invariably, we found that one or two ideas never do dominate the advance, practically speaking, but that at least five or ten are essential, and often a hundred are necessary for the full performance of the advanced system. To me, this was a very surprising thing. I always felt that one or two ideas was really it, and all you have to do is build a working model demonstrating this new essential ingredient and you were off. But this is *not* the case in weapons systems. Instead, it is clearly the case that a large number of advances are needed that come from a diverse number of fields—and respect all aspects of a system. One must probe into the electronics, the aerodynamics, the structures, and the supporting equipment in an airplane or missile system or whatever it may be.

Another very important item that we found in this study in our setting was that a very clear recognition of the need on the part of the innovator was the motivating factor in the large majority (over 90%) of these events. These people were not working in an ivory tower. Almost invariably, they had a governmental problem or need (mostly military) in mind and, actually, a particular system in mind in which they thought it would apply. In other words, they saw their part, their invention, as a piece of something that would be useful in a bigger sense, and they were motivated by this. In a great majority of the cases, they had a direct understanding of this—they were told this problem. They were usually in an organization which was directly in contact with a tough problem or which needed some end product.

Often the invention they made ended up in a different system, but it was intended for an application with which the organization where they were working was heavily involved and they had a direct exposure to the need. They were forced to see the problem because they were involved in an organization that was faced with it. Not only did they see what the problem was, they also invented the solution. The solution was not handed to them; they created a way to do it. And even more important, in the great majority of the cases, in over 80 percent of the cases, by hook or crook they financed the initial demonstration of feasibility out of locally controlled funds. They didn't wait for approval up the line. They didn't get it coordinated at the higher levels of the government. They charged in. Sometimes it took a little digging to find this out, since they often bootlegged funds to get the initial financing. In some cases, they were fortunate and they had money that was legitimately deflectable. Often they would get approval by a telephone call one level up the line. They might call somebody and say, "Look, we have a hot new idea and we have to put another $50,000 in—how about it?" And the other fellow says "O.K., go ahead." There was a very short chain of approval for innovative ideas, and the people who approved it had the authority to approve it and didn't bother to check out with anybody else.[2]

In my opinion, the idea producer is a disappearing person in the United States government, I am sorry to say. It is, I think, because of the tendency to produce central planning in too much detail and with too much rigidity and crystallization. Nonetheless, these are the things that we found which formed the environment in which the technology, which has in *fact* proved to be useful, has grown. The thing we don't know is what fraction of all the people that were working in the defense-related technology enjoyed the conditions mentioned here. If maybe 90 percent of all the people were in this state, actually, and if they produced 90 percent of all the ideas that turned out to be useful, then we haven't proved anything except that we want to be sure to maintain that 90 percent state.

Another finding in Project Hindsight should be of interest to creativity researchers and to those funding research and to others seeking to understand and facilitate scientific progress. We found that only two-thirds of the scientific and technical knowledge needed to successfully construct and complete a new weapons system was available at the time that the military was willing to

---

[2] Editor's Note: One wonders from the statements in Andrew Kay's chapter (10) whether this kind of flexibility in functioning (this ambiguity) might have been difficult for some accountants with certain personality characteristics to cope with, and if their natural tendencies might not be to resist seeing things done at this speed and in this way.

formally initiate the project. The other one-third of the knowledge needed to successfully complete the project was generated during the course of the project. Since this was an average figure, about half of the projects had to create more than one-third of the know-how and capabilities needed. Thus there was a large amount of applied science, technology, and innovation needed to be created during the engineering development itself.

Taylor: To me, such remarkable growth and development will not occur in projects in cases where people will only initiate or support projects when all the knowledge and capability needed to complete this project are available at the start. Nor will this great growth be likely to occur in projects where people feel they must have a very high probability of verifying their hypothesis before they will undertake a study—in other words, in what will likely be merely verification projects. So, to me, the projects in the military are to be commended, not only for successfully leading to official implementation of superior machines and systems, but especially for having contributed in just a few years such an increase in knowledge and technology in the process, on each project.

S: In a different study, another interesting phenomenon emerged. We asked the research officers in the three military departments to tell us what invention and discoveries they knew about which had come out of universities which have been useful to the Defense Department. They came back with 50 examples which were examined by us. It turned out that over 40 cases (over 80%) came out of what we call "programs." To us, a program is a goal-oriented research activity at a university, involving several hundred thousand dollars a year or more, with a locally determined program. The details are locally administered and it is related to the Defense Department. The Joint Service Electronics Programs, of which there are ten at the present time, are a very good example. They exist at a number of universities—Stanford Electronics Laboratory has one, and has had for many years. Research Laboratories for Electronics at M.I.T., is another case. Columbia University, for example, has an outfit called the "Hudson Laboratory" which does research work on undersea phenomena. Collectively, then, these programs produced 80 percent of all the university generated utilized ideas with which the military research people identified. Yet we know that these programs have only about 30 percent of the money the Defense Department spent at the universities. These results are from one study—admittedly, a very crude one. But we only expect to bring out phenomena like this if they are very large, which this one is. The people in the most fruitful programs of research had a sense of identification with government needs. They were broadly concerned with applications; they invented things which they realized have a good chance of being useful.

One of these things was the invention of the maser by Charles Townes, a Nobel Laureate. He was trying to make a more sensitive detector for an experiment. He was working on the Joint Service Electronics Program which the Defense Department supports at Columbia.

Project Hindsight has been a pioneering one in the defense setting, but we feel it has important implications for other research settings. Though we are confident of our general findings, we nonetheless realize that all of our findings may not generalize to every other setting, so we hope they will provoke other studies in different situations to see what the outcomes there will be.

SOME VIEWS AND SPECULATIONS

Let me now give some of my philosophical views and speculations on the subject of climate for creativity. Most people are anxious to see research ideas become useful in some way, of having some influence in society. When we look through our study to see how this has happened in the past in our setting, we discover that this has not, primarily, been accomplished by independent people having independent ideas. Instead, it usually involves an organization which is working on what we call a "focused project"—one which tries to do something very difficult on a very big scale and, invariably, involves more than one discipline. Take, for example, a very large scale demonstration of automated interactive teaching devices. They must use all the resources of modern research —instrumentation and technology and psychology—all working toward a defined goal. It is clear that this is the way to make the effort have a successful impact on a five to ten-year time scale. First, to accomplish this usually means that the people who are involved in this activity have to reduce the personal "private effort," and increase the amount of focused group effort toward eventual implementation. Second, the focused project must have clear exposure to the real needs. Third, it must have enough resources to show working equipment to operational production managers who have the ongoing responsibilities. It must demonstrate feasibility, clearly and convincingly, on a fairly large scale. Generally, nobody can do this except the people who have the ideas. Enough of them have to somehow get together, focus their efforts, bring together the disciplines needed, and then wrangle the finances to carry them to the point of feasibility demonstration. The idea must work in such a way that it cannot be denied by even the most unimaginative of managers, of which, I might add, there are still a few left around. Even an unimaginative manager or operator will be impressed by dramatic demonstrations on an adequate scale.

C: Can you produce ideas on the same basis as you produce hardware? This is the theoretical point where, I think, the everybody-ought-to-get-together-in-a-programmed-approach falls down in the area of experience.

S: We found that if competent people are exposed to need and given funds, they will invent efficiently and effectively.

Taylor: To me it seems that your emphasis here is much more on the D part than on the R part of the total R and D program.

S: Yes. About two-thirds of our innovations were closely related to development. let me make one more observation. I believe that you have to have competition. You should not have only one outfit that has a monopoly to solve the problem. The competitive motivation in the technical organizations of the Defense Department, in fighting for their ideas, their solutions, has had a powerful and good effect. One of the greatest dangers in government, as I see it, is the tendency to become so efficiently organized that monopolies on problem-solving are actually granted.

Recently, I visited the Air Weather Service. I found they are doing much research in the frontiers of weather prediction as part of their support of the Air Force. There is a tremendous competitive drive in that organization, and they look upon the Weather Bureau as their prime competitor. One of the worst things in the world would be to have a single weather service in this country. It would probably be very poor. It is perfectly obvious that these two organizations are each striving to do a better job than the other one. In a bureaucracy, competition can be just as powerful a motivation as it is in private industry. I don't think many people realize this. The thing that is missing in a bureaucracy, but which exists in private industry and is the only thing needed, is the willingness to have competition and to defend it. You have to prove that it is efficient—something that a Congressman sometimes would have trouble believing when he is worried about duplication—but I am confident it could be proven. You have to have a fair and wise judge, somebody who will reward the performers[3] and not reward the people who drag their tails and, if you build up a set of judges who can observe performance and all the appropriate measures of effectiveness and efficiency, and then reward people or organizations, the drive for competition in a bureaucratic structure, according to my observations, can be just as powerful as it is in a free enterprise and just as needed. So it is clear that this sense of competition must be maintained in all parts of our economy and in all parts of our government.

I would also say that half of the real research (not technology) in the Defense Department, which was eventually used, was motivated by a clear understanding of need. There are so many things you can do in research, many of which may prove to be largely irrelevant to real world problems. If you have a problem to solve, however, you tend to work on a certain class of things and there is strong motivation. There can be a sense of urgency about your work, if you have focused efforts.

One trouble with many top managers is that they worry about the wrong things. The top management is worried about superficial efficiency rather than where the great payoff lies, namely, in the use of new technology. The problem for the technical people is to prove this payoff point. Once you prove it,

---

[3]Editor's Note: Like in the Parable of the Talents—though I suspect that few management and personnel systems have the courage to give greatly differential rewards for such great individual differences in performances.

management will listen. Let me give you an example of worrying about superficial efficiency. Recently, I read in the paper that the Defense Department is upset because they can only buy margarine instead of butter, because butter costs 19 cents a pound instead of 17. Yet consider some calculations from our studies. If the Defense Department had not invested in research and technology in the last 20 years, but instead, we had to buy the same defense effectiveness that we now have in our present inventory, we would have had to have invested 100-billion dollars more in equipment, and also have military forces at least twice as large—at least twice. Against that background, they worry instead about margarine, you see.

C: In this point of the payoff, I believe the basic, underlying undirected research is so important, although this doesn't come out in an obvious way, but only in terms of certain basic research that gets singled out.

S: This is a very interesting point. It looks like about 95 percent of all the research, the basic science and the undirected research that the Defense Department now *uses* was done *before* 1930. This seems surprising to many people; however, there are only a few cases since 1940 which as yet have really paid off. We discovered that only when science is very well-organized is it really used. It has to be beautifully organized so people can understand. If it isn't that way, then elegant papers may impress colleagues for decades, but nobody else may really pay attention. But if it is reduced into a textbook, or even a handbook, so that it can be understood and applied, it will get used. We discovered, furthermore, that at least half of the inventions used came from Edisonian methods and from what we call "Edisonian research."

C: Apparently there is a great need for more "bridging" or "coupling" efforts to get the information from the elegant papers of the scientific literature into usable form and into the working handbooks used in the technological fields. Otherwise some person may end up writing papers just to impress colleagues. If we go back into history, even back to the primitive man, every year since primitive man existed, when he finds out something, he wants to tell somebody about it.

S: Yes, and if there was nobody to tell, many of them wouldn't do it. They want to be admired for their ingenuity.

C: But let us not present a gross misunderstanding of the whole creative mind, for the whole thing is not just need—or not solely that necessity is the mother of invention.

Taylor: I think we can get usable contributions in at least two different ways from people. One extreme would be to look at the system needs and at real live problems in the official operations; whereas the other extreme would be to let those who can readily create ideas on their own have them in mountain retreats or in ivory towers. And the approaches and motivations for these two extreme types are not exactly the same—and, in both cases, the motivations would prove to be highly complex in their nature.

C: There is a difference in the kind of needs of these people. You are talking about a concrete kind of military need which you can specify and call a system, for instance, a weapon system. There can be another kind of need that is much less concrete, and possibly most people don't feel this need. That's what the problem is—it isn't as explicitly a felt need to begin with. So we can't set up this as a target in the concrete sense that you are talking about. This is one of the problems.

S: Why can't we? Isn't it potentially possible?

C: Maybe you are right. At least I would like to see us try.

S: As far as I can see, we are inundated with second-rate basic research in this country. At this time, I feel we should take half of that so-called free undirected research (much of which, let's face it, is not profound) that is going on in this country and get that into focused projects, and maintain the other half of the free research in physical communicative associations with the focused projects. To us, our project proved that the place for free money is where people have real problems in the sense of motivation. Then we feel that we will get a lot more usable results and that even the basic research will move ahead faster.

C: I suspect that if you did take the money and put it into more focused research, you would not attract the other kind of people that are doing the unfocused research—many of them are the kind who just won't get into that other kind of a program.

Taylor: I feel the main point is to emphasize the *development* (D) part of the R and D so it is functioning more effectively, and to have better bridging and coupling and linking efforts working in both directions. That is, we should ensure, first, that someone is picking up the new ideas and findings from basic researchers and is developing them so they have a greater chance to become usable and used. We should also ensure good communication linkages in the opposite direction so that operational problems will flow back, probably through D people, to the basic researchers who will, then, not be unaware of the present practical problems and needs. At present, too many linkings when they occur, especially between basic R and D, appear to be unsystematic—even almost fortuitous.

Stated otherwise, my strongest of convictions is that if you want a basic R (research) program to be most solidly founded and with the greatest hope for sound long-range support, you should ensure that a very effective D (development) program is functioning in connection with it, so that noticeable portions of the basic research results are continually being implemented. Yet many of our basic researchers and far too many of our newly research-trained graduates of universities have not caught the vision nor the soundness of this point. Such effective bridging will permit all types of R workers to keep functioning—ranging from those highly focused on operational needs to those not so focused, but free to follow their own research interests and leads sheerly for basic research purposes.

Part II
Other Creativity Settings and Studies

CHAPTER 12

Predictors and Criteria of Creativity: — A Utah Progress Report

Calvin W. Taylor and Robert L. Ellison*

TWO THINGS will be covered in this chapter. The first will be a general progress report on our various research activities on predictors of creativity. And second, the all-important criterion problem and the great challenges and complexities that we have found therein will be dealt with briefly, though technically.

COMPLEXITY OF THE PREDICTOR PROBLEM

At an earlier (1962) creativity research conference, reported in *Widening Horizons in Creativity* (Taylor, 1964), our work on the predictor problem was presented, covering the identification and the characteristics of creatives. The results clearly indicated the great complexity of this predictor problem. As Guilford once said, "Creativity is a many splendored thing," and our evidence shows that to predict creativity to a high degree, one must get at a large number of different characteristics collectively to account for very much of the total creative performance. No single measure of any characteristic will likely predict as its own distinctive contribution anything as high as ten percent of the criterion of creative performance (except in a rare instance). The present picture, then, shows the need to measure a great variety of characteristics, both intellectual and non-intellectual, if we hope to account for very much of the total criterion. To date, non-intellectual scores have tended to be more promising as predictors than intellectual scores, perhaps because the intellectual tests have been too short, too speeded, and too verbal for creativity in science and in other less verbal fields. Many tests, a long battery of them, will be required, as well as a willingness to pay the price, if we really want to go after the prediction or identification problem in more than just a beginning way. Of course, we believe that creativity is well worth such a price.

Some of our work has been focused on a single prediction approach in the form of non-intellectual scores from a biographical inventory. It is misleading, however, to believe that this use of biographical items is a singular or simple

---

* Robert L. Ellison is Director of Research, Institute for Behavioral Research in Creativity, Salt Lake City.

approach. For example, Elwin Nielsen's dissertation (1963) indicated the great complexity of the biographical approach—at least 30 different dimensions were measured by a set of 150 biographical items. We have seen this same result in many other ways.

We have constructed what someone recently called a "dynamic biographical inventory"—it isn't the same from one time to the next when used for research because we are always trying to get rid of the deadwood and put in new live-wood items. This is a continuing attempt to overlap more and more of the criterion target, as indicated in our *Science* article (Taylor and Ellison, 1967). We are fortunate to have had the support of the Richardson Foundation in moving ahead further on biographical studies. Some very promising leads have been cultivated toward working with certain large organizations in doing further research on the biographical inventory, as well as providing scoring services for increasing its availability. As an outgrowth of all this work, we have published the *Alpha Biographical Inventory*, especially for use at the high school and beginning college levels. [1] This inventory yields two scores—an academic performance score and a creativity score based on studies of adult scientists and engineers. These scores are based on extensive research and both of them, surprisingly, have shown no correlation with black versus white races, so they are race unbiased and color fair according to all evidence to date. A *Beta Biographical Inventory* is also being produced, especially for use on graduating college seniors.

It is a personal persuasion of mine that in the identification problem, at the present stage of our measurement capability in this difficult field, we greatly need length and variety in our measuring instruments. Thought on this has led me to come up with a pet statement that is not always welcomed by all people. One of the longest tests I have ever seen is our educational program which covers 12 to 16 or more years—and yet the grades that come out of this long and expensive test, as our studies have found, in many cases have surprisingly low validities—sometimes even zero validities—as predictors of future performances. These performances are just in "unimportant" things like the total career performances in the sciences or in the professions—high level activities of this sort.

We have over 800 correlations in the areas of physicians' performance. Each one of these correlations is between performance in the academic world and performance in the professional world. We obtained these 800 correlations by pooling them across four samples. The distribution of these correlations gave us an almost perfect random error curve around zero correlation,

Q: Really!

S: Yes. This is reported in the *Journal of Medical Education* (Price *et.al.,* 1964) and our Dean of Medicine gave the oral report of this at a research

---

[1] Available through the Institute for Behavioral Research in Creativity, 1417 South 11th East, Salt Lake City, Utah, 84106.

meeting of the Association of American Medical Colleges so that we, as psychologists, would not get tarred and feathered.

Q: What were your performance characteristics?

S: We had only 80 performance measures on each of four groups: medical faculty, certified specialists, urban general practitioners, and rural general practitioners. Across these four samples we pooled all our correlations between the two worlds—academic and professional performances. This yielded essentially a random error curve around zero correlation, with only three percent of the correlations significant—two percent in the negative direction, and only one percent in the positive direction. That is the only way the distribution of correlations varies from a random error normal curve. So current grades are inadequate as predictors.

We contend that one of the best ways to get at the identification problem is to do it through this test of considerable extent called "education," in which we have a long chance to have these people try to display the characteristics desired. We are now obtaining only a single grade with comparatively little validity. Instead, we can potentially get a long profile of scores—within grades, maybe one that is creativity or several that are related to creativity. If there is a more extensive test than the educational program, it is the entire career performance of a person, which still can be seen partly as a prediction and also strikes fully at the criterion problem. So to really identify people who are creative, you have a prolonged period in the educational and training programs and then you have an even longer period in the world of work.

Suddenly, we are faced with the serious problem of seeking to identify creativity in educational programs directly in the classrooms. We must also try to find it in the world of work. If we can develop the capability of setting the stage right and asking for appropriate kinds of performances in these two areas, then the problem of identification will become much simpler and we won't have to put such a heavy burden on short tests—and only a few short tests—but put the burden right into the official system where more creative processes, experiences, behaviors, performances, and products could justifiably be more often called for, encouraged, and developed.

An Institute for Behavioral Research in Creativity has recently been founded, with Leroy Robertson, Thelma Thurstone, and Kenneth Beittel as trustees. This new trusteeship will help handle, in a sound research-based manner, the snowballing of interest and activity in creativity. It is being staffed by my former doctoral students and it may be said that this Institute will try to create a more ideal organization and climate for research and development work on creativity—a nice challenge in itself.

In 1965, I was briefly involved in what, in my opinion, was the best news story of the year, but it unfortunately never quite caught the attention of the national news people. In April, I visited the campus of the Utah State University. The student body had a revolution going on, but their revolution was for creativity— a very healthy focus, as Lester Beck characterized it. It was led by two beautiful girls: one was Linda Zollinger, a sophomore, who ran on a creativity platform for student body social vice-president. The other girl, Marilyn Hovey, whom Linda recruited as a teammate, was the homecoming queen that year. After winning the contests, these two charming young ladies led a revolution for creativity and worked all year on it so that in April the student body had a week-long "Festival for Creativity." What a marvelous pictorial and otherwise contrasting story to the student revolution that occurred the same year on the Berkeley campus!

They brought their efforts as close as possible to the official system by holding their activities in the Student Union Building. Their creativity went "across the board," including as wide a variety of events as possible. They ran into a lot of early resistance from some faculty members who were sure that students wouldn't know what they were doing in creativity—only the faculty would. But, as the year went along, some of the faculty who had resisted most bitterly finally joined them to help. A highlight of their attempts may have been a little booklet they produced called "Profiles of Creativity." It featured faculty members from each part of the university, thus setting the stage remarkably for creativity on their campus. In one or two cases, students added the necessary push and spark so that certain teachers or departments, not quite ready to do something officially about creativity in their own system, started making these things part of their regular classwork in order to produce materials for the spring festival. This student movement did happen and it was a most healthy thing.

In September, the National Inventor's Council and several other organizations, including the National Science Foundation, joined in a conference on Creative Engineering Education at Woods Hole, Massachusetts. One reason for holding such a conference, as described by Assistant Secretary of Commerce Holloman, was that engineering is growing more fully into a doctoral field and, as this occurs, many do *not* want to repeat certain patterns of some other fields, such as English. He said that many people obtain Ph.D.s in English, but the creative writers do not necessarily or often come out of this group. Therefore, they do not want to have the same thing happen in engineering. It was amazing to note the high caliber of the engineers who participated. In chairing one of the sub-groups, I only had to be their recorder, as they had a good feel about what creativity researchers are finding and did not need all of the information on the subject that had been anticipated. One of the many interesting things was the report of one subgroup on "Ways and Means" that, as far as creativity in engineering education is concerned, their situation is sick. What must be done as soon as possible is to give *first aid to teachers*—that was their recommendation. This may require working against the usual habit patterns of teachers and of students, too. This conference report has been produced in a book entitled *Education for Innovation* (De Simone, 1968).

As an outgrowth of groundwork laid down over a few years by Dean Kistler, Frank Williams, and myself, our College of Engineering finally managed to obtain support from the Esso Educational Foundation for identification and especially for educational attempts in the creativity area. Since its inception, however, none of us has really been active on the project, but we do hope it is a very fruitful one. Another area of interest on our campus is creativity in dance, or more appropriately, creativity through dance. Virginia Tanner is deservedly attaining a top national reputation in this area. Some films were recently produced to illustrate the techniques she uses to have her students learn to express themselves through dance. If there were ten students in her class, you would simultaneously see ten different ways of how they expressed themselves with their bodies. Getting anything like this into the official system is always a difficult infiltration problem. Lester Beck's comment after seeing these youngsters demonstrate was intriguing for us. He said that Virginia's demonstration was the best course in physical education he had ever seen. So there is plenty of room in the curriculum for these new things. We have a graduate student doing her research in this area, in connection with Virginia's teaching program, to get at these problems. We hope eventually to see to what degree this creative dance instruction and experience affects the total life careers of these girls. Lowenfield said earlier that he was trying to teach creativity *through* art and Tanner says she is trying to teach creativity *through* dance, and she thinks she builds up confidence in her dancers which will develop even more strongly as they encounter the stage of the world, the stage on which they will live their total lives.

C: I wondered how you might visualize measuring what she saw taking place in their careers.

S: In our biographical inventory, this notion of more self-confidence has shown up as a favorable indicator related to career creative performance. Self-confidence is an important characteristic. Tanner teaches her students how to use their own inner resources and ways of expressing these inner thoughts and feelings. She has them think of all the different ways they can express a given idea with their body. When you stand back and watch ten girls showing ten different ways of expressing the same general idea, it is really wonderful. She sees that her students experience a variety of ways of physically expressing themselves, to avoid teaching them all to follow a single pattern someone else has created, and to try to prevent their being highly self-restricted and nonexpressive. In contrast, I recall a Catholic sister telling me about a child who came to their nursery school program. This child, tense away from home, hardly ever moved but just stood still in one spot in the room. The teachers had difficulty getting the child even to sit down: that's the other extreme.

I think Ellison should add his comments on how self-confidence scores are obtained from a biographical inventory.

Ellison: The inventory has been empirically keyed. We have also factor-analyzed the inventory and eyeballed the items carefully. When you look at the items that have validity and are therefore keyed against criteria of career performance, items concerned with this feeling of self-confidence and favorable self-perception and integrity have come through.

S: Let me add to my earlier comments about the educational world. In our study on Air Force scientists, one of our best predictors, and certainly our best in terms of the amount of time it consumed, was the rating obtained when we asked the scientist how creative he was. This may seem a little strange, but if in education you give students ample chance for creativity and other talents to be displayed through their entire academic careers, they will become quite well-aware of their own characteristics. I see Owens nodding his head positively, and he is studying intensively in the biographical area, too. This is a strong recommendation to let them become acquainted with their talents and develop them in the educational system, possibly as the main focus, while they are adding to their knowledge. We would have them focus much more on this and we would thereby expect to get more transfer of training, more spread effect to later careers from this than from a lot of educational things students now do (which may yield low or zero correlations and little transfer to life situations).

Youngsters probably aren't very much aware of their inner thinking and learning processes, of their multiple talents, of their inner resources. This came out of our last conference of Instructional Media and Creativity. When Lester Beck shows students his lively film about a squirrel, he has found that none of the youngsters particularly write or talk about the learning processes in the squirrel. They talk about more external matters, not the inner learning processes in the squirrel.

C: John Holland has very good evidence on this at the American College Testing Service. They developed a number of scales in the area of leadership and interpersonal competencies, as well as creative scientific activity and artistic activity, and recently he checked out the validity for this on a sample of over 190,000 cases against actual outcomes in the college years and the validities are running from about .40 to .45 for an eight-item scale.

C: With the outcomes being what? College grades?

C: No, not college grades. Of course, with their batteries they predict college grades in the usual way but, in this case, he is predicting what he calls non-academic accomplishments.

S: He is using these types of items as predictors of later non-academic accomplishments.

C: That's right. These scales are given at the point of entrance, that is the senior year of high school, and the criterion information is accumulated from the college record, but not grades.

S: If I understand correctly, what is being said is that what Holland is looking for are the things which typical predictors are not usually looking for, but which are being displayed by the students parallel to the official systems. If these characteristics could be welded into the official system, they might probably work even more strongly as predictors.

We have started a series of annual summer creativity workshops on our campus through the assistance of Frank Williams. We have rotated research people like you through these workshops to make this research information about creativity directly available to potential users. Teachers and others have attended from nearly all states in the Union. For example, we have been fortunate to have Roger Stevens, the Broadway producer, as a featured speaker. He is the first White House Chairman of the National Foundation in the Arts. This new program is a counter-action to the money that is being spent on creativity in sciences. This is very healthy because the sciences can and do learn about creativity from the arts and humanities, who, in turn, have learned from the creativity research on scientists. A forthcoming book from our first five workshops will be appropriately entitled *Creativity Across Education* (Taylor, 1972).

Another area of our activity is trying to bridge from our research into practice in various settings (Taylor, Ghiselin, and Wolfer, 1962). Recently, we have started a serious attempt to bridge into classroom practice in our Granite School District where Bill Hutchinson and Elwin Nielsen, two of my former doctoral students, are now in key positions. Interestingly enough, the poverty program for the economically, culturally, and educationally deprived is worried about the people who are at the bottom of what we call the "academic totem pole". In contrast, past focus has been at the top of the same pole where one finds those with the highest amount of the currently most favored kind of talent. The poverty program is trying to reach those who are not now being reached, the educationally deprived. A teacher can focus upon other intellectual characteristics, other thinking and learning characteristics, so that this kind of classroom is not highly related to the typical classroom in terms of the characteristics stressed in top performance. In so doing, new people will emerge as star performers in the "thinking" classroom and these star performers may come from all levels of this previous academic totem pole.

Likewise, one can get new people to settle to the bottom of the new totem pole. They probably came from all parts of the initial totem pole. An interesting thing is that the people who are at the bottom can rise and move up as a group more towards the average in a "thinking" classroom. We have been using some of the things initially developed to spot top talent of new kinds in the educationally deprived. By these same methods, we are now drawing these previously deprived students upward from the bottom and more toward the average. This is a very hopeful message because it says that there isn't just one kind of talent, but that there are multiple types of talent. Each time you dip, you don't reach and get the same group of people, but you get a somewhat different group. So we are struggling successfully with this and are also encountering the problems of teacher readiness, teacher resistance, and teacher change. In one instance of this, there was no alternative but to walk away from a group of teachers.

Last year I had an interesting experience working with a team on "Project Compass" for the Navy. We tried to get a computer into the personnel program and eventually did so with success. The Navy has about 60 schools which are the entrance pathways into Navy jobs. With the help of the computer, we could handle 1500 people who had come into the Navy during one week. By processing the profiles of characteristics and then investigating a variety of Navy schools, it became possible to try to place everyone into one of the better places for them, though not necessarily absolutely the best. It's called "differential prediction," to try to place each person into a job where he would have a good chance of success and so the entire set of placements would yield a maximum in terms of total predicted success for those entering the Navy. The computer kept the final placement problem open until it had made 60 forecasts for each of the 1500 people as to how well he did in the school. We checked back and found that something over 80 percent and, if we worked at it harder, something approaching 90 percent of the people would get into areas where they are above average, which is great news for education and the world of work and the manpower situation. There are many kinds of talents and with these modern facilities we can use techniques which previously have theoretically been available, but are now also practically available through computers. This argues not only for those on an upward lift who were previously at the bottom, but to new groups rising to the top as each new kind of giftedness is focused upon.

The Navy doesn't realize fully what a good thing they have, nor have they adequately told the nation about it. If there were only one kind of talent, there obviously would be no differential predictors on which to capitalize in this way through use of the computer. But since there are multiple types of talent and since jobs likewise differ widely in the types of talents they require, differential prediction and placement can be used to great advantage. Similar ideas have been applied to classroom practices and they can be very effectively visualized in the form of Taylor Talent Totem Poles and in a dynamic Multiple Talent Wheel.

Roe: Cal, this is terrific. Where can we read more about this?

S: Nothing has been written yet about this differential prediction and personnel assignment solution, but I will be writing about it in terms of its application to classroom practices. (Editor's note: See the "Highest Talent Potentials of Man" and other talent articles by Taylor listed in the References.)

C: Maybe they are above average in terms of past groups, but what about the groups that they move into? Do you place them so that they get into places where they will be above average? You are going to raise your averages all around the line. It looks like kind of an endless spiral to me.

S: But it's onward and upward. It's a great message of hope, individually and also in terms of total manpower.

C: You get upward movements for everybody?

C: Everybody is going to get moved up, and then there is always going to be somebody below average in some group, as the average moves upward.

S: That's the comparison in terms of the after-group, not the former group. We must keep our thinking straight about norm groups. The Navy doesn't realize fully what a good thing they have in terms of a national message with widespread implications and they are sitting on it until they feel they can release it.

C: I understand what you are saying. I'm just looking to see what the picture is at the next step.

S: These computers are becoming more and more available and this message is a tremendous one for the present and oncoming manpower situations. And we completed this project almost in spite of the system. We finished it to the stage of making it operational just a month before the number of enlisted men going into the military doubled, but we met this deadline only through putting sustained strain on the system, because the system had not budgeted nor otherwise planned to have all this done that year. We also have at least a local three-pronged attack for trying to get creativity findings into education. We will try as many-pronged attacks as we can think of and try to get each of the attacks functioning. One of them is that we would like teachers to find just one thing they would like to do differently than they did last year. We encourage them to be like scientists—keep everything else going as before, but change one thing and then see if this makes a difference toward greater creativity in students. I also recently gave a speech to administrators, the secondary principals in the nation, called "Cultivating Creativity within the New Curriculum" (Taylor, 1966).

We have an AFOSR project on communication abilities and creative abilities which has been published by the U.S. Government Printing Office (Taylor, Ghiselin, and Yagi, 1967). This is a volume covering more than a decade of sustained research. It is worthy of a full report, in itself, at one of our conferences and its potential value was foreseen in my report at our first (1955) creativity research conference (Taylor and Barron, 1963).

We may be starting another project which is fascinating in terms of the criterion problem. This project in nursing may be generalizable to other fields. They do not want us to select nurses who are entirely like the nurses of today, but to help them learn how to select nurses with certain things phased out and other things, such as creative leadership, phased in more strongly. They are not sure they can go out and find enough nurses who already display enough creative leadership so that we merely then have to find more like them. Instead, they are trying to select and produce nurses with more creative leadership than yet exists. We call it the "problem of the moving criterion target," which also has an effect on the predictor side. It's a bootstrap operation of building a new kind of professional group with a new emphasis. All our world is faced with this to some degree; the need for more creative leadership poses a very realistic problem in the area of supervisory and management leadership of every kind.

Another project, a fascinating one, is with the Peace Corps—a very young and alert organization. We often marvel at the Peace Corps for its receptiveness and alertness to new ideas and its ability to try to do something immediately, if not sooner, about these ideas. This project grew out of our being questioned and our advising the Peace Corps concerning creative and related characteristics. They recognized and openly admitted that they had not yet selected volunteers in terms of certain characteristics that are needed overseas, nor trained them in these characteristics. They describe some of these as: ability to sense problems, ability to initiate action, resourcefulness (dealing with different resources than they have in our country, or sometimes almost doing without resources when they get overseas), innovativeness, and creativeness.

In our discussions I suggested a situational testing approach to which they reacted with interest. Joe Colmen said that potentially there could be a double payoff, because situational testing might not only display things for selection and assessment but the approach could catch the attention of the training people who might find new ways in the Peace Corps to try to elicit some of these characteristics which had not been elicited in training before. We hoped that after the project was completed we might catch their attention, but what has happened is that training people found our project much sooner. This shows how alert they are. In midstream, we had to set aside our research in order to put on a training demonstration for nearly a week, to try to awaken these training directors from universities on new ways of running educational training programs that are more lifelike regarding the problems faced by the volunteers overseas. Our project was most timely for Peace Corps training, because the training directors had just been officially encouraged in their contracts "to experiment with their training programs." Our approach was quite different from the usual academic programs prevalent at colleges and universities.[2] Top Peace Corps officials are well-aware of the tendency of university professors to settle back into that rut. So we became a catalyst for change, to swerve Peace Corps training, and we held up our situational tests and training approaches as targets and let them experience our materials and procedures. In other words, we put training directors through our situational training approaches. A sizable number of the top Peace Corps people from Washington, D.C. went through our training program, too. We told them all we would be *pleased* if they would consider our materials and procedures; we would be *more pleased* if they would consider *revising* our materials and procedures; and we would be *most pleased* if

---

2 Mimeographed copies of our large 455-page Peace Corps final report (Taylor, Yagi, deMik, Branum, Tucker, and Wight, 1967) are available in our laboratory.

they would throw out our materials and procedures and build better ones of their own to replace ours.

This training demonstration became a real catalyst toward change in the Peace Corps training programs at a most timely period—when they were thinking along new lines themselves—and ours was the first Peace Corps research project that had made any impact on the vast Peace Corps training programs. We did use a wide variety of approaches: situational, paper-and-pencil devices, development of ideas from research on creativity and on communication abilities, new training ideas from our project staff, and instrumented laboratory training modified from creativity and other management development programs from Aerojet General, in Sacramento. My staff of four graduate students, Kan Yagi, Mike Tucker, Gary de Mik, and Al Wight, deserve a lot of credit for their ideas and materials which led to this impact on Peace Corps training directors.

C: Are you training the people who went to the training centers and who, in turn, train the Peace Corps people? Is that what your demonstration training institute was?

S: We trained a set of the training directors and a sample of their staff who train their group of Peace Corps volunteers. About 20 key persons from the central Peace Corps office in Washington, D. C. also went through our demonstration training program to learn about our procedures and to experience them themselves. In general, we were training the directors of training..

Let me add two more things. Midstream in our own research we made almost a 180 degree switch ourselves. We got some clues for this change from certain Peace Corps personnel. We decided that we weren't sure that we really wanted the Peace Corps volunteers to show these characteristics of resourcefulness, initiating action, innovativeness, and creativeness but, instead, we wanted the host country people with whom the volunteers worked to show these characteristics. We wanted to have the Peace Corps volunteers selected and trained to be subtle catalysts so that these characteristics would show up in the people with whom they worked. This is why we talk about three or four steps removed—we demonstrated to the training directors so they would train their staff to train their volunteers in new ways, with the hope that the volunteers, in turn, would then set the stage so that these characteristics would emerge in the people with whom they worked in the host countries. We wanted the resourcefulness, innovativeness, initiating action, and creativeness to be developed and strengthened in the local people so they would then gain confidence in their own potentials and could develop and do things in their communities that had never been done before. But they would do these new things themselves; the Peace Corps volunteers would not "do it for them." This is the latest thinking in Peace Corps community development work.

C: Is there a difference in the type of training approach you need at each level when you start at this top level and work down to the different groups at different levels? Do you train all of them by the same system, or do you differentiate in some special way at each level?

S: We have no answer to that. In fact, we do not have a training research project; we have a situational testing research project. In midstream, we have had to switch and try to modify our materials and become trainers of training directors. By midstream, I mean this calendar year. We are now being tentatively signed up to train Peace Corps volunteers who returned and want to hire into the Peace Corps as training people for their "second hitch." We are trying to figure out the best thing we can do for them. We saw the main training question to be: "What can we do with training directors that will swerve Peace Corps training out of old ruts and hopefully into new and more promising directions?" A recent idea is that we, or at least someone, should do more of this research and developmental work on training approaches, periodically feeding new materials and procedures to training directors as a counteraction for natural tendencies to settle back and train in the old way. No one has yet followed through with new training at each of these series of levels, including the working level process. We did our training demonstration only two months ago. That was our first and only experience in training the directors. We were supposed to have had a dress rehearsal with about 20 persons from seven or eight training programs, but our demonstration proved to be the "real McCoy" because about 50 people turned up, including the top training people from Washington, D. C. The Peace Corps really hits fast and hard when they want to get a new idea or program considered.

Last summer, at six training centers, we did insert from 8 to 40 hours of our own training as experimental procedure with Peace Corps volunteers. From the beginning we had the general notion of setting situations with "booby-trap features," such as a statement from an authority figure that "it's impossible." Thus Peace Corps trainees would be faced with a difficult situation to which they could respond by saying, "It's impossible—it can't be done." And the sooner they took this way out, the lower their score. If a candidate would buy this way out of our situation, then our hunch was that his test scores would validly forecast that he was not a good prospective overseas volunteer.

Elsewhere (Taylor, 1962) I have argued that the creativity research findings call for revisions of the typical textbook description of the scientific method. The direction suggested is to add the groping, but effective, exploratory work at the frontiers, and the creative processes in generating new ideas and creating new paths and new fields for others to enter. We were fascinated to find an analogous argument occurring in another context, namely, in a Peace Corps training program. One of the abilities important to the Peace Corps volunteer is to be able to scout a new community thoroughly and effectively when he first arrives there. (We describe it as "casing the community.")

In one training program, they had this task as a situational exercise for which the trainees could map out some plans in advance. The poorest performers, as scored by the training directors, were the volunteers (1) who knew in advance exactly the one or two sources where they would go for their information and (2) who had quite clear "hypotheses," in advance, as to exactly the information they would find when they went to these one or two sources. They were highly focused and were largely prepared to verify (to another decimal point) what they felt they already knew about the town or community. In effect, they proved to be relatively incapable of searching and exploring widely for all kinds of information from all kinds of sources. In sharp contrast were the persons who could do this kind of exploratory work most successfully. The latter were judged to be the most promising volunteers, whereas those who could verbalize in advance exactly what they were going to do and what they were going to find—and generally found no more nor less than what they expected—were seen as the poorest risks for successfully cultivating effective actions in these community situations.

COMPLEXITY OF THE CRITERION PROBLEM

One thing we have demonstrated is the complexity of the criterion problem in creativity. We reported this early in our creativity conference series (Taylor et al., 1959, 1963). The scientists recommended that we not use anything resembling only a single criterion for their total career accomplishment in science. Instead, they suggested a large number of different criteria of performances and achievements. As a consequence, we obtained over 50 criterion measures for each scientist by going to eight different sources to collect our information. Several of these criteria measures fully or partially involved creativity. When we finally factor-analyzed these multiple measures of contributions of scientists, we found at least 14 dimensions were required to account for their various contributions and accomplishments. At least five of these dimensions were creative factors or had some creative features, as reported earlier, so that creativity on the criterion side is certainly not a simple single-dimensional concept, even when one focuses only upon creative work in science. Two tables are included to further illustrate the complexity of the criterion problem, as found in our first intensive criterion research on scientists.[3]

Table I is a condensation of a correlation table between our 52 criterion measures, reorganized according to the eight main sources of criterion information (with control variables separated out and treated as if they represented a 9th source). In each case in the table, we have shown the median correlation

---

[3] Since that time, we have even more intensively analyzed 80 criterion measures for each of three different samples of physicians: namely, medical faculty from one college, medical specialists, and general practitioners. We have found even greater complexity of total physician performance than we have yet found for total performance of scientists. We have also synthesized these 80 criteria in different ways to form several different sets of overall criteria (Taylor et al., 1969).

TABLE I

Median and Range of Correlations Between Scores from Different Sources of Criterion Information on 166 Scientists*

No. of Scores	Source Title	Source No.	I	II	III	IV	V	VI	VII	VIII	IX
11	Supervisory ratings	I	55 (32 to 84)								
4	Monitor ratings	II	07 (-09 to 39)	51 (24 to 85)							
6	Peer ratings and ranking	III	26 (01 to 73)	18 (-03 to 37)	31 (02 to 63)						
4	Ratings from project researchers	IV	08 (-23 to 28)	10 (-16 to 36)	04 (-16 to 34)	09 (-07 to 63)					
9	Scores from official records	V	13 (-04 to 37)	10 (-01 to 30)	12 (-08 to 46)	04 (-19 to 26)	04 (-15 to 81)				
13	Scores on reports and publications	VI	04 (-23 to 29)	10 (-11 to 27)	08 (-21 to 46)	04 (-19 to 29)	02 (-20 to 37)	10 (-14 to 55)			
1	Membership in professional societies	VII	13 (02 to 23)	14 (09 to 20)	12 (01 to 18)	13 (01 to 18)	04 (-05 to 24)	14 (00 to 26)	— (—-—)		
4	Control variables	VIII	03 (-10 to 22)	04 (-10 to 22)	09 (-10 to 28)	04 (-11 to 17)	13 (-28 to 29)	-02 (-22 to 35)	-02 (-15 to 39)	33 (-09 to 83)	
4	Self-ratings	IX	18 (-08 to 32)	02 (-08 to 16)	11 (-02 to 22)	04 (-16 to 21)	01 (-17 to 19)	06 (-16 to 33)	22 (19 to 30)	10 (-07 to 24)	50 (35 to 53)

*Decimal points have been omitted. A correlation of .20 is significant at the .01 level.

between a pair of criterion scores, one from each of the two sources. Printed in parentheses below this median correlation is the range of the correlations between a pair of scores from the two sources, from the lowest (or most negative) correlation to the highest (most positive) correlation. The top numbers down the diagonal of this matrix indicate the median correlation between the various criterion measures from the same source, together with the range of correlations between pairs of measures from the same single source. The table also permits one to determine the number of correlations obtained between any two pairs of sources, simply by multiplying together the number of measures from each of the two sources. In addition, we obtained four measures which we have called "control variables" to see whether we should partial out the effects of these four variables, which were age, years of education, total years of experience, and total number of months of experience in the research center studied.

Table II lists 13 scores that to some degree contain some creative features, together with six scores from four sources that have some overall features to each of them. However, the various overall scores do not pretend to cover entirely the same components nor to have the same weighting of each of the components. By looking at the three types of sections in Table II, one can find the correlation among the creative criterion, among the overall criteria, and between pairs of criteria, with one, in each case, being a creative criterion and the other one being an overall criterion. A quick inspection of this table again indicates a great complexity in the criterion problem. For example, overall criteria and the creativity criteria were correlated by considering the relation of one overall and one creativity criterion at a time. These correlations ranged from -.16 to .54, with an average (median) correlation of .20 for the 78 correlations. The highest correlation between pairs of overall criteria was .73, the lowest was .08, and the average was .35 for the 15 correlations. Similarly, typical (median) correlation among the 13 "creativity" criteria was .12 and the intercorrelations ranged from -.15 to .83 for the 78 correlations. Even if the last so-called "creativity score" in the list of a non-conforming, non-complying type was deleted as being an irrelevant score, the median correlations would not change very much; only the bottom of the range would move away from the negative value, closer to zero.

The results of these tables again indicate the great complexity of the criterion problem of total scientific performance and how creativeness is somewhat of a different concept as seen through the products of a person or when viewed by high-level supervisors, immediate supervisors, peers, or by the person himself. These are not, necessarily, entirely different views because they do overlap to different degrees, but any overlap is generally minor. So we feel we have illustrated the complexity of the performance criterion problems in scientists, as well

TABLE II

Correlations Among Creative and Overall Criterion Measures on 166 Scientists*

Source	Name	No.	Creative Criteria													Overall Criterion					
			11	8	6	2	44	14	15	55	28	21	31	26	20	1	16	47	48	12	17
I	Creation	11	—																		
I	Flexibility	8	58	—																	
I	Indep., discovery	6	83	67	—																
I	Drive, resource	2	60	60	77	—															
III	New problems	44	27	33	35	47	—														
II	Creat. cklist.	14	07	-01	03	13	09	—													
II	Sci. char. cklist.	15	09	-01	08	11	11	85	—												
IX	Creation: self	55	24	08	26	19	13	11	11	—											
V	Patent rate	28	12	-02	12	16	05	17	16	19	—										
V	Awards	21	17	13	17	14	16	00	06	01	06	—									
V	Suggestions	31	-04	00	08	06	12	10	05	02	03	-03	—								
VI	Orig, reports	26	08	-03	08	12	16	18	14	13	24	-15	24	—							
IV	Noncomply, alter.	20	-21	-09	-21	-23	-09	-07	-06	-02	08	-10	09	09	—						
I	Prod. rnk., super.	1	39	35	47	54	45	18	14	23	29	18	14	19	-08	—					
III	Prod. rnk., peer	16	30	25	36	44	46	21	16	18	22	10	15	15	02	73	—				
III	Lab nomin.	47	32	18	34	31	39	28	19	18	35	25	12	25	-14	60	52	—			
III	ERD nomin.	48	30	01	29	19	11	35	30	15	20	25	13	10	-16	31	31	62	—		
II	50% retention	12	23	20	32	28	16	24	28	16	18	21	10	07	-16	39	35	37	32	—	
IV	Prod. predicted	17	27	10	28	19	20	26	22	21	-02	-04	11	12	01	18	22	-26	28	36	—

* Decimal points have been omitted.

as the complexity of the creative portion of that total performance problem. We are also well aware of the further complications possible if criterion studies of creativity are completed and compared, not just in science, but across different fields of human endeavor.

In general, ours is a strongly criterion-oriented approach in each area of creativity, hinging our work, as much as possible, in the predictor, education, and climate areas all upon multiple criteria developed through intensive and extensive measurement, analysis, and synthesis work. We are always struggling to improve the goodness and coverage of our set of criteria so that we will have more sound criterion bases for our work on the identification and development of and on the climate for creative and other talents. [4]

---

[4] Our statements on the complexity especially of the predictors where each characteristic typically contributes far less than 10% (see p. 149) are intriguingly analogous to those by Sherwin (p. 142) in which many cumulative events are needed, each event typically making only a small (1% or 2%) difference.

CHAPTER 13

Maintenance of Creative Output Through the Years

Anne Roe*

BETWEEN 1947 and 1950 I made studies of 64 of our leading research scientists in biology (n=20), physics (12 theorists and 10 experimentalists), and social sciences (14 psychologists and 8 anthropologists). In 1963, I reinterviewed 52 of the 54 who were still living. The other two were abroad at the time and, although a long report was received from one of them, I did not reach the other. My object in revisiting them was quite simply to find out what had been happening to them in the intervening years. Many had retired, and I was particularly interested in finding out what happens to a man of great stature after official retirement.

At the time of the second study, their ages were from 47 to 73. The biologists are the oldest group and more of them had retired. One biologist had retired twice, at 65 from one university and at 70 from another. One of the physicists had retired at 65 from one university and was then on the staff of another, with a later retirement age. The oldest man in the group, 73, has not yet retired and was not even considering it, as far as I could see.

I have published a fairly full account of what they had been doing, their sources of support, their families, etc., but this report will concern only some of the material on their written productions over the years. For various reasons, I have complete bibliographies for only 45 of them. The problem of measuring and reporting on their productivity, even limiting it to writing, is a tricky one as you may realize. One reason for bringing these data to you is to ask if you can think of something better to do with them. In the tables, all the biologists have been put together; they include botanists, zoologists, geneticists, anatomists, bacteriologists, but not enough of any subgroup to separate them. Theoretical and experimental physicists have been kept separate since they are quite different in many ways; and for this purpose, I have also separated the psychologists and anthropologists. General data on total publications are shown in Table I.

Also kept separate are scientific and non-scientific publications; there are relatively few of the latter. Scientific publications have been separated into books, research reports, other technical publications, and book reviews. "Other technical papers" include such things as symposium papers, general review papers, all technical publications that are not reports of specific, limited re-

---

*Anne Roe is now a Consultant in Tucson, Arizona. She was formerly Professor, School of Education, Harvard University.

search. Category assignments, especially as between research reports and other technical publications, were usually made with the help of the subject. Book reviews, as prepared by most of these men at least, are not just abstracts, but may require much thought and even research. I used one other category, "notes and abstracts"; but these totals are not included in the tables. It is usually the case that material in papers recorded by title or abstract will appear in some form in a fully published work. Notes and letters to the editor are generally excluded, except that letters to the editor of *Physical Reviews,* and notes in journals such as the *Maize Genetics Newsletter* or the *Drosophilia Information Service* are included in the category research reports.

Non-scientific publications include quite a variety of things: non-technical presentations of scientific material (such as encyclopedia articles or articles in journals with general circulation) memorials, committee or directors' reports, discussions of educational problems, and so on.

The number of years covered in the table varies with each man. In every case, it is the time from the first publication to the last one listed, except for the war years. For the men who were active in governmental research during the war, and whose non-classified publications are, therefore, very few, I have simply eliminated the war years from the calculations. This will be seen more clearly in the figures later.

In an attempt to arrive at a measure of total productivity, some adjustments have been made by giving different weights to different kinds of publications. A major problem concerns the relative weight to be given to book publication, since the time required for preparation of a book is usually considerably more than that required for preparation of a research report or a technical paper. As a measure of output, then, each book is given a weight of 10. A weight of 5 is given for material revision of a book or for editing one. Translations, and editions without change have not been included in the tallies. Book reviews, as prepared by most of these men, are not just brief abstracts, but may require much thought and even research. Each book review is given a weight of 0.5. (There may be a few who have done some book reviews but have not listed them in their bibliographies. These are probably routine reviews which are chiefly reports of what the book contains.) The other two categories used, "research reports," and "other technical papers," are each given unit weight.

Productivity, both scientific and non-scientific, is reported in Table I, in terms of weighted total per year. The number of years used in the calculation, in each case, is that which elapsed between the last full year for which a record was available and the year of the first publication, minus the period lost because of the war (hot and cold). Time deducted for this varied from none to seven years for different subjects, with few of the biologists and social scientists and most of the physical scientists involved in defense activities. There is some relationship between age and total productivity, as will be shown later, since on the whole it tends to fall off with increasing years. There are also considerable differences

TABLE I
Data on Publications

N	Biol. 15	Th. Ph. 6	Exp. Ph. 8	Ps 13	An. 4
Scientific					
Total Per Year					
Range	1.11-7.57	2.00-9.24	1.72-6.50	2.41-11.76	1.83-5.52
Average	3.75	4.73	3.77	4.95	3.54
% Books					
Range	0-38	0-66	0-31	0-52	0-56
Average	9	20	7	27	23
% Research					
Range	39-90	26-97	34-99	11-95	11-49
Average	70	70	79	48	32
% Tech.					
Range	4-36	3-20	1-35	5-39	16-52
Average	18	9	14	22	32
% Book Reviews					
Range	0-14	0-1	0-2	0-15	0-36
Average	3	0	0	4	14
% Joint Authors*					
Range	10-93	22-72	22-89	9-70	0-35
Average	34	45	62	44	17
Non-Scientific					
Total Per Year					
Range	1.54-8.70	2.05-10.06	1.79-6.69	2.67-11.88	2.03-7.32
Average	4.29	5.05	3.94	5.46	4.78
% of Total Output					
Range	0-29	1-14	0-9	0-22	7-47
Average	12	6	5	10	22

*The denominator is the sum of books, technical papers, and research papers. Book reviews are not included.

across fields in the form in which different groups choose to report their work. Although the subgroups are very small, these differences are probably representative of the work in the fields generally.

Book publication is most popular with the social scientists and the theorists among the physical scientists. Other technical papers are commonest with the social scientists, while the biologists and experimental physical scientists do most of their publishing in terms of straight research reports.

Percentage of scientific publications with joint authorship is based upon an unweighted count of books, research reports, and other technical reports (book reviews are practically never written jointly and they are, therefore, omitted here). It is clear that joint efforts are most characteristic of experimental physicists and very uncommon among anthropologists. Some attempt was made to check on the collaborating authors, to see what proportion were students and what proportion, colleagues, but I do not have complete data for all of the subjects. The range is from none to about 90 percent, and there seem to be no consistent differences among fields, except that very few students share authorship with the anthropologists, who have few joint publications anyway.

Non-scientific publications all have unit weights, except books, which have been given the same weight in non-scientific as in scientific publications. It was difficult, in some instances, to be sure how to classify a book. As the table shows, except for the anthropologists, the percent of total output which is non-scientific is quite small in most instances.

Of considerable interest is the flow of productivity over time. This has been analyzed for each man for successive five-year periods, beginning with the year his doctorate was granted, although 29 of these men have earlier publications. It is difficult to categorize the ensuing patterns, which are quite varied and complicated, in part, because of the time devoted to defense activities and the varying periods in the professional life histories at which these activities occurred.

One way of looking at the data is to observe the period in which productivity was greatest. This is shown in Table II. Clearly the physicists reach their peaks earlier than the others. This is not inconsistent with the general consensus that they also make their major contributions earlier. It should be noted, too, that more physicists have moved into administration which seriously curtails scientific productivity. The figures that follow have been selected, in part, as examples of different peak periods.

One may also note, however, that there is no justification for the sometimes expressed opinion that rapid advancement in the academic hierarchy will somehow reduce motivation to produce. Ten years after the doctorate most of them were well up in that hierarchy and, as the figures show strikingly, they have not stopped producing.

The graphs also show that there are changes in the relative productions of scientific work which appears in different forms. There is some tendency for straight research reports to diminish with respect to other technical publications as time goes on, but this is not consistent.

In all of the figures that follow, the first graph shows the weighted totals for scientific and non-scientific publications; the second graph shows unweighted

TABLE II

Distribution of Periods of Peak Production

	Biol.	Th. Ph.	Exp. Ph.	Ps	An.	Total
N	15	6	9	11	4	45
Period						
1	0	1	1	0	0	2
2	3	2	3	2	0	10
3	1	1	3	1	0	6
4	5	0	1	1	1	8
5	0	0	0	1	0	1
6	2	1	1	5	0	9
7	1	0	0	0	1	2
8	1	0	0	0	0	1
9	1	0	0	0	0	1
Two or more peaks	1 (3 & 7)		1 (2 & 4)	1 (4 & 5)	2 (3 & 4), (1 & 3 & 6)	
N with Predoctoral Publications	9	6	6	6	2	29 (64%)

frequencies for scientific publications. The figures have been selected to show the great variations in patterns, in approximate order of increasing lateness of the peak production of each man. Descriptions of the subjects are included in the captions.

Note that the war years intervened at different ages for different men. . . also, the usual effect of taking administrative duties. (The subject represented in Figure 1 is a rare exception.) When the last period shown includes fewer than five years, the number of years is given. It would probably have been better to make some adjustment for this, either by using a dotted line, or by multiplying by an appropriate factor.

Perhaps the graphs will have given you some idea of the intricacies of dealing with this kind of material. There was no attempt to make an evaluation of the quality of the work, but I did ask the men what they considered their major contributions with a view to noting the age at which these were made. Most of them were unwilling to give any answer at all; some noted that there had been a

A. Total Productivity

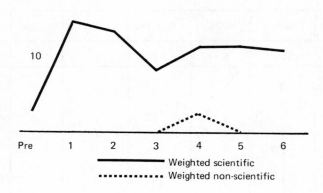

B. Scientific Publications

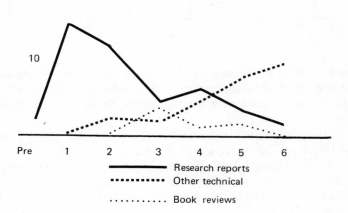

Fig. 1. Psychologist. Three years during the 3rd period were spent chiefly on war work. Became department chairman early in the 6th period. Average productivity per year = 2.5. Papers: 33 (47%) with co-authors of whom three were students.

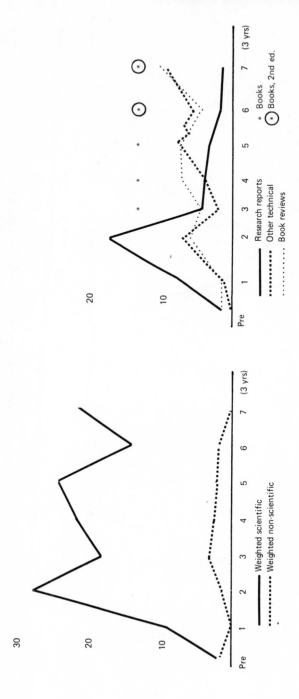

Fig. 2. Psychologist. During the 3rd period, two years were spent on wartime activities. He became a department chairman in the middle of the 3rd period, and spent five years in the 5th and 6th periods as Dean. Average productivity per year = 4.1. Papers: 38 (49%) with co-authors, of whom 19 were students.

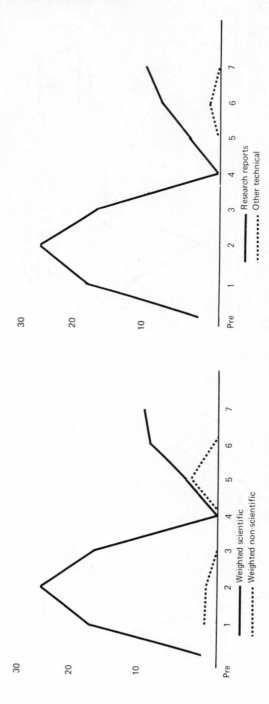

Fig. 3. Experimental Physicist. The 4th period was entirely devoted to wartime activities. After that he became Director of a research institution. Average productivity per year = 3.4. Papers: 68 (77%) with co-authors, all colleagues.

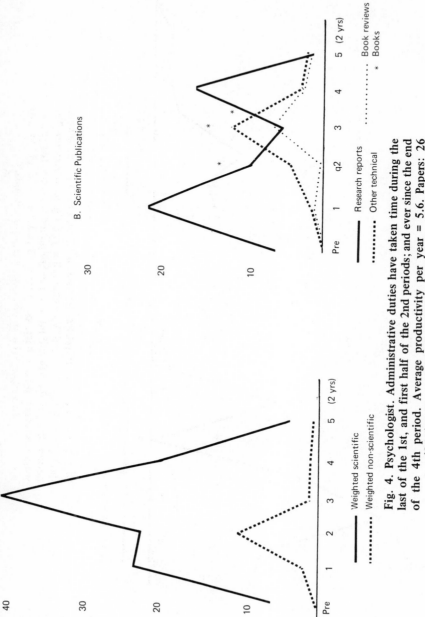

Fig. 4. **Psychologist. Administrative duties have taken time during the last of the 1st, and first half of the 2nd periods; and ever since the end of the 4th period. Average productivity per year = 5.6. Papers: 26 (26%) with co-authors, of whom 14 were students.**

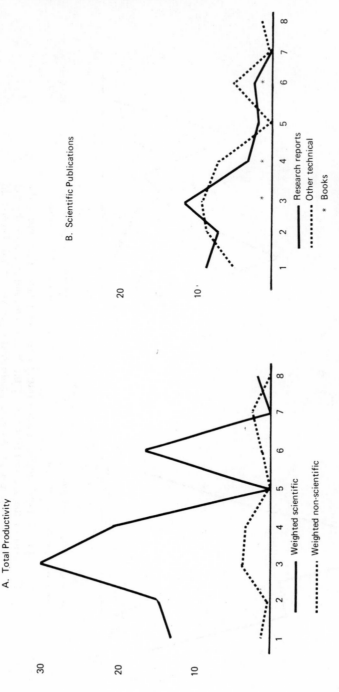

A. Total Productivity

B. Scientific Publications

—— Weighted scientific

·········· Weighted non-scientific

—— Research reports

········· Other technical

* Books

Fig. 5. Experimental Physicist. He became Dean of a graduate school during the 3rd period, and Vice-chancellor and Chancellor in the 7th period. Part of the 4th and most of the 5th period were devoted to war work. Average productivity per year = 3.1. Papers: 23 (33%) with co-authors who, in one case, were two students.

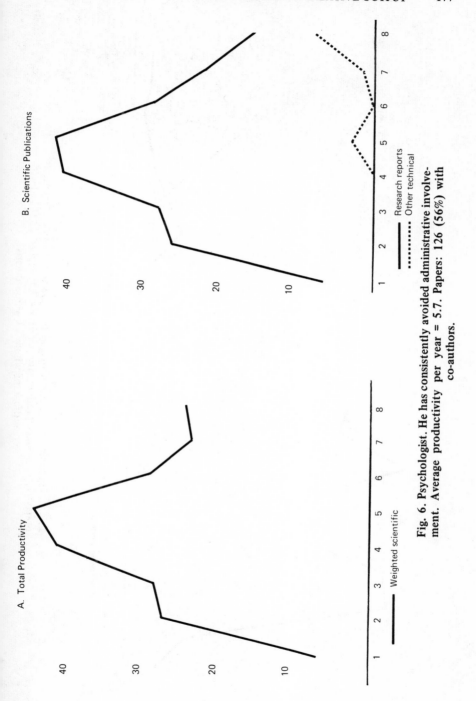

Fig. 6. Psychologist. He has consistently avoided administrative involvement. Average productivity per year = 5.7. Papers: 126 (56%) with co-authors.

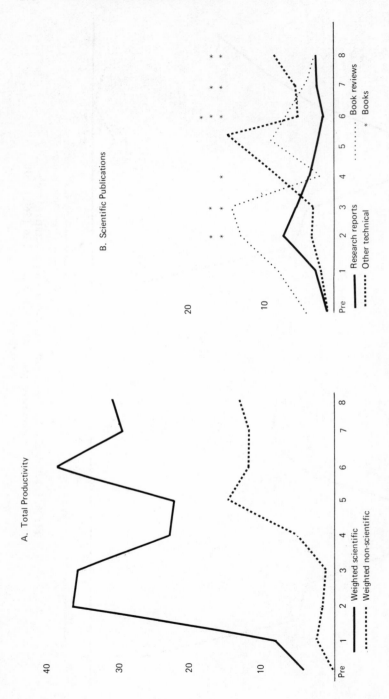

A. Total Productivity

Weighted scientific
Weighted non-scientific

B. Scientific Publications

Research reports   Book reviews
Other technical   * Books

Fig. 7. Psychologist. He has managed to avoid administrative functions pretty fully. Average productivity per year = 7.1. Papers: 23 (15%) with co-authors, of whom 13 were students.

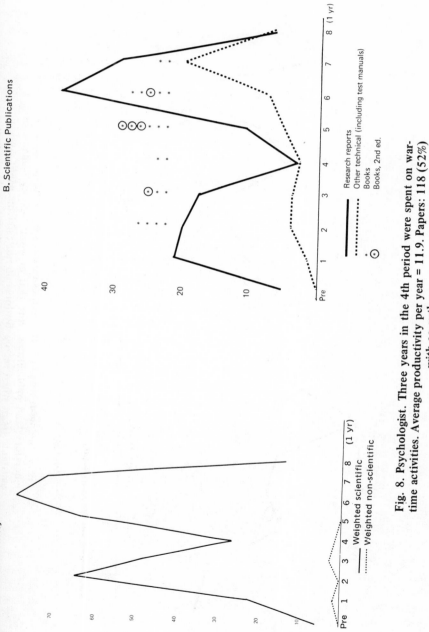

Fig. 8. Psychologist. Three years in the 4th period were spent on war-time activities. Average productivity per year = 11.9. Papers: 118 (52%) with co-authors.

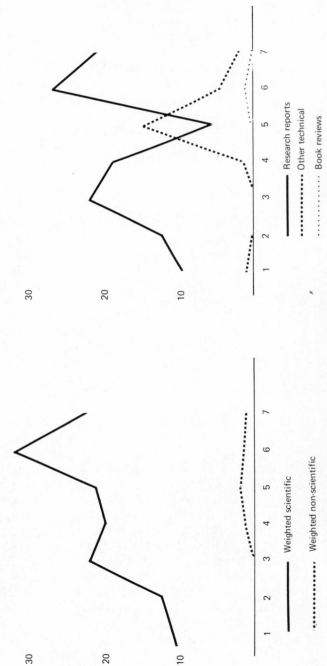

Fig. 9. Biologist. Administrative duties have centered around a research laboratory, and publications from that of work done by students or assistants (even when set up by him) do not carry his name. Average

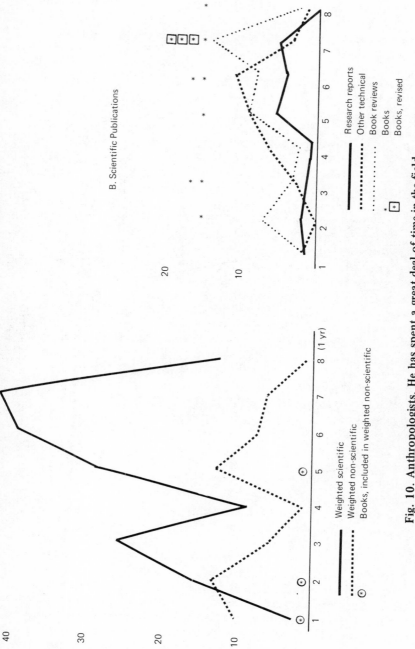

Fig. 10. **Anthropologists. He has spent a great deal of time in the field, as well as three years in war service in the 4th period. Average productivity per year = 7.7. Papers: 23 (17%) with co-authors, none of whom were students.**

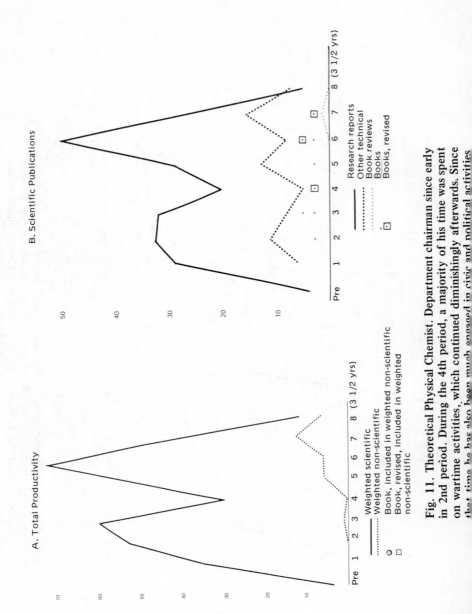

A. Total Productivity

B. Scientific Publications

Pre 1 2 3 4 5 6 7 8 (3 1/2 yrs)

Weighted scientific
Weighted non-scientific
Book, included in weighted non-scientific
Book, revised, included in weighted non-scientific

Research reports
Other technical
Book reviews
Books
Books, revised

Fig. 11. Theoretical Physical Chemist. Department chairman since early in 2nd period. During the 4th period, a majority of his time was spent on wartime activities, which continued diminishingly afterwards. Since that time he has also been much engaged in civic and political activities

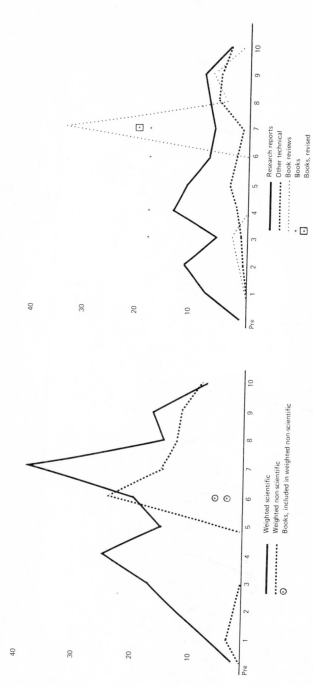

Fig. 12. Biologist. He has been productive in two different fields, which are combined in the graphs. He was department chairman from the middle of the 6th period until the last year of the 9th, and has served as administrative officer of a society during the last 4 years of the 10th period. Average productivity per year = 4.7. Papers: 24 (12%) with co-authors.

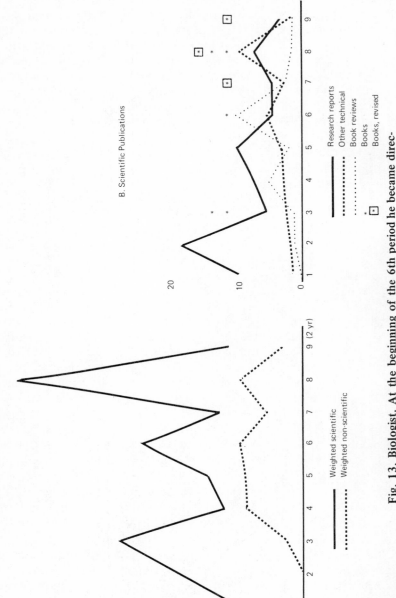

Fig. 13. Biologist. At the beginning of the 6th period he became director of a research institution. Average productivity per year = 5.36. Papers: 10 (10%) with co-authors.

series of papers over a long period when they were working toward something in particular. One of them said, "The biggest thing I ever did, I did as a graduate student and I haven't come up to it since." I'm not sure such an evaluation would be made by his peers.

There are some who have been so productive in ideas that they shift from one thing to another, although frequently it is true that, as they get older, they tend more to continue on the same line they have been following than to institute a new one. This seems to have been particularly true among the geneticists. The field was moving so fast that their early work has tended to become outmoded. One of them described this situation and said quite frankly, "This is why I became a college president. I didn't have to work so hard to keep up. Maybe I could have but, anyway, I can do this" (and successfully).

In general, after retirement these men can expect to retain laboratory and office facilities at their universities if they wish to do so. Any of them who have wanted research grants have continued to get them. One thing they do have a problem with—their universities do not provide them with secretarial help which most of them need. They have tended to gain large numbers of correspondents over the years (students and colleagues particularly) and still keep in touch with them.

C: I'd like to make a comment on the implications that you have made. I would like to point out that this is studying a particular type of creativity which is citing research publications. There are many and varied remarks made about the poor fellow who has given up research for administration. And this, I think, is a really fundamental problem. The scientific community in this country has moved into a new era in their relation to society and they simply have not recognized the importance of taking part creatively in administrative matters.

S: I don't think that is a fair comment.

C: Emotionally and psychologically. There is no way to measure it by counting papers, books, and what have you, as creative contributions in this area. I think one of the reasons they do not have the impact they could have been getting in view some of the things they have discovered by publishing is because they're unwilling to organize a situation which is meaningful. They feel obligated to the administration in universities and colleges. Many of them do not participate in government responsibilities. In short, they have stuck narrowly to a particular form of creativity or to "where the action is." This is all right as long as it is labeled with the assumption that the production of a paper is a measure of creativity. It is a measure, but it is only one.

S: That's quite correct. Some of the others have gone into administration and maintained creative research. All I'm saying is that if you do a lot of administration, you don't do a lot of research. I'm not saying it's bad. I'm sorry if I have conveyed this.

C: No, not necessarily from you, but from around the room. The assumption is that administration is a fate worse than death and this assumption really kills me. It isn't just you; it's the whole community. It's a very poisonous attitude which has got to go in the society of the creatives. They've somehow got to devise means of organizing themselves first, and this just producing one paper after another and admiring each other, and so forth. . . .

S: There are research laboratories which have facilities for a number of people. Some scientists feel that one way to do this is to have a non-scientific administrator to take a lot of the detail off of their hands. One or two of them have been successful in getting someone to do this. In the university community, this can be very difficult. A non-professional administrator has a problem because his position in the university area is very much like that of a warrant officer. He may not be a member of the faculty club, for example. Now this kind of thing happens.

As far as research productivity goes, you do not get this kind of productivity at a high level along with administration. Their time is taken up with other things. Most of these men have served on government committees, particularly the physicists. A large number have told me that there have been periods when they were running to Washington every two weeks. Most of them have served five or ten years this way and then they say that they've done their share and let somebody else do it. Because of the final presentations, I think that they've underestimated the amount of their efforts in civil and professional services. . . .

C: You haven't tried the method of putting in that information?

C: We have done studies not only of scientists, but of physicians in practice, including our medical faculty, specialists and general practitioners. We have profiles of their contributions, accomplishments across about 80 activities, e.g., faculty members, physicians, researchers, teachers, and communicators to the public, and other services. Now this profile is jagged, so all men cannot be good in the use of their energies and different talents in all things. We do have such profiles. Some of them put a lot of effort into a few things and some a lot into others. One challenge is the problem of weighing these things.

C: I'd like to raise a voice in support in view of Sherwin's statement, because I think he was reflecting a feeling that many people have, which is that government is'in a tough spot in getting able people into some of these programs and have this feeling about the permanent list now on the NASA program. I'm very grateful when some of the really able people go in and take these jobs, which are not very rewarding in money, and make these kinds of contributions. These are not directly relevant to the study, but it's, in my opinion, a top number one national problem.

C: I am aware of Dr. Sherwin's approach with the military in which he tried to reduce the number of administrative people over the research effort, so that researchers won't be used wrongly and they will be reporting more directly, in person, to the top. Then they can concentrate more on their contributions

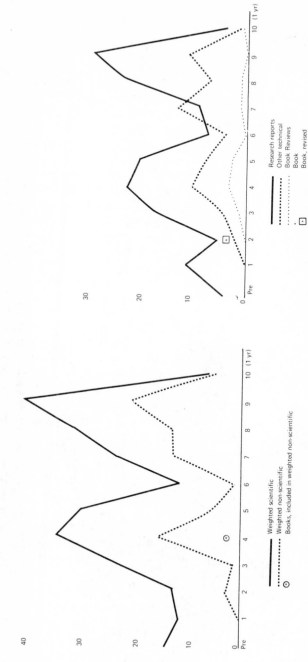

Fig. 14. Biologist. The drop in the 6th period reflects a stint at a college not encouraging of research. Since then he has had all the facilities he needs and in recent years a large research group under him. He has had some heart trouble since the 8th period. Average productivity per year = 6.5. Papers: 84 (39%) with co-authors.

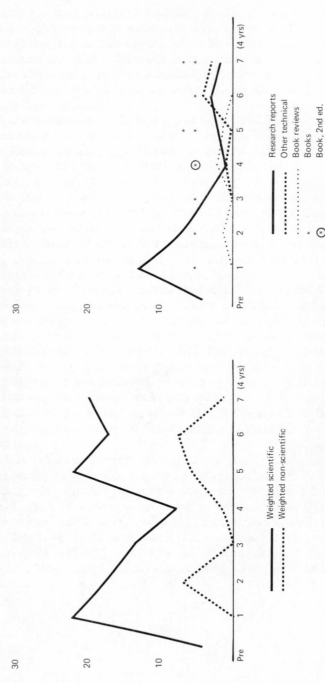

Fig. 15. Theoretical Physicist. Within periods 3 to 5, 8 years were spent on wartime activities. Since the middle of the 6th period, administrative activities have increased steadily. Average productivity per year = 4.8.
Papers: 29 (50%) with co-authors.

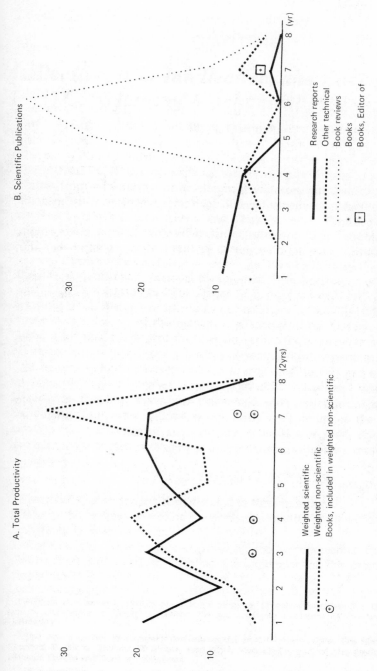

Fig. 16, Anthropologist. He became department chairman about the middle of the 4th period and has continued in this position. Average productivity per year = 6.0. No papers with co-authors.

rather than spend their energies thinking about communications, complications, and problems, week after week after week.

C: Anne mentioned, in regard to four anthropologists, that they tended not to have regular joint publications. Maybe the character of anthropological research could have changed over the last thirty years. Thirty years ago, the idea was to go live with some primitive tribe and write about one's experiences. It might be kind of interesting to analyze the contemporary publications in anthropology and see whether there is more joint authorship, and more team effort. We may be reflecting past anthropology rather than the present, so that it's not in the nature of the paper so much as the change in the nature of anthropological research.

S: I don't think that tells very much.

C: You've raised an interesting question about demonstration. In a field like experimental physics, you may need a team to do something that's not so simple. I would just conjecture that the people in the field of communications research and also, I'm happy to suggest, creativity, have an awfully tough time writing joint papers.

C: I think we have a lot of erroneous ideas floating around about this matter of basic research. In the field of education, we always have some people sniping by saying that some people who spend all that time in research just want to be rewarded; they should spend more of their time in teaching.

I have a not completely verified hypothesis: people who are most productive in research spend more time with students and have more demands made on them for service than those who are not doing it. There is a limit to innocence, but within those limits where I have been able to agree with the universities, it seems to be the people who are most deeply involved in research who are giving more to their community, to the international situation. They also spend more time with their students than those who are not doing research.

C: Both of your comments remind me of another, that is, the person who is highly productive in Shockley's IRE paper; that fewer and fewer people produce more and more and these highly productive persons have never been paid what they are worth by their organizations and it might be difficult for most people in organizations to conceive of paying them what they are really worth, even though the total input costs for them, including overhead, may not differ much from the input costs for other scientists.

Another hunch that I have is that professors, who are doing both research and teaching, are better teachers in many ways than non-researcher teachers, including giving the students a feel for everything about the state of knowledge. The professor should not only keep abreast of knowledge, yet the output differences may be manifold, even of a different order of magnitude. In fact, one scientist we studied suggested that the less talented often require greater facilities to do the same job, and that when you get below a certain level of talent, no amount of facilities could be added that would enable such a person to cope with and contribute to a problem, but he may be able to produce new knowledge and have his students learn much more about knowledge production and working at the fringe of knowledge and with unknowns than the non-research teachers can do. We heard once that there had been a report from a study indicating that researchers were better teachers than non-researchers, but, unfortunately, we never were able to locate it.

C: I'd like to break in with a story about my freshman seminar. I got involved in a research job in Palo Alto. One of my customary ways of getting some familiarity with a thick stack of papers that were stapled together with dates on them, before I tried to develop these new approaches, was that I thought along the line of the "pass-the-scissors game," and I thought I ought to give these fellows a realistic impression. So I grabbed a handful of the stuff that I was going to throw in the ash can and I took it in to pass it out. I said to look at all the time they had wasted, and I found that several of them were plagiarized—that is what they had written up and gotten out of courses. This made an impression on them when I let them know that some of them had learned how to plagiarize in other courses.

C: It seems to me that possibly your most important point is that the persons who earlier in life have learned how to turn on their own internal productive processes and creative processes in their scientific work can and generally do continue to be productive and creative throughout their careers. 'Tis not true that they build up to one major contribution, usually fairly early in life, after which they then fade away almost into unproductivity.

S: Yes, I agree thoroughly. A first-rate man remains first-rate, barring most unusual circumstances. I don't know how widely held is the notion that people quit after one major contribution. It seems odd to me, and I am sure it is not correct. Perhaps it developed, so far as it has, because individual scientists get into the history books on the basis of one or a few contributions. People don't realize perhaps that any one contribution, as finally summarized in a brief historical statement, may be only part of years and years of work, and that other contributions may be of equal importance in terms of what they led to, rather than in terms of what they rounded off. It's the rounded off bits that get into the histories.

CHAPTER 14

Programming Creative Behavior [1]

Sidney J. Parnes*

THE PRESENT research to develop auto-instructional materials capable of developing creative behavior in students (based on materials developed in a creative problem-solving course) is the first stage of a contemplated long-range period of research activity designed to ascertain the following: to what extent can auto-instructional materials provide for deliberate development of students' creative behavior and at the same time assure mastery of subject matter? The *total* project would thus couple the creative trend in American education, advocated by leading educators, with the requisite acquisition of course content. In later stages, it is anticipated that incremental programs which already exist in subject-matter courses will be modified in such a way as to permit their integration with creative thinking principles and procedures.

A substantial foundation for the present project had already been provided at the State University of New York at Buffalo, where the principles and procedures of creative problem-solving had been developed and taught for over twelve years. During the latter half of this time, the validity of these principles and procedures had been scientifically confirmed by research projects at Buffalo State University and at a number of other institutions of higher learning. The specific purpose of the present research, the first stage of the contemplated long-range project, was to program these evaluated principles and procedures.

CREATIVITY DEFINED *Read*

Creative behavior is herein defined as behavior which demonstrates both uniqueness and value in its product. The product may be unique and valuable to a group or organization, to society as a whole, or merely to the individual himself. Thus, in behavioristic terms, creative behavior is: (1) a response,

---

[1] The author is indebted to Hayne Reese for providing the detailed statistical analyses required in the study, as well as for his collaboration in the design of the research.

*Sidney J. Parnes is Professor of Creative Studies, State University College, Buffalo. He was formerly Director of Creative Education at The State University of New York at Buffalo.

responses, or pattern of responses which operate upon (2) internal and/or external discriminative stimuli, usually called things, words, symbols, etc., and (3) result in at least one unique combination that reinforces the response or pattern of responses. In general, such creative behavior may be classified as discriminative, manipulative, and evaluative.

Creativity is thus a function of knowledge, imagination, and evaluation. Bruner (1962) describes learning as encompassing "acquisition, transformation, and evaluation." He is referring to *creative* learning—not learning in the usual sense of the word. Conant (1963) emphasizes the need for better knowledge on the part of teachers, more *acquisition*. Without knowledge, there can obviously be no creativity. But as Whitehead (1929) emphasized long ago, education should aim at "the effective *utilization* of knowledge." Conant argues particularly for the tools; Bruner and Whitehead emphasize all three elements involved in learning.

By way of analogy, we might consider the kaleidoscope, wherein the more pieces we have in the drum, the more possible patterns we can produce. Likewise, in creative learning, the greater our knowledge, the more patterns, combinations, or ideas we can achieve. However, as in the kaleidoscope, merely having the knowledge, the bits and pieces, does not guarantee the formation of new patterns. In the kaleidoscope, it requires the revolving of the drum; in the mind, it requires the manipulation of knowledge, the combining and rearranging of facts into new patterns in the form of ideas. The effectiveness of creative productivity also depends, of course, on the evaluation and development of the embryonic ideas into usable ideas.

Without knowledge, imagination cannot be creatively productive. With abundant knowledge, but without manipulation thereof, we again achieve no worthwhile creativity. Even with both imagination and knowledge available, but without the ability to evaluate, synthesize, and develop our potential ideas, we again achieve no effective creativity. Thus creative productivity is a function of knowledge, *manipulated, evaluated,* and effectively *developed* into usable ideas.

For development of creative behavior, we teach students to observe facts and to discriminate what *is,* what exists; then we teach them to manipulate—to create many new hypotheses as to what *might* be—before they decide what *should* be. How can one be sure what *should* be until he knows what *might* be? I think this alternative-searching stage gets relatively little emphasis in our educational system. What do you think about that? Does that seem reasonable to you?

Taylor: We tried this approach before making a final decision on one of our research projects. After we had thought about it one day, we said, "Let's incubate on it and not accept the best decision found so far." So we thought about it the next day and again said, "Let's worry about it tomorrow." We kept this up daily until about four days later. The quality of one proposed decision that emerged on the fourth day was far better than anything we had generated up to that date, and we were quite willing to settle for that new one because it was so much better than anything from the days before.

S: Yes, this is the notion. We find this over and over again in our research and other experience. Let me also point this out: while we emphasize that we want to get students to "manipulate" between the "observing" and the "evaluating", it is also important to stress that the imagination—"manipulating"—actually has much to do with how carefully we observe and what kinds of viewpoints we get from what we observe. And as to evaluation, it is obvious that here, too, imagination has a great influence on our effectiveness in terms of the potential consequences we foresee for our ideas.

Taylor: To manipulate and to sense what might be, you have to allow yourself some time on the problem—either time in the curriculum or time in the organization. You may have to challenge existing deadlines. You may have to make some value judgments to decide that even though there is a deadline, even though there are a lot of things pressing, this particular point is too important for you to make a fast decision, when much better ones may be possible by adding more time to think on the problem.

S: Yes, but it is a matter of relativity. Obviously, you can't delay the decision forever. There has to be a happy compromise. You have to ask, "What is the ideal time?"

EFFECT OF PROGRAMMING ON CREATIVE DEVELOPMENT

Research suggests that incremental teaching of subject-matter can be more efficient than conventional teaching methods. For example, Galanter (1959) reported that students could master a programmed course in spelling four times faster than a conventionally taught course. The first comprehensive source book on programmed learning reported a number of pilot research projects which indicate an increase in teaching efficiency (Lumsdaine and Glaser, 1960). Schramm's (1964) annotated bibliography cites 36 studies, of which 17 showed significant superiority for students who completed programs as compared with those in conventional classes. In all but one of the remaining 19 studies, no significant differences appeared. In the one exception, the classroom students proved superior to the programmed ones.

As a result of the encouragement of research, auto-instructional programs are appearing at a rapid rate in practically every academic field. Inasmuch as the effective programming of a textbook is a costly and time-consuming process, many forward-looking educators are asking themselves whether they should reconsider the entire curriculum before developing programs. This would enable them to incorporate the benefits of any improvements into the new programs from the start. By the same token, it seems opportune and appropriate to seek ways of programming the much-sought creative development of students and ultimately, in later stages, to attempt to incorporate this into the newly emerging auto-instructional materials in all fields. Thus an opportunity may be provided to *plan* for the creative development of students through the new programs.

Many auto-instructional authorities are concerned about development of creative behavior. Kendler, of New York University, has stated, "We are faced with a serious threat to our national scientific creativity," and claims this is because our language habits are becoming less abstract, more concrete, and more standardized (Galanter, 1959). Stone, of the Department of Health, Education and Welfare, has voiced a common concern of many educators in his statement: "There is a need for more research in the effects of the new media on creativity and on higher thought processes" (HEW, 1961).

Can Creative Behavior Be Programmed?

Many psychologists who conduct research in teaching-machine programming think that this can be done. Skinner (1961) has written that "teaching machines are by no means confined to imparting explicit repertoires of behavior." That is, programmed learning can require the student to produce more than "right" or appropriate answers. Klaus, of the American Institute of Research, writes:

> The third level of instruction involves the teaching of such capabilities as creative thinking and judgment. This last level of education may be the area in which auto-instruction will yield its greatest fruits. The possibilities of developing a program in this area are derived from two simple observations. First, we have sufficient data to indicate that creativity and judgment are examples of learned behavior. Second, we have evidence to indicate that these behaviors can be taught. What is left is simply a matter of mechanics: that is, identifying exactly those behaviors to be learned and then finding the means to successfully establish these behaviors in the student's repertoire with auto-instructional methods and devices. (Klaus and Lumsdaine, 1960)

Other psychologists provide further emphasis. Guilford (1961) wrote, "It has seemed to me that it should be possible to introduce training for creative performance by means of modified programs for the machines." Maltzman *et al.,* (1959) have already found that reinforcement can strengthen originality. Cowen (1952) discovered that reinforcement by praise resulted in less rigidity in problem-solving. Carl Rogers told a symposium that, although programs are well suited for shaping people to "fit" into society, they can also be used to *release* creative potential.

RESEARCH ON PROGRAMMING FOR CREATIVE DEVELOPMENT

Authorities emphasize the value of creative thinking in programming, but give much less attention to programming deliberately for creative development. Very little of the teaching machine research reported in the literature deals with creative thinking. Barlow (1960) conducted a project in which students were presented alternatives, neither of which was correct. By allowing the students to discover this, and then having them develop a third correct form, he hoped to teach them to think for themselves. Klaus (1961) has been developing programs for teaching independent thinking and judgment, as well as creative writing. Crutchfield initiated a project on auto-instructional methods and creative thinking for fifth and sixth graders under a grant from the Carnegie Corporation. He obtained strong positive results which are summarized by his associate, Olton (1966), as follows: "in general, children who went through the program scored more than *twice* as high on the posttest as the control children . . . . This very large difference existed over a broad range of creative thinking skills . . . ."

IMPLICATIONS FOR BASIC RESEARCH

Auto-instructional research is usually aimed at ascertaining factors in learning efficiency and determining to what degree each factor or variable can be varied, alone or in combination, in order to develop optimum efficiency in learning. Some variables are functions of the machines; some are functions of the program; some are functions of the students or their environment; and some are functions of all four.

Such learning variables are also creative variables; i.e., the more we learn, the more ideas our imaginations have to manipulate. This does not mean, however, that factors which affect learning will necessarily have the same relative effect on creative behavior and vice versa. It seems obvious, however, that while certain aspects are stressed more in creative behavior than in learning and vice versa, the optimum situation would be a happy balance between the two.

It follows that research regarding creative behavior should closely accompany auto-instructional research. Any future research which reveals that a certain procedure has impact upon learning effectiveness should be checked to ascertain whether it is also helpful or detrimental to creative development. This, of course, opens up new fields of basic research in creative behavior. For instance, if reading speed, eyespan, speed-of-association, and other such factors increase retention and comprehension, this does not necessarily mean that they also enhance creative development. When one considers the part played by incubation in creative thinking, one realizes that the variable "time" may bear so complex a relationship to creative thinking that much research will be needed on this point. Incidentally, research has already indicated that "uncommonness and remoteness of response" increase with time, while "cleverness" has been found to be independent of time (Christensen *et al.*, 1957).

OBJECTIVES OF THE RESEARCH

General Objective

The hypothesis tested was that scores on creative ability tests can be significantly increased through a program developed to present incrementally the principles and procedures of a creative problem-solving course. As a by-product, the effect of such a program on student attitudes toward the course was also studied.

Specific Objectives

1. To reduce various creative abilities—fluency, flexibility, originality, elaboration, and sensitivity—to their manifestations in defining and solving problems creatively. That is, using the principles and procedures of a creative problem-solving course, creative abilities were reduced to actual behavior which manifests these traits and abilities. In behavioristic terms, fluency is defined as the ability to generate many responses (ideas) in response to one discriminative stimulus (problem). Flexibility is defined as the ability to generate many different *classes* of responses (ideas) in response to one discriminative stimulus (problem). Originality is defined as the ability to create a response that is statistically uncommon. Elaboration is defined as the ability to generate many responses (details) that implement or spell out an idea which serves as the discriminative stimulus. Sensitivity is defined as the ability to generate many problems or challenges as responses to a situation or observation that serves as the discriminative stimulus.

2. To devise means of immediately reinforcing any response showing any slight tendency towards such creative behavior. Such reinforcement was constructed so that it was not limited to only one correct response. Rather, reinforcement was provided for any response that was considered acceptable and met criterion standards.

3. To conduct error-analyses and revise the program as necessary for optimum effectiveness.

4. To ascertain, by using experimental and control groups in a pretesting and posttesting design, to what degree this "optimum" program increases the students' creative behavior as measured by various creative ability tests. The purpose of the control groups is to provide a base line for differentiating between improvement due to the treatment effects and that due to general growth and practice effect.

5. To determine, by the use of experimental and control subjects, whether or not subjects receiving creative problem-solving training by programmed methods alone show increases in creative ability to the same extent as do subjects receiving the same error-free programmed materials by instructor-taught methods, and

whether or not either or both of these groups show a significant gain in creative ability when compared with control subjects receiving no training.

6. To study the attitudes toward the course of students taking the programmed version alone as compared with those receiving the programmed material via an instructor.

PROCEDURE

A Chronological Outline of the Development and Evaluation of the Programmed Materials

Fall, 1963

Completion of first set of five pilot-programmed booklets on the following phases of the creative process: Orientation (two booklets), Observation, Manipulation, and Evaluation.

Experimentation and error-analysis of the above with three groups:

1. Fifty day and evening students of creative problem-solving courses at State University at Buffalo;

2. Fifteen engineers and other personnel in a value engineering course at Sylvania Electronic Systems;

3. A volunteer Creativity Programming Committee made up of about ten faculty of SUNY/B and several evening instructors from education and industry.

Spring, 1964

A. Pilot testing of above at Sylvania, using Guilford creativity tests on experimental and control groups. The control group received comparable training from an instructor of creative problem-solving of Sylvania's central staff. Although proper sampling and experimental controls were lacking, and although rigorous statistical tests were not computed, results did indicate that the posttest scores of students taking the program were approximately equivalent to those of students who had instructor training. There was even some indication of greater originality and sensitivity on the part of the program students.

B. First and second major revisions of Observation and Evaluation booklets, based on all error-analysis and feedback mentioned above.

Summer, 1964

A. Experimentation and error-analysis on Observation and Evaluation booklets with 250 new enrollees in Tenth Annual Creative Problem-Solving Institute, June of 1964, plus 150 faculty and leaders at same Institute.

B. Analysis and critique of above by consultants during and after above Institute, as well as by special group of leaders at the Institute.

Reactions were most encouraging with respect to participants' attitudes toward the program. These experimental materials were introduced in place of the skilled and enthusiastic instructors who would otherwise have conducted the particular sessions. In spite of this, and in spite of the fact that the participants had not expected to be given any programmed materials, 87 percent found the experience from "acceptable" to "highly enjoyable"; only 13 percent found it "distasteful" or "very distasteful."

As to the effectiveness of the programmed instruction, 52 percent of the participants felt it was "capable" or "superb," 33 percent "passable," and 15 percent "poor" or "terrible." Significant improvements were made in the newer versions, based on the reactions and recommendations. Of course, the comments herein refer to participants' reactions only, rather than to measured effectiveness in improving creative ability. However, the experimenters were much concerned with participants' attitudes because of the widespread feeling among creative problem-solving instructors that "you cannot program creative behavior."

C. Experimentation and error-analysis on Observation booklet with 50 students in psychology class at Cornell University. (Half were administered Revision 1, half Revision 2.)

Results, as to student preference, were inconclusive. Each version received comparable feedback in terms of preference of those who took it at Cornell. (The same was true at the Institute.) However, based on a posttest on a creative task given to the Cornell students, the first experimental version appeared more effective. Hence, the decision was made to follow that style of programming for the present research.

D. Experimentation with Observation booklet with a group of 22 supervisors at Headquarters, U.S. Army Tank-Automotive Center, Warren, Michigan.

Fall, 1964

Third major revision of Observation and Evaluation booklets, based on error-analyses and feedback from 400 Institute members and 50 Cornell students. First major revision of Orientation and Manipulation booklets; construction of remaining booklets.

A. Construction of five consecutive Observation booklets and two consecutive Evaluation booklets.

B. Revamping of Manipulation booklet into six consecutive booklets, based on experiences with Observation booklets.

C. Reconstruction of two Orientation booklets into series of six booklets, based on (1) error-analyses described earlier under Fall, 1963, (2) experience with other booklets, and (3) feedback from about two dozen individuals.

D. Construction of remaining booklets to make a total of 30.

E. Experimentation and error-analysis with 25 students (SUNY/B day students in a creative problem-solving course).

F. Feedback from the students. This confirmed the need for the resequencing of the course.

Spring, 1965

Major revision and resequencing of entire 30 booklets, based on student reactions and error-analysis mentioned in E above.

A. Error-analyses of all 30 booklets on three new groups: (1) three paid college students; (2) 15 SUNY/B day students in a creative problem-solving course; (3) 20 college-bound high school seniors at one of Buffalo's city high schools.

B. Editing and revising of booklets by staff and eight consultants, in preparation for testing of the experimental hypotheses. Special attention was paid to necessary changes in timing so as to allow the slower students to complete the basic material in a single class period, yet to provide enough supplementary exercises to challenge the faster ones for the entire period. The booklets were thus designed so that each student could "stretch" his imagination for a full 40 minutes on each one. This is important because the course is concerned with *relative gains* of each individual. There are no *absolute* standards against which he is measured.

Summer, 1965

Preparation for major experimental evaluation of finished booklets.

A. Restructuring of 30 booklets into 26 course sessions. Some booklets were combined as a result of the last error-analyses. The final set includes 28 booklets for the 26 sessions. (Two booklets each—a Part A and a Part B—are designed for two particular sessions—thus 28 booklets instead of 26.)

B. Printing and preparation of the final booklets.

Fall, 1965

A. Setting up matched experimental and control groups from 1086 volunteers for the final experiment. Six academic high schools in the Buffalo Public Schools were included in the major experiment; the remaining two academic high schools were used for additional pilot-experimentation.

B. Conducting pretesting, experimental courses, and posttesting.

C. Computing reliability of scorers.

D. Scoring of tests.

E. Revision of booklets into two additional forms: (1) a "long form," which provides all "convergent" responses but leaves blanks for all "divergent" responses; (2) a "no-response" form, which leaves blanks for all responses as did the original set, but which does not provide the printed response as reinforcement.

F. Preparations for the control students of the present experiment to take the course in the spring as they had been promised. The different types of program format (described in E above) were then available for pilot experimentation in the spring classes. Thus preliminary evaluations will be possible of the relative effectiveness and student preferences of different booklet formats, as well as of different modes of instructor involvement with the presentation of the materials.

G. Completion of another error-analysis on the booklets used by the experimental students. Even though all of the booklets had been thoroughly error-analyzed before, minor modifications were suggested by the feedback from the large group of students who took the programs. All of these changes were incorporated into the revised copies prepared for the spring classes.

H. Preparation of a final questionnaire to obtain thorough feedback on student reactions. Session-by-session feedback had also been obtained through brief questionnaires in each of the booklets.

Spring, 1966
A. Analysis of results of major experiment.
B. Pilot-experimentation in all eight schools with respect to the three types of booklets and with respect to different modes of teacher involvement in the learning process.

THE EXPERIMENTAL METHOD

The Groups:

Control	Program Alone	Program Instructor-Presented [2]
62 subjects	62 subjects	62 subjects

These three groups (randomly selected from 1086 who requested to be included in the experiment) were matched on the basis of the Lorge-Thorndike IQ. Students eligible for the experiment were seniors who intended to continue their formal education after graduation. The majority of those eligible volunteered for the experiment. All were students in the eight academic high schools of the Buffalo Public Schools.

In order to increase the accuracy of the matching and to insure an adequate number of subjects for each group, as well as to provide the additional "in-school" control groups explained later in the report, the initial number of subjects that were selected and tested was 335. Students with ten or more absences per semester in the previous year were excluded as poor risks, except in a few cases where subjects with one or two extra absences were needed for better matching of groups.

---

[2] Instructors presented in conventional fashion *exactly* the same material as in the incremental program, with no deviations being allowed. This worked a hardship on instructors, but made possible a more controlled experimental comparison. Students had the opportunity to interact on all divergent responses rather than merely to write their ideas as did those taking the program alone.

Took course in Spring of 1966[3]	Took course in Fall of 1965[3]	Took course in Fall of 1965[3]
Tested at beginning and end of fall, 1965; i.e., both pre- and post-tests given *before* taking course.	Tested at beginning and end of fall, 1965.	Tested at beginning and end of fall, 1965.

Pretesting: One week—two full periods—was used for the battery of 11 psychological pretests for all three groups.

All testing was divorced from instructing; i.e., the instructor or program-proctor for an experimental section never tested his own class. Each tester introduced the pre-tests with the following istructions:

> I am _____ of the staff of the Creative Education Office. This is "blast-off" hour for the very significant experiment of which you are now an important part.
>
> As was explained to you in the earlier material you read, the tests you will now take will have nothing to do with your grades or school records. They will not be shown to your teachers or administrators. However, they are an important part of the research project in which you are participating.
>
> I think you will find interesting what you are asked to do. Sometimes the nature of the task may seem strange or silly. Nevertheless, please cooperate to the fullest extent inasmuch as everything you are asked to do is highly significant. Do the very best you can on each test.

Before the second period of pretesting, the following instructions were read:

> These tests, like the last ones, will not be used other than for research purposes. No individual scores or papers will be shown to anyone other than the University research staff, who will be identifying your papers by a number rather than a name.
>
> This second set of tests are as vitally important as those you took earlier. Again you may find some parts of the test unusual or strange; but please cooperate fully inasmuch as everything you are asked to do is highly significant. Do your very best on each test.

Treatment:

Control	Program Alone	Program Instructor-Presented
None	13 weeks—two periods per week—for course. Students were assigned to classes, in their own high schools, during their study periods. Each class met twice a week during the entire semester. There was no required outside work.	

[3] One quarter unit of high school credit was given.

Posttesting: One week—two full periods—was used for the battery of 11 psychological posttests for all three groups.

The schedule of testing was so arranged that for each section, the same tester who conducted the pretesting was assigned to carry out the posttesting. Before the posttests, these instructions were given:

Please print your name and homeroom number on the outside flap of the envelope. *Do not* put your name on any test paper. I was with you a semester ago for "blast-off" on the very significant experiment. We might call the testing you will now undergo the crucial "recovery" phase of this experiment.

As explained earlier, the tests you will now take will have nothing to do with your grades or school records. They will not be shown to your teachers or administrators. However, they are an important part of the research project in which you are participating.

All of you are subjects in an experiment designed to measure changes which may have occured in your thinking as a result of all your course work this semester.

During today's period you will be given the posttest, consisting of a series of tests similar to the ones given the first time.

It is crucial to discover whether those who haven't yet taken the creative thinking course can increase their scores on these tests as much as or more than those who did take the training last term. Otherwise, we will never know how effective the course actually is, and how worthwhile it is to offer it to students in high school generally. Therefore, you are providing data as important to the future of education as the astronauts' data was to the future of space exploration.

If you would like to have a summary of the general results of this experiment when it becomes available, put your home address on the envelope of tests. Individual test results will not be included in the summary—only conclusions based on group averages.

I think you will find interesting what you are asked to do. Sometimes the nature of the task may seem strange or silly. Nevertheless, please cooperate to the fullest extent inasmuch as everything you are asked to do is highly significant. Do the very best you can on each test.

In the tests you will now take, you may use any appropriate answers which you may have used before and/or any new answers. The important point is to get as high a score as possible on the present test.

Be sure you have ready a pen or pencil and your test envelope *only.* No other notes or materials may be used during these final tests.

The second period of posttesting was introduced as follows:

These tests, like the last ones, will not be used other than for research purposes. No individual scores or papers will be shown to anyone other than the University research staff, who will be identifying your papers by a number rather than a name.

This second set of tests are as vitally important as those you took earlier. Again you may find some parts of the test unusual or strange; but please cooperate fully inasmuch as everything you are asked to do is highly significant. Do your very best on each test.

Schools were assigned to Type I or Type II as a result of ratings by a panel of three professional members of the experimental staff. Schools were rated on the

Posttesting (continued)

Control	Program Alone	Program Instructor-Presented
Tests determined to what extent creative behavior increased without any training in creative problem-solving.	Tests determined degree to which the creative behavior increased due to training in which the students used only the programmed books.	Tests determined degree to which the creative behavior increased due to training in which the students were taught by instructors who presented the materials in the programmed books.
	Both of these groups were given an extensive questionnaire at the end of the course to assess their attitudes toward the experience.	

School Types:

Control		Program Alone		Program Instructor-Presented	
School No. 1 Type I 31 Students	School No. 2 Type II 31 Students	School No. 3 Type I 31 Students	School No. 4 Type II 31 Students	School No. 5 Type I 31 Students	School No. 6 Type II 31 Students

extent to which both the school and the neighborhood show an academic emphasis and an interest in education as a whole, including cultural and enrichment opportunities. Type II schools were rated higher in this regard than Type I schools. Within each type, the schools were randomly assigned to the three different treatments.

Type I schools were very similar to one another. However, the Type II schools were less homogeneous. Hence the comparisons among Type I schools are more valid. However, there was only one test among the 11 in which there proved to be a consistent effect of school type on treatment means. Therefore, the Type II data are, in effect, a replication of the Type I data.

In-School Controls: Six different schools[4] were used to prevent contamination, i.e., to eliminate discussion between groups, and to minimize possible replication

---

[4]Six schools are needed for the type of experimental design used. However, all eight academic high schools were used so as to provide equivalent opportunity to all college-bound students. The data from the extra two schools are being used for additional studies. Likewise, the data provided in the spring (as a result of the course offerings then to all control subjects) will be used for further studies regarding a variety of methods of presenting the course.

error. However, additional "in-school" control groups were also used for comparison purposes. Since there turned out to be no evidence of contamination, the results to be reported include these "within-school" comparisons.

Thus, in addition to the control students mentioned above in the two separate "control" schools, the "in-school" control groups served as a "double-check" in the experiment. The fact that, as will be shown later, both the "outside-school controls" and the "in-school controls" gained, in general, significantly *less* than did the experimental (trained) students, increases the confidence that may be placed in the results of the experiment. This is especially reassuring inasmuch as the experimental subjects in a particular school are even more certain to be equally matched with "in-the-same-school" controls than with their control subjects in other schools.

Scoring: All measures were scored by two independent raters. Protocols were coded so that no rater was aware of what type of subject or school he was rating.

Pearson correlation coefficients between the scores of these raters were computed for all ability measures. Computations were based on a randomly selected sample of 50 subjects, *after* each rater had done an initial group of 50. In posttests, whenever alternate forms were used and the raters were already trained and experienced, a random sample of 35 protocols was used for computation of reliability.

All test measures were scored in accordance with standard scoring instructions provided by the various authors of the tests.

Reliability of Scoring

Test	
Associational Fluency	.94
Other Uses — Quantity	.99
Consequences — Total	.97
Product Improvement — Toy Dog-Fluency	1.00
Product Improvement — Toy Monkey-Fluency	1.00
Alternate Uses	.96
Product Improvement — Toy Dog-Flexibility	.82
Product Improvement — Toy Monkey-Flexibility	.74
Consequences — Remote	.68
Product Improvement — Toy Dog-Originality	.78
Product Improvement — Toy Monkey-Originality	.81
Planning Elaboration — Part A	.88
Planning Elaboration — Part B	.99
Apparatus — Items 1-9	.80
Apparatus — Items 10-18	.78

Guilford Measures. In order to allow for a wider range of testing, abbreviated forms of four of the Guilford tests were used. The experimenters were informed by J. P. Guilford's offices that the reliability of the tests was not seriously impaired by shortening them as follows:

Apparatus—Items 1-9 for pretest, 10-18 for posttest
Planning Elaboration—Part A for pretest, Part B for posttest
Alternate Uses—Part I and II only (same for pre and post)
Consequences[5]—Items 1-3 only (same for pre and post)

AC Test of Creative Ability. Only one item from Part V of the AC Test was employed because of the time limitation (listing all possible uses for a wire coat hanger). This item only had been used in several previous studies (Meadow and Parnes, 1959; Parnes and Meadow, 1959; Meadow, Parnes and Reese, 1959; Parnes and Meadow, 1960; Parnes, 1961).

California Psychological Inventory. The CPI Dominance Scale was scored according to standard instructions provided by Gough[6](1957).

FINDINGS

The results of the tests will be summarized first, and then presented with detailed statistical analyses. An analysis of student reactions will follow.

Summary

The experimental students, on almost every test, made greater gains than did the control students. In almost all of the measures, the gains of the instructor-taught programmed groups were significantly superior to that of both control

---

[5] In Guilford's Consequences test the *total* score was used for fluency instead of the *obvious* score. This was done for the following reason: After creativity training, subjects tend to give relatively more of the "remote" responses (originality) and relatively fewer of the "obvious" ones (fluency). Therefore, if fluency of ideas were computed by counting only the number of "obvious" ones, it would appear that a subject's fluency decreases as a result of training. When summing the two scores, however, the *total* score almost invariably increases. For example, suppose a subject gave two obvious ideas and five remote ones in his pretest (total − 7), but gave one obvious idea and ten remote ones in the posttest (total − 11). In Guilford's scoring system the subject would have increased in originality but decreased in fluency. In relation to other types of fluency tests, however, he has increased his fluency as well as his originality; for other tests used to measure fluency in the experiment derive these fluency scores from the *totals*.

In conversations with the investigator, Guilford recommended caution in interpreting the "total" score (on his factor-analyzed test) as a pure fluency score, inasmuch as there is the strong impact of the originality factor being reflected in the total. The Consequences Total as a fluency measure, however, seems to provide essentially the same results in the present experiment as do the other fluency tests.

[6] We wish to thank Harrison Gough for providing the individual-item key for the scale used. We also wish to express acknowledgement to the Consulting Psychologists Press, Inc., Palo Alto, California, for permission to use the scale.

groups. In the case of the groups who took the program alone, the students were significantly superior to the control students in gains on most tests, but not to as large a degree. In other words, the instructor-taught groups tended to be more *markedly and consistently* superior to the control groups than did the students who had the program without an instructor.

Qualities of Creative Behavior Measured

Fluency	Flexibility	Originality	Elaboration	Sensitivity
ability to generate many similar ideas; i.e., in thinking up uses for a paper clip, examples are: clip money together, clip tie to shirt, clip name-plate to pocket.	ability to generate ideas outside of usual category and in many categories; i.e., in thinking up uses for a paper clip, examples are: connect dry-cell batteries, clean pipe, shoot from rubber band, etc.	ability to generate statistically uncommon responses; i.e., in paper clip uses, an example is: a race track for fleas.	ability to implement or spell out ideas; i.e., in paper clip uses, an example is: use as a tie clasp, gold plate it, add wire initials and sell for $2.98.	ability to sense problems; i.e., in thinking of *improvements* for a paper clip, an example is to rubberize the wire to give it a firmer grip (sensitivity to the problem of papers slipping out of their paper clips).

The most clear-cut effects of the training were on Flexibility and Elaboration.

Instructor-taught ≥ Program-Alone > both Controls.

The next most clear-cut effects of the training were on Fluency and Originality.

Instructor-taught ≥ Program-Alone ≥ both Controls.

Another test of originality, mentioned earlier, has not yet been statistically analyzed. This is the test concerning the effects of extended effort upon originality. From a preliminary analysis of the data on this additional test, the effects appear to be even more strongly in favor of *all* experimental students than were the effects of the originality tests summarized above.

The least clear-cut effect of the training was on Sensitivity.

Instructor-taught = Program-Alone ≥ both Controls.

The ability to think of improvements for common objects was illustrated earlier as a measure of sensitivity. "Improvement" exercises were used constantly throughout the course (different ones, naturally, from the items in the test). It is surprising to the investigators that this "sensitivity" gain was the smallest. From examining the results of periodic exercises throughout the course, it is apparent that the experimental subjects should have been able to do much better than they did on this test. As a matter of fact, in the students' questionnaires, almost half of them reported *perceived* gains in sensitivity at the *high* end of the scale. Inasmuch as students had complained frequently during the course about the repeated emphasis on improving common objects, it may be that they were poorly motivated for that particular test. Further study is thus indicated on this factor.

One personality factor was measured, in addition to the abilities discussed above. This was the "dominance" trait, on which increases had been reported in an earlier investigation with older subjects in day and evening college classes (Meadow and Parnes, 1959). No changes were observed on this measure in any of the experimental or control groups.

In general, results were similar for both types of schools studied. The School Type made a consistent difference on gains on only one test—Associational Fluency—a test of the ability to list words that bear some relation to a given word. In this test, results were ambiguous. Where there were any differences, these differences were always in favor of the experimental students. However, in some comparisons there was no difference between experimental and control students on this test.

Detailed Statistical Analyses of Data

The pretest data were analyzed in order to ascertain whether the School Types differed initially, whether the schools within each Type differed initially, and whether the groups within each Experimental school differed initially. (It might be noted that the third kind of difference would represent sampling error, since the subjects were assigned to the Experimental and In-the-Same-School Control groups in a random manner.) The logic of the experiment required the use of three separate analyses, each with a two-by-three factorial design. In each analysis, the factors were School Types with two levels, and Groups with three levels. In "Run A," the Program-Alone, With-Instructor, and Control School groups were compared; in "Run B," the Program-Alone, Program-School Control, and Control School groups were compared; and in "Run C," the With-Instructor, Instructor-School Control, and Control School groups were compared. (The Program-School Control groups were in the same schools as the Program-Alone groups; and the Instructor-School Control groups were in the same schools as the With-Instructor groups.) School Types I and II were represented in all three analyses. Each "run" tested differences between School Types and differences among schools within Types. Runs B and C also tested differences between groups within schools (e.g., Program-Alone group versus Program-School Control group).

Table I gives the cell frequencies (group sizes) for the analyses of variance and covariance, and shows how 31 subjects were obtained in each of the major groups. The analyses of variance and covariance require equal numbers of subjects in corresponding groups in the two School Types. The numbers of available subjects were examined, and the numbers to be omitted were determined in such a way that the numbers retained were maximized within the imposed restriction. Insofar as possible, subjects to be omitted were selected on the basis of some kind of "contamination," such as having an excessive number of absences from school, having an Otis IQ score instead of a Lorge-Thorndike IQ score, or having taken the tests in an unusual way—for example, because of being absent on the scheduled testing day. (In no cases were test data examined in making the selection.) When necessary, additional subjects were omitted by selection from a table of random numbers.

Table II presents the mean pretest scores of the various groups, and Table III summarizes the analyses of variance of the pretest data. As can be seen in Table III, the School Types of Groups interaction was statistically significant in almost every "run." The interactions indicate that there were differences among schools within each School Type, and that the directions of difference were not the same in both School Types. The differences were fairly large, as can be seen by inspection of Table II.

Because the magnitudes of the differences among the groups on the pretests were fairly large, the posttest data were analyzed by means of analysis of covariance techniques. Three runs were used, with the same comparisons as in the three pretest runs. The means of the adjusted posttest scores are presented in Table IV. In general, the With-Instructor groups had higher adjusted posttest means than the Program-Alone groups and both control groups (i.e., the Instructor-School Control and Control School groups). With somewhat less consistency, the Program-Alone groups were superior to the corresponding control groups (i.e., the Program-School Control and Control School groups).

The results of the analyses of covariance are summarized in Table V. The Run A analyses, comparing the Program-Alone, With-Instructor, and Control School groups, indicated that the main effect of Groups was significant on every test of creativity but was not significant on the personality test (CPI Dominance). The School Types by Groups interaction was not significant except in the three runs on Associational Fluency and in Run C on Other Uses.

Tables VI and VII summarize the results of t tests comparing individual groups, and Table VIII summarizes the interpretations of the outcomes of these tests. In Tables VI and VII, a negative value of t means that the second group listed in the row had a greater mean than the first group, and a positive value

TABLE I

Sample Sizes for Analyses of Variance and Covariance

	Type I Schools					Type II Schools				
Sample Size	Prog. Alone	Prog.-School Control	With-Inst.	Inst.-School Control	Control School	Prog. Alone	Prog. School Control	With-Inst.	Inst. School Control	Control School
All tests except Other Uses	31	10	31[a]	12	31	31	10	31	12	31
Other Uses	31	10	17	12	27[b]	31	10	17[b]	12[b]	27
Number of Omitted Subjects										
All tests except Other Uses	0	1	a	0	1	0	0	2	12	0
Other Uses	0	1	13	0	0	0	0	0	0	4

[a]Includes one fictitious subject (group means) (See Lindquist, 1956, p. 148.). [b]Data lost because of expiration of available testing time (Other Uses was last test in battery).

TABLE II
Pretest Means

Test	Type I Schools					Type II Schools				
	Prog. Alone	Prog.-School Control	With-Inst.	Inst.-School Control	Control School	Prog.-Alone	Prog.-School Control	With-Inst.	Inst.-School Control	Control School
Assoc. Fluency	12.1	13.0	11.6	10.9	13.4	14.0	15.0	13.4	13.5	11.8
Other Uses	8.0	8.1	7.6	6.2	9.3	9.0	10.4	9.9	7.8	8.5
Conseq. Total	15.6	16.3	13.0	15.4	15.8	16.5	15.7	17.4	14.6	13.6
P.I. Fluency	11.3	11.7	10.6	11.3	12.9	13.6	11.2	13.6	12.8	10.1
Alt. Uses	13.4	15.0	14.4	14.6	15.7	17.0	16.8	16.3	14.1	14.3
P.I. Flexibility	6.6	5.9	5.8	6.8	6.7	6.6	6.6	7.0	6.5	5.8
Conseq. Remote	5.7	4.3	5.0	5.6	6.3	6.6	5.7	7.2	6.9	4.3
P.I. Originality	9.3	10.6	8.4	9.2	10.8	11.9	10.1	11.5	10.3	8.2
Planning Elab.	10.2	11.0	8.9	9.8	10.5	10.4	10.8	11.7	12.7	9.9
Apparatus	6.4	7.3	6.9	5.7	7.4	7.1	5.9	8.6	7.2	5.7
CPI Dominance	27.4	25.2	26.9	22.0	24.1	26.9	27.6	27.6	28.9	26.2
IQ	116.4	114.8	113.6	114.8	116.7	118.2	120.6	118.8	117.2	117.1

TABLE III

Pretest—Results of Analyses of Variance

Source of Variance	df	Assoc. Uses	Other Uses	Conseq. Total	P.I. Flu.	Alt. Uses	P.I. Flex.	Conseq. Remote	P.I. Orig.	Plan Elab.	App.	CPI Dom.	IQ
Run A													
Schools (S)	1	1.32	2.10	2.01	2.03	3.75	<1.00	<1.00	2.44	2.87	<1.00	<1.00	5.30**
Groups (G)	2	<1.00	<1.00	1.20	<1.00	<1.00	<1.00	1.47	<1.00	<1.00	4.83***	2.19	<1.00
S x G	2	3.40*	1.82	6.96***	10.34***	4.58**	6.37***	6.75***	7.99***	4.79***	8.97***	<1.00	1.74
within cells	-	17.27 (179)	10.30 (144)	24.63 (179)	14.90 (179)	22.41 (179)	2.45 (179)	10.35 (179)	18.85 (179)	10.25 (179)	5.26 (179)	40.34 (179)	53.70 (179)
Run B													
Schools	1	<1.00	1.31	<1.00	<1.00	2.08	<1.00	<1.00	<1.00	<1.00	2.53	<1.00	2.35
Groups	2	<1.00	<1.00	1.11	1.03	<1.00	<1.00	1.54	1.14	<1.00	<1.00	1.41	<1.00
S x G	2	2.94	1.52	1.29	6.71	4.17	2.43	3.61*	6.32***	<1.00	4.40**	<1.00	1.15
within cells	-	17.61 (138)	9.93 (130)	29.33 (138)	14.63 (138)	24.12 (138)	2.28 (138)	10.77 (138)	16.62 (138)	10.70 (138)	5.55 (138)	44.33 (138)	47.71 (138)
Run C													
Schools	1	<1.00	1.96	<1.00	<1.00	<1.00	<1.00	<1.00	<1.00	6.43***	<1.00	5.04**	5.40**
Groups	2	<1.00	4.06**	<1.00	<1.00	<1.00	<1.00	1.41	<1.00	<1.00	5.30***	2.03	<1.00
S x G	2	3.50	2.12	7.53***	8.91***	1.93	6.53***	7.30***	7.22***	4.63**	9.87***	2.29	1.74
within cells	-	16.77 (141)	9.64 (106)	23.96 (141)	15.23 (141)	22.78 (141)	2.47 (141)	9.71 (141)	16.93 (141)	11.36 (141)	5.16 (141)	37.36 (141)	51.10 (141)

*p < .05; **p < .025; ***p < .01. Note: The "within cells" rows give mean squares and in parenthesis df.

TABLE IV

Average Posttest Means Adjusted for Pretest Differences (by Covariance)

Test	Type I Schools					Type II Schools				
	Prog.-Alone	Prog.-School Control	With-Inst.	Inst.-School Control	Control School	Prog.-Alone	Prog.-School Control	With-Inst.	Inst.-School Control	Control School
Assoc. Fluency	16.0	12.7	13.3	13.7	14.1	16.3	16.1	16.1	13.0	12.2
Other Uses	12.7	9.4	13.2	8.8	11.3	13.3	9.2	17.3	9.2	11.1
Conseq. Total	17.8	15.6	19.0	14.6	16.1	18.0	18.1	20.9	15.9	15.3
P.I. Fluency	14.6	11.4	17.0	11.9	12.4	14.6	12.8	17.8	12.6	13.6
Alt. Uses	18.9	18.0	19.0	15.9	15.9	20.3	16.6	19.1	16.0	15.7
P.I. Flexibility	7.5	5.9	8.5	6.0	6.9	7.9	6.7	8.7	6.9	6.1
Conseq. Remote	7.2	7.1	8.1	5.7	6.3	7.6	6.5	8.6	7.1	7.1
P.I. Originality	4.8	1.7	4.6	3.0	3.9	4.9	2.3	6.4	4.0	3.1
Planning Elab.	12.8	10.2	14.0	10.2	11.8	13.0	10.8	14.2	11.1	10.6
Apparatus	8.2	7.8	8.5	8.0	7.2	8.4	7.1	8.7	8.3	7.2
CPI Dominance	28.2	27.9	27.7	27.0	26.9	28.1	26.8	27.1	26.2	26.7

Note: Means for Prog.-School Control and Inst.-School Control are from Runs B and C, respectively. The other means are means of adjusted means from Runs A and B (Prog.-Alone), A and C (With-Inst.), or A, B, and C (Control School). Cell frequencies for analyses of covariance as for analyses of variance of pretest scores.

TABLE V

Posttest—Results of Analyses of Covariance

Source of Variance	df	Assoc. Flu.	Other Uses	Conseq. Total	P.I. Flu.	Alt. Uses	P.I. Flex.	Conseq. Remote	P.I. Orig.	Plan. Elab.	App.	CPI Dom.
Run A												
Schools (S)	1	<1.00	2.53	<1.00	1.11	<1.00	<1.00	1.32	<1.00	<1.00	<1.00	<1.00
Groups (G)	2	9.07***	10.49***	17.80***	16.23***	14.01***	22.98***	3.69*	6.99***	12.52***	4.00**	1.32
S x G	2	5.73***	2.66	1.75	<1.00	<1.00	2.24	<1.00	2.95	<1.00	<1.00	<1.00
within cells	-	14.85 (178)	16.56 (143)	16.29 (178)	18.98 (178)	18.83 (178)	2.97 (178)	11.51 (178)	9.22 (178)	10.79 (178)	7.06 (178)	19.81 (178)
Run B												
Schools	1	<1.00	<1.00	<1.00	1.05	<1.00	<1.00	<1.00	<1.00	<1.00	<1.00	<1.00
Groups	2	8.55***	7.51***	4.35**	3.39*	12.01***	10.24***	<1.00	8.44***	7.14***	3.25*	1.34
S x G	2	3.55*	<1.00	1.35	<1.00	<1.00	2.86	<1.00	<1.00	1.09	<1.00	<1.00
within cells	-	15.61 (137)	15.79 (129)	14.90 (137)	18.91 (137)	18.66 (137)	2.78 (137)	10.69 (137)	8.06 (137)	9.29 (137)	5.87 (137)	15.57 (137)
Run C												
Schools	1	<1.00	3.43	1.11	1.85	<1.00	<1.00	2.09	1.55	<1.00	<1.00	<1.00
Groups	2	3.25*	23.48***	22.14***	21.09***	11.58***	28.55***	5.05***	8.85***	15.80***	3.88**	<1.00
S x G	2	6.82***	4.56**	1.82	<1.00	<1.00	2.99	<1.00	2.76	1.06	<1.00	<1.00
within cells	-	13.05 (140)	12.22 (105)	15.72 (140)	18.24 (140)	16.49 (140)	2.81 (140)	10.83 (140)	8.03 (140)	11.03 (140)	7.23 (140)	19.87 (140)

$*p < .05$; $**p < .025$; $***p < .01$. Note: The "within cells" rows give mean squares and in parenthesis df.

TABLE VI

Comparisons of Adjusted Posttest Means (from Analyses of Covariance):
I. Comparisons of Groups in Combined School Types

Groups Compared	Run	Test							
		Conseq. Total	P.I. Flu.	Alt. Uses	P.I. Flex.	Conseq. Remote	P.I. Orig.	Plan Elab.	App.
With-Inst. vs. Prog.-Alone	A	3.04**	3.04**	<1.00	2.74**	1.53	1.29	2.05*	<1.00
With-Inst. vs. Control School	A	5.96**	5.64**	4.24**	6.74**	2.71**	3.67**	4.98**	2.58*
With-Inst. vs. Control School	C	6.08**	5.73**	4.56**	6.97**	2.82**	3.91**	4.93**	2.75**
With-Inst. vs. Inst.-School Control	C	4.80**	4.97**	3.17**	5.32**	2.40*	2.91**	4.35**	1.00
Inst.-School Control vs. Control School	C	<1.00	<1.00	<1.00	<1.00	<1.00	<1.00	<1.00	1.39
Prog.-Alone vs. Control School	A	2.90**	2.08*	4.86**	3.99**	1.19	2.39*	2.93**	2.30*
Prog.-Alone vs. Control School	B	2.95**	2.06*	4.90**	4.05**	a	2.59*	3.16*	2.50*
Prog.-Alone vs. Prog.-School Control	B	1.10	2.23*	2.04*	3.33**	a	3.91**	3.04**	1.20
Prog.-School Control vs. Control School	B	<1.00	<1.00	1.38	<1.00	a	-2.08*	<1.00	<1.00

Note: For each test included in this table, analysis of covariance showed a significant Group effect and a non-significant Schools by Groups interaction (except as indicated by Note[a]). The body of the table gives values of t computed with denominator based on within-cells variances of indicated run (Lindquist, 1956, p. 327). The df of t is the same as the df of the within-cells variance of the indicated run. *$p < .05$; **$p < .01$.

[a] Fs for Groups and interaction in analysis of covariance not significant.

TABLE VII

Comparisons of Adjusted Posttest Means (from Analyses of Covariance): II. Comparisons of Groups in Separate School Types

Groups Compared	Run	Assoc. Fluency		Other Uses	
		Type I Schools	Type II Schools	Type I Schools	Type II Schools
With-Inst. *vs.* Prog.-Alone	A	-2.57*	<1.00		2.58**[a]
With-Inst. *vs.* Control School	A	<1.00	4.05**		4.70**[a]
With-Inst. *vs.* Control School	C	<1.00	4.40**	3.12**	6.02**
With-Inst. *vs.* Inst.-School Control	C	<1.00	2.43*	1.58	5.78**
Inst.-School Control *vs.* Control School	C	<1.00	<1.00	-1.91	-1.44
Prog.-Alone *vs.* Control School	A	1.79	4.17**	2.34*[a]	
Prog.-Alone *vs.* Control School	B	1.83	4.02**	2.48*[a]	
Prog.-Alone *vs.* Prog.-School Control	B	2.35*	<1.00	3.65**[a]	
Prog.-School Control *vs.* Control School	B	-1.09	2.56*	-1.83[a]	

Note: For both tests included in this table, analysis of covariance showed a significant Schools by Groups interaction (except as indicated by Note [a]). The body of the table gives values of t computed with denominator based on within-cells variances of indicated run (Lindquist, 1956, p. 327). The df of t is the same as the df of the within-cells variance of the indicated run. $*p < .05$; $**p < .01$.

[a] F for interaction non-significant, F for Groups significant.

TABLE VIII

Summary of Results of Analyses of Covariance and *t* Tests

Test	Significant Effects	Interpretation of Significant Effects
Assoc. Fluency	A G(.001), G x S(.005)	Type I Schools: Prog.-Alone > With-Inst. and > Control School (.10); With-Inst. = Control School. Type II Schools: With-Inst. = Prog.-Alone; both > Control School.
	B G(.001), G x S(.05)	Type I Schools: Prog.-Alone > Prog.-School Control; neither diff. from Control School. Type II Schools: Prog.-Alone = Prog.-School Control; both > Control School.
	C G(.05), G x S(.005)	Type I Schools: no sig. diffs. among With.-Inst., Inst.-School Control, & Control School. Type II Schools: With-Inst. > Inst.-School Control & Control School; Control gps. =.
Other Uses	A G(.001)	With-Inst. > Prog.-Alone > Control School.
	B G(.001)	Prog.-Alone > Prog.-School Control & Control School; Control School > Prog.-School Control at .10 level.
	C G(.001), G x S(.025)	Type I Schools: With-Inst. > Inst.-School Control, but not diff. from Control School; Control gps. =. Type II Schools: With-Inst. > Inst.-School Control & Control School; Control gps. =.
Conseq. Total	A G(.001)	With-Inst. > Prog.-Alone > Control School.
	B G(.025)	Prog.-Alone > Control School; Prog.-School Control = Prog.-Alone & Control School.
	C G(.001)	With-Inst. > Inst.-School Control & Control School; Control gps. =.

(Continued)

TABLE VIII *(Continued)*

Test	Significant Effects	Interpretation of Significant Effects
P. I. Fluency	A G(.001) B G(.05) C G(.001)	With-Inst. > Prog.-Alone > Control School. Prog.-Alone > Prog.-School Control; Control School = Prog.-Alone & Prog.-School Control. With-Inst. > Inst.-School Control & Control School; Control gps. =.
Alt. Uses	A G(.001) B G(.001) C G(.001)	With-Inst. = Prog.-Alone; both > Control School. Prog.-Alone > Prog.-School Control & Control School; Control gps. =. With-Inst. > Inst.-School Control & Control School; Control gps. =.
P. I. Flexibility	A G(.001) B G(.001) C G(.001)	With-Inst. > Prog.-Alone > Control School. Prog.-Alone > Prog.-School Control & Control School; Control gps. =. With-Inst. > Inst.-School Control & Control School; Control gps. =.
Conseq. Remote	A G(.05) B No sig. effects C G(.01)	With-Inst. > Control School; Prog.-Alone = With-Inst. & Control School. No sig. diffs. among Prog.-Alone, Prog.-School Control, & Control School. With-Inst. > Inst.-School Control & Control School; Control gps. =.
P. I. Originality	A G(.005) B G(.001) C G(.001)	With-Inst. = Prog.-Alone > Control School. Prog.-Alone > Control School > Prog.-School Control With-Inst. > Control School = Inst.-School Control.

(Continued)

TABLE VIII *(Continued)*

Test	Significant Effects	Interpretation of Significant Effects
Planning Elab.	A G(.001) B G(.005) C G(.001)	With-Inst. > Prog.-Alone > Control School. Prog.-Alone > Prog.-School Control & Control School; Control gps. =. With-Inst. > Inst.-School Control & Control School; Control gps. =;
Apparatus	A G(.025) B G(.05) C G(.025)	With-Inst. = Prog.=Alone; both > Control School. No sig. diffs. among Prog.-Alone, Prog.-School Control, & Control School (but Prog.-Alone > Control School at .10 level). With-Inst. > Control School; Inst.-School Control = With-Inst. & Control School.
C. P. I. Dominance	A, B, C No sig. effects	No sig. diffs. among With-Inst., Prog-Alone, Control School, & the Prog.-School & Inst.-School Controls.

G = Group
S = School Type
> = better than (sig.)

means that the first group had the greater mean. Table VI summarizes comparisons of the separate groups in each run in which the main effect of Groups was significant and the School Types by Groups interaction was non-significant. These comparisons showed that the Instructor-School Control groups were not significantly different from the Control School groups in any of these runs; and the Program-School Control was significantly different from the Control School group only in Run B on Product Improvement Originality. The With-Instructor group was significantly superior to the Control School group in all ability tests. The With-Instructor group was also superior to the Instructor-School Control group on all of these tests, significantly so on all but the Apparatus test. The Program-Alone group was superior to the Control School group on all ability tests, and the difference was significant on all tests except Consequences Remote. The Program-Alone group was also superior to the Program-School Control group on all ability tests, significantly so on all except Apparatus, Consequences Remote, and Consequences Total. The With-Instructor group was significantly superior to the Program-Alone group on Planning Elaborations, Consequences Total, and Product Improvement Fluency and Flexibility, but was not significantly different from the Program-Alone group on Alternate Uses, Apparatus, Product Improvement Originality, and Consequences Remote.

On the two tests on which there was a significant School Types by Groups interaction, the groups were compared separately within each School Type. These comparisons are summarized in Table VII. In general, differences were more often significant in the Type II schools than in the Type I schools. In the Type I schools on Associational Fluency, the Program-Alone group was significantly superior to the With-Instructor group and the Program-School Control group, and was superior to the Control School group at the .10 level of significance. No other differences approached significance. In the Type II schools on Associational Fluency, the pattern of results was essentially the same as for the tests on which the interaction was not significant, except that the Program-Alone group was not significantly different from the Program-School Control group, which in turn was significantly superior to the Control School group.

On Other Uses, the interaction was significant only in Run C and, as shown in Table VII, there was no discrepancy between the comparison of the With-Instructor and Control School groups based on Run A and the comparisons of these groups based on Run C. The interaction in Run C apparently resulted primarily from a difference between the School Types in the comparison of the With-Instructor and Instructor-School Control groups. The difference between these groups was significant only in the Type II schools.

In summary, the pattern of results on the various tests of creative ability permits the generalization that the With-Instructor groups were superior to the Program-Alone groups and to both Control groups; and the Program-Alone groups were superior to both Control Groups. The tests most representative of this outcome were Planning Elaboration, Product Improvement Fluency, and Product Improvement Flexibility; and Alternate Uses, Other Uses, Product Improvement Originality, and Consequences Total gave essentially the same pattern of results. Associational Fluency yielded different results in the two School Types. On this test, the experimental treatments were more effective in the Type II schools than in the Type I schools. The Consequences Remote test showed results that were partly consistent with the generally obtained pattern, since the With-Instructor group was significantly superior to the Control groups on this test. On the Apparatus test, the Experimental groups were not significantly different from each other, nor from their respective In-the-Same-School Controls, but each was significantly superior to the Control School group.

Taylor: I just want to make a comment that you are using tests as what might be called immediate criteria. We need the ultimate-criterion problem solved. In a sense, you are saying the training is doing the same kind of thing that the testing is doing, so you have two kinds of consistent performances. It occurs that maybe those performances in themselves are things lacking in the background in most of our people.

C: I have one reservation here. In New York City they have a number of people who train children to take achievement tests in schools. I am just wondering to what extent your program is training people to take these tests.

S: I have been doing a lot of thinking about this very point. We would like to use Guilford's entire testing battery for his Structure-of-the-Intellect model in a pre-post experiment designed to measure what is happening to all these test factors as a result of our training. In contemplating how I might further strengthen our training program toward that goal, I have asked myself what would be wrong with designing a program where I took every one of Guilford's tests and studied the particular mental trait that was being developed in each one. Then suppose I gave students practice exercises of all types without giving them the actual test items. How would that differ from teaching someone arithmetic by giving practice in every way possible, and then giving him as a test a set of problems different from the actual figures on which he practiced? Is this the same thing?

C: The only reservation is that you don't know what is carried beyond the specific paper and pencil exercise. You don't know what else, if anything, is affected.

S: Oh, with that I'll agree. I have that definite reservation, too.

Taylor: I wanted to make something explicit. When you think of the Structure of Intellect with 120 different cells, would you feel that your training program would influence each and every one of these 120 cells?

S: No, not necessarily; but what I was also saying was that I would like to develop ways to train for the others as well. I've been asking myself this question: Is intelligence to a large extent an accidentally-acquired set of traits? In other words, are there certain experiences a person has that accidently lead him to certain understandings about analogies, logical relationships, classification systems, etc.? And if so, when you specifically and deliberately teach these concepts to those who didn't accidentally have the experiences, might we be able to help them acquire the same mental traits that the more fortunate person has reached "accidentally"? Does this make sense?

C: In relation to IQ scores and intelligence, there seems to be some general factor of intelligence that is very stable over time within the individual and is inherited to a substantial degree. All the studies go in this direction.

Analysis of Student Reactions

Regarding students' own reactions to the course, it is interesting to note that, even though the instructor-taught students found the course more interesting and felt they gained more from it, *both* groups, in their total comments, appeared to report equal application of what they had learned and seemed to feel they would apply it equally well in the future.

A few specific reactions are particularly interesting. For example, 59.7 percent of the Program-Alone students expected something of the course which didn't materialize, while this was quite dissimilar for the With-Instructor students. The "something" that didn't materialize was the class discussion with an instructor. This was mentioned repeatedly in the comments. Evidently, the Program-Alone students had all hoped (and perhaps assumed), when volunteering, that they would end up in an instructor-taught class. Regarding another specific reaction, it appears that the With-Instructor students are not in as much need for "progress-feedback" as are the Program-Alone subjects. The Program-Alone subjects reported more encouragement from the feedback on the periodic five-minute test exercises than did the students with an instructor, even though the latter made greater progress on the exercises!

Hundreds of pages of comments by the students have been amassed as a result of three sources of "open-ended" feedback from the experimental students: (1) the "comment" sections and open-ended questions in the final questionnaire; (2) session-by-session "reaction" questionnaires completed by all students at the end of each of the 26 sessions; (3) one-page summaries by all students of their overall reactions to the course at approximately one-third and two-thirds intervals through the course. All of this material is being studied further by various members of the staff.

DISCUSSION

The results show that the instructor-presented program was more effective than the program taken alone by the student, but that both increased creative behavior significantly.

The principal investigator felt, as the experimental course proceeded, that the students who worked on their own would do better because of the intense effort they appeared to exert, page by page. He felt so in spite of the fact that these students, in general, showed less interest in the course than did the instructor-taught students. It was thought that the interaction benefits of the instructor-taught class would heighten interest but would not necessarily produce greater gains in creative ability. The latter gains, it was felt, would be greater for the students who did every page and exercise laboriously on their own.

However, the interaction benefits in the conventional classes evidently contributed more to the learning than did the seemingly intense effort on the part of the subjects who took the program alone. On reflection, it may well be that each of the interacting students was *thinking* just as intensely as the programmed subjects, but simply not making constant overt responses. And recent programming literature indicates that active responding does not *necessarily* lead to better learning (Schramm, 1964).

It should be noted that certain students enjoyed the programmed booklets immensely. For example, one commented enthusiastically, "This puts me in the driver's seat!" It is also important to point out that no discussion at all was allowed between the proctor and the students who took the program on their own. This was done in order to get a picture of the results where there was no teacher influence. The proctor merely greeted the students on arrival. Any questions were related back to the booklets. The only comments made about the material were a few general announcements. Many times the proctors wanted very much to discuss something with a student, or to make an appropriate comment, but did not do so because of the rigid experimental situation. In normal usage, the programs could be dealt with much more flexibly, as has already been done in the pilot work in the classes in the spring following the major experiment.

It is highly interesting with respect to the above comments to study the following discussion of James *et al.,* (1962) regarding the creativity-development course they evaluated in their Cooperative Research Project with the U. S. Office of Education:

> As noted elsewhere in this report, our cognitive-skills approach, on its simpler levels, reduces the role of the instructor to that of an administrator who presents practice devices to participants. Thus we see few obstacles, other than development costs, to the development of auto-more complex levels the need for discussion and personal attention appear indispensable. A combination of two approaches, an automated cognitive-skills method, and a personality-insight focus might be used simultaneously. Such a course ought to involve the characteristic opening-closing phasic alternation we discussed above. 'Closed' practice would alternate with 'open' instruction and participant interaction.

Variations and Improvements

In college classes the principal investigator has done what James advocates; i.e., he has provided the programmed booklets as *homework* assignments and has used the class time for discussion, amplification, and interaction experiences. This has seemed to work out exceedingly well, although it has not been subjected to rigorous scientific testing. It has the further benefit of not limiting students' time to one class period for each booklet. Many of the college students spent as much as two or three hours each on some of the booklets when doing them at home. Furthermore, when they receive them as homework, they are able to work on the booklets at the time and place that feels most comfortable for them. Many report taking extended "incubation" breaks—others report beneficial effects of music while working on the booklets. Students mention many other special techniques that are suggestive of interesting and potentially valuable studies.

In improvements that are suggested session-by-session by students, there are many other leads worth exploring. For example, there may be definite value in providing more materials to handle, as well as more illustrations and cartoons. These ideas are used in several booklets and appear to be very successful. Research needs to be carried out to test out their effectiveness and, if confirmed, to develop ways of integrating the ideas more fully with all or most of the booklets.

It is appropriate to note that the task of programming teaches the instructor a great deal about his course, and raises scores of new questions as well. For example, because of what was learned, it became apparent that it was important to rearrange the sequence of the course. Originally, all of the principles were taught first, using practice exercises; then the students were taught how to apply the principles to their own problems. The course now allows for intermingling of problem *exercises* with student's practice on their *own* problems. It makes the program much more meaningful to the student.

Future Research Questions

There are many future questions to be answered. For example, there are scores of alternate sequencing patterns to try. Also, there are many specific booklets to refine further and test individually. Considerable pilot work in this respect was carried out with SUNY/B classes, but no attempt was made to do this under the rigorous experimental procedures that were followed for the *total* group of booklets that were evaluated (as an entire course) in the final experiment.

Fred Amram, an instructor at the University of Minnesota, gave the single booklet on "Evaluation" to students in one of his speech classes as a homework assignment. He found, in subsequent testing, that the students could not intellectualize about "criteria" for evaluation, but that they could *think up* criteria and *apply* them in evaluative tasks. He claims that the students reacted very well to using the self-instructional booklet. Many controlled experiments could be designed around specific booklets already available in the series.

The research provided much more abundant data than could be fully evaluated at the present. There are many interesting questions raised by the specific items in tables of correlations that were computed. Other correlations can also be computed between the test data and the data provided by the questionnaires. Results of the extended effort on originality can be studied, as mentioned earlier. Also, all of the pilot data provided by both the spring classes and the extra two schools are available for study.

The abundance of additional information obtainable pertains not only to the test data but also the raw data (responses) within each programmed booklet. For instance, no attempt was made to determine which particular booklet increased a particular creative trait. In effect, the full program is a "shot-gun" approach to the task of nurturing creative ability. A "rifle" approach will now take years of experimentation with individual booklets, plus modifications and changes of sequence of same.

It is intended to make further analyses of the test data from the present experiment in order to attempt to explore the following: what type of person *gains* most from the course, and what are the different *reactions* to the course on the parts of different personality types? An entire series of experiments could be designed to adapt the programs to younger levels and to specific types of students, such as the gifted, the retarded, senior citizens in adult education courses, etc.

Additional questions for further research might include the following:

1. How does the poorer reader fare in such a program? What side effects may it have on his reading ability?

2. What would longitudinal studies show regarding both the retention and transfer of the training? (Additional test results are already available from groups of the experimental subjects who repeated the ability tests again a full semester after completing the course.)

3. What additional factors in Guilford's "Structure-of-the-Intellect" are being affected by the training?

4. What are the differential effects of verbally vs. non-verbally oriented programs?

5. What effects would occur if students' booklets were returned to them to keep, or if the students were allowed to keep them without even turning them in?

6. What would be the effects of a team approach (without teacher) wherein students showed one another their responses to certain exercises and discussed them with one another as they worked through the booklets?

Conclusion

Thurstone (1924) wrote: "That teacher is more fortunate who realizes that the starting-point for the educative process is in the child's own mind, and that the tools of education are merely the means whereby we attempt to induce the child to express its own self in a direction that may be ultimately advantageous."

The present study provides data which show the effectiveness of such education in creative problem-solving at the high school level, as well as a tested program for application in high schools. Thus secondary-school educators who would like to offer entire creative problem-solving courses, or aspects of these courses, will have tested materials available to them when the booklets can be made available in published form.

Plans are being made to suggest alternative ways of introducing the self-instructional programs, so as to allow for interaction of students with an instructor who is not highly trained in the creative problem-solving instructional methods. With the help of the instructional booklets, such instructors may be able to conduct effective courses that also allow students the opportunity for discussion and group participation—an important element in any study of creative problem-solving. Also, ideas will be suggested for incorporating parts of the materials *as is* within present academic subjects, as in the example of the "Evaluation" booklet cited earlier. These ideas will be spelled out in detail in a manual to accompany the final programmed course when it is published. And last, but far from least, there remains, of course, the huge task of finding ways to integrate the programmed principles of creative thinking within emerging programs in subject-matter courses. This was stressed early in this report as a next stage for subsequent research.

Meanwhile, the majority of the material has been integrated into the *Creative Behavior Guidebook* and *Creative Behavior Workbook,* by Parnes (1967). These publications are in a form similar to that used by the instructors who used the programmed approaches in the "instructor-taught" groups of the present experiment.

Taylor: One thing I am worried about is the highly verbal nature of education. I remember Provus said at our sixth conference that we have to get rid of words if we really want to develop creativity. You haven't dropped this possibility that a person can solve a problem without ever having stated it—or perhaps without ever having used words at all in the process.

S: You mean sensing it without stating it? It's a very good point and I think it could be done. For example, I would like to do a programmed booklet in which we would test this out without students writing anything. They would be forced to *think* on every page. I don't know how we would get them to do this or how it would work.

Taylor: Maybe just have them poke a hole through the paper whenever they are thinking but have nothing verbal to write. It would be a non-verbal but effective mark.

CHAPTER 15

Dynamic Dimensions of Teacher Learning

Robert C. Burkhart*

A DISTINGUISHING quality of lasting drama is its primary concern with character, rather than plot. Plot is too specifically situational to create understanding in depth, but human relatedness developed through character seems a significant feature of persistently valuable drama. Education is in many ways analogous to drama and, while the more ordinary teaching may induce understanding of situational specifics, any profound education must develop character. We sometimes sense the drama in good teaching and see the classroom as a stage, the teacher and pupils as actors, and the daily sequence of lessons as acts or scenes. This sense of live drama is particularly vivid in student teaching, where the problems of role definition and character formation are most visible.

The decision to educate for character development rather than for understanding of specific situations is, therefore, a critical one in student teaching. However, student teaching has not generally emphasized processes essential for developing one's character as a teacher; the emphasis has been rather on the situation, or plot. We have recently tried to specify a teacher learning system for integrated character development; this report embodies research on the functioning of this system, and on the struggles of students who were learning to become themselves in the classroom. And, at this point, the limitations of our "drama" metaphor become obvious: an actor's commitment to a role is partial and, however serious, he is playing a temporary part.

But the dramatic dimensions of student teaching are real and permanent, and profoundly significant for both the professional and personal life of the teacher. We teach what we are, without always knowing what we are. The individual teacher achieves integrity in teaching through self-knowledge, through self-motivation, self-direction, and self-evaluation. If the operating modes of good teachers have anything in common which can be generalized and communicated to student teachers, it arises from their own understanding of particularized experience, not from imposed theory. Self-knowledge promotes individual integrity, and the more truly individual we get, the more universal we may become.

---

*Robert C. Burkhart is Coordinator of Research in Art Education, State University College, Buffalo.

Most students' perceptions of what they are conflict with their concept of what a teacher should be. The drama of student teaching is generated by the resulting tensions and their resolution. However, stereotyped role definitions, derived from theory or authority, tend to insulate the student teacher from the realities of himself and his pupils. Consequently, the tensions are never faced or resolved. The "method" teacher faces the same problems as the "method" actor. Integrated self-knowledge is as essential for an ultimate personal style in teaching as it is in the other arts.

We have, therefore, developed a new set of criteria, aimed at helping the student to know himself as a teacher. Instead of authority being or controlling the criteria, the student teacher himself sometimes creates and always determines the relevance of criteria in the classroom. This process not only allows for individual differences among teachers, but for variation in teacher behavior in similar situations. In fact, some teachers in the program have enjoyed teaching the same lesson, to the same age level, in different ways, and then discussing the effects and value of these differences.

Thus the supervisor need not necessarily be the model for the student teacher. Our assumption is that looking into one's own character helps develop character. And the word "develop" suggests that comparative reviews are needed to determine how we may have changed in responding to the challenge of the classroom, and what it is we may have learned as teachers. Such systematic reviews should enable us to visualize ourselves as individual teachers with unique abilities and responses. Recording our performance helps us to see and hear ourselves in action. These, then, are the requirements of a self-evaluative teacher learning system: (1) self-knowledge, rather than knowledge of externals; (2) individual teaching experience, not theory or authority; and (3) self-motivation, self-direction, and self-evaluation, rather than externally imposed controls.

A comprehensive picture of ourselves requires some information on how we *acted,* how we *felt,* and on what we *said* as we taught. Action is one significant dimension of classroom behavior. How did we act? We need some descriptive information which shows us how we moved our body, hands, and face, and how our pupils responded to our action patterns. Our inner responses are another dimension. How did we feel? We need some way of recalling what we felt as we taught. (How did we feel about our students, our materials, and ourselves?) But as we look at ourselves externally, our picture has no sound. We also need to know what we said.

However, simply to see ourselves is not enough. To learn from what we have seen, we must make meaningful evaluative distinctions about ourselves as teachers in all three of these dimensions. The genuine need for objective evaluation, and the frequently threatening character of evaluation by authority, combine to suggest a fourth dimension in the teacher learning process: shared peer-evaluation. Sometimes we can see others' mistakes and virtues better than our own, and vice versa. We can develop effective evaluative criteria by sharing with others our judgments about ourselves as teachers.

We believe that visualizing the teacher's learning in these four ways clarifies the complexities of evaluation. The student teacher sees himself and is seen in a way in which his full struggle is taken into account in determining his achievements. These four dimensions all lead to the fifth dimension of teaching—the most mysterious dimension to the teacher: what the pupils learn.

RESEARCH

Our student teaching sequence was divided into an eight-*day* orientation period, followed by an eight-*week* experiment in actual classroom teaching. We wanted student teachers to understand the dimensions of teaching operationally. The orientation period included a three-day introduction to the program, a three-day teaching experience, and a final two days in which students discussed problems they had encountered.

Students were grouped in pairs for the whole program, so that each student had a peer partner who observed his teaching and whom he, in turn, observed. Our purpose here was to enable students to help each other, and to give a better balance to the student teaching situation, in that three people (including the cooperating teacher) were interacting rather than two. We also hoped to increase the educational dialogue and to reduce the threat inherent in authority or the cooperating teacher. These arrangements also provided more conference time for the peers with each other (when the cooperating teacher was teaching), and with the cooperating teacher (when either peer was teaching). More time was also available for planning and trying new ideas without neglecting essential work. In addition to these three principal actors, a fourth—the college supervisor—visited the classroom four times during the eight weeks.

During the orientation period, each student role-played what he expected would be his actual patterns of behavior in presenting his lesson. A public school cooperating teacher worked with the students, who went through each dimension of learning separately. As they dramatized their activities, the rest of the student teachers acted as an audience, analyzing the teachers' difficulties and tape-recording their comments.

In trying to discover what is needed to prepare a student to teach, we discovered that the traditional type of lesson planning was insufficiently dynamic. Formulating goals and procedures usually didn't help the student visualize the lesson as it would actually occur. Such analysis is not operational and too abstract. We broke each lesson cycle down into three stages: introduction, studio, and evaluation. Then we asked the student to visualize his actions in each of these stages, and to describe how he thought his pupils might react. We learned that beginning students had great difficulty in anticipating and describing pupil reactions. We hoped teaching experience would improve their performance in this area.

Then, starting with their plan, we had each student teach a lesson while the other student teachers acted as pupils. The lesson was recorded and the student's peer recorded a description of the physical actions involved. (The speech and actions during the orientation teaching were similarly recorded for review and analysis.) After the lesson, each student evaluated his own lesson according to previously determined criteria. The cooperating teacher and the peer also evaluated the performance, and then the three met to discuss their evaluations. This session was also recorded. At this time, the students also examined their pupils' work. In the two-day follow-up period, the class reexamined the parts of the lesson cycle and tried to determine what they had learned from them.

Ordinarily, if students are asked to evaluate any one aspect of this cycle, they have difficulty determining what is relevant. They cannot tell which of their actions are effective and which ineffective. Experience is helpful here. Our experience as observers of teachers suggested some descriptive categories which would help students sort out various kinds of actions and distinguish among them. As far as possible the categories are exclusive, so that when the student looks at all of his acts, he can determine the proportion in each category. We have thus developed categories for actions, feelings, talk, and shared evaluation—the four dimensions of student teaching.

For the naïve, self-evaluation isn't useful without a structure; they do not have the tools to describe themselves in order to determine what is important about what they did, or to think about specific factors in terms of cause and effect. To acquire these habits is to become disciplined as a teacher and this, we think, is the educational function of student teaching. We need categories to describe ourselves, to see causes and effects, and to evaluate ourselves in terms of intent. We believe our program is a meaningful reorganization of the student teaching program, one in which the student teacher becomes conscious of self-knowledge as a key to a professional discipline.

One useful way of discussing the four dimensions is to start inside the person and work outwards. The "Confidence" dimension is a matter of relative certainty or uncertainty—the degree to which the student knows or doesn't know what to do. For our purposes, three points on a scale seem needed, ranging from *confident* to *hesitant* to *fearful.* In order to evaluate degree of confidence, we look at actions rather than words. Much of human recall ability seems kinetic rather than verbal. If someone describes our actions fully, we can usually remember how we felt internally, but we are not so apt to do this merely on the basis of what we said. Characteristically, human beings don't say what they feel. We may *hear* someone say (with apparent confidence), "One thing I know for certain"; but observation of his demeanor, bearing, and movements suggests strongly that inside he is really saying, "Gee, I'm frightened." Confidence, to a large degree, determines the student's readiness to teach.

Although we use "Action" to estimate confidence, we also regard it as a somewhat more externalized dimension in its own right. We distinguish three kinds of action: *integrated, alternating,* and *disassociated. Integrated* action is positive in that some appropriate connection exists between what we do and what we say. The rhythms of speech and action tend to coincide and to reinforce each other. There is no strain in the rhythm of simultaneous integrated action, and it is reflective rather than intense. The improvisational actors and their subjects on *Candid Camera* provide an illustration of what it means to speak with your body. Deaf persons can understand what the actors and subjects are saying through total body cues, not merely from reading lips. But deaf people cannot do this on interviews and person-to-person programs which are "just talk."

Alternating action, on the other hand, is transitional and intentional. It can be a dramatization of what we want to say, and skilled actors frequently use it in this way. Jack Benny will say, "Well," and turn his head abruptly; or a singer will stretch out his arm just before singing "out there."

Alternating action precedes or follows verbalizations, rather than being simultaneous, and shows emphatic use of single body movements, with actions rhythmically switching from one body part to another. It is useful in gaining pupil interest and participation, and stimulates excitement rather than extending control. It also has a negative aspect. When the action is desperate or excited, it may have no real connection with what is being said. A teacher who waves her hands frantically while asking for quiet *contradicts* herself and creates excitement—speech and action don't correspond, although the teacher's actions and feeling may.

Disassociated action, on the other hand, has nothing to do with what is being said and is not suggestive of what the teacher feels either. It may include nervous habits like pulling one's tie, scratching one's head, low eye contact, perfunctory use of the mouth in speaking, or restricted and repetitive body gestures.

In response to such movements, students act in disassociated ways—drum their fingers on the tables, stare out of windows, and sit with their arms folded. When the teacher isn't sure he is saying something worthwhile and interesting, and doesn't know what to do with his hands, this kind of action occurs and the teacher seems personally non-involved. Pupils either lose attention, or fail to respond. Ed Sullivan's movements, for example, often seem disassociated, both from the meanings of his words and from his feelings. Just as confidence is related to the instructor's readiness to teach, so the quality of teachers' actions probably establishes the form of pupils' reactions and the level of their readiness to learn. If the teacher can utilize actions and integrate them with what he is saying, emphasizing the main points with alternating action, the pupil will be ready to listen. Then the teacher needs to say something.

We have distinguished four kinds of teacher "Talk," characterized as *now, what, how,* and *if. Now* statements are used to order the classroom; such remarks as "Come in and sit down," "Now look in this direction," are essentially management statements and help to get the job done. The naval, "Now hear this," is another example. *What* statements are connected with the material at hand, and constitute subject matter orientation. They refer to concepts that need to be discussed in working with the particular subject matter. *How* statements tell the pupils how the teacher wants pupils to work. They deal with methods or procedures that will help the pupil solve the kind of problem he is working on. *If* questions both begin and end units. They get pupils' interests, their imagination, and make them look at things in unusual ways. *If* questions are great promoters of originality and may involve the word *suppose*. In any kind of problem-solving where there is no one right answer, or where the answer may differ from one pupil to another, the answer doesn't exist and must be *supposed*. Suppositional thinking is at the heart of the creative process.

The "Evaluation" dimension typically occurs after teaching, and is an indicator of the degree to which sharing actually exists; frequently it tests whether sharing needs to exist. It involves the student teacher, the peer, and the cooperating teacher. Being attitudinal, it is present in *any* evaluative relationship, and is not peculiar to the present situation. We distinguish three sorts of evaluative attitudes: *defensive, privately prejudicial,* and *positively sharing. Defensive* evaluation does not merely try to ward off attack, but is deliberately aggressive. It involves bringing in authority for support, and is like saying, "I can't hit you, but he can, and you know he is the champion." Defensiveness uses authority as an assertion of being right, and its intent is to make the other person feel wrong. Evaluation which is *privately prejudicial* operates by exclusion, by not allowing the other person admission. It is like saying, "In my house, this is the way I want it; that's the way I feel; this is my belief and I don't care what you think."

Both defensive and privately prejudicial feelings are negative ways of isolating the self from other people so as to avoid being self-evaluative. *Positive sharing,* on the other hand, is an inquiry process. Though it may begin by agreeing with another person, it never stops there; it always goes on to inquiring and examining. It represents search and a request for common exploration with others.

The appropriateness of the drama teaching analogy was evident from the very beginning of our program. Role-playing developed a heightened sense of the dynamics of shared evaluation, and produced some exciting training methods. We found it quite difficult initially, for example, to describe another person's actions from simply watching him. However, when the narrator partner performed the actions together with the actor teacher, he was able to describe them much more vividly and used two to three times as many descriptive words. Apparently, kinetic internalization is essential for detailed observation and description. In *Phoenix Park,* the poet Thomas Kinsella remarks: "Whatever we know, we know bodily." By "becoming" the actor, the narrator seemed to sense more fully the affective meanings of actions.

This awareness was reinforced when the narrator described the actor's behavior, using "I" rather than "he" or "she." Saying, "I walked slowly, stopped, and looked down," is quite different from saying, "He walked slowly, stopped, and looked down." Most important, first person narration appears to help student teachers recall what they felt as they taught. Listening to the narrator's first person description of their actions, they can more easily recall and classify their feelings (concomitant with those actions during actual teaching) as confident, hesitant, or fearful.

The trial classroom teaching experience, which was part of the orientation program, was taped on small shoulder-holster recorders. Although these instruments might have been psychological blocks to the naturalness of their instructional methods, some students used them as sources of stimulation. One teacher suggested to his second-grade pupils that the small light which kept blinking on and off was powered by two fireflies trapped inside. He then asked the children to imagine that one firefly was wise and one was foolish, and to compare the escape paths that each might take.

Perhaps the most exciting use of dramatic techniques occurred in the evaluative session following the trial lesson. With the whole class acting as an audience, the teacher and his peer each discussed their respective ratings of the student teacher's performance, using criteria designated by the teacher for himself. Two other students acted as "consciences"—one for the peer and one for the teacher. They acted as inner voices and attempted to verbalize what the peer and teacher were *really* thinking as they discussed the evaluation. The consciences thus magnified the defensiveness, private prejudice, or genuine attempt at sharing of the peer and teacher simply by saying what they thought was going on inside the speakers. Student teachers and peers later agreed that the consciences had described accurately the real peer and teacher reactions. Thus the sharing dimension was made alive.

To determine what each teacher had learned, we formulated a quantified composite profile for their eight weeks of work. Their accomplishments and problems were designated at the end of the first three weeks, and again during the last two weeks. Independent assessments were made by peers, cooperating teachers, college supervisors, and the students themselves. These profiles included ratings on each of the dimensions already discussed, and a rating of their pupils' progress. The pupils also rated the student teachers' effectiveness on a brief questionnaire they received at the end of each class.

Since the intercorrelations among raters were significant and reasonably high—somewhat above the .800 level—we could divide our student teachers into *high*, *average*, and *low* thirds, of seven, nine, and six members, respectively. These groups were defined according to students' standing at the end of student teaching, as shown by ratings of pupil learning. We hoped to clarify the differences between student teachers, and the extent to which such differences were the result of the self-evaluative learning program. We wondered whether the better teachers were simply better to start with, or had learned to be better on the job. We wondered also how much those who started poorly had learned. These questions were prompted by colleagues who pointed out that there was little evidence that students learned to teach, especially in as short a time as eight weeks.

Our groups, then, were defined by ratings of their classroom accomplishment, and we wanted to see how the behavior of each group differed on each of the four dimensions. We wanted to see if our theory of how teachers ought to behave was supported by evidence derived from actual practice. What follows is a report of what we learned.

Looking at what actually happened in each dimension gave us some insight into the systematic differences between teachers of varying ability. We then examined the backgrounds of each group for evidence which would make our distinctions dubious or invalid. The two types of validation measures employed were academic records and scores on creativity tests, before and after student teaching. Such basic measures are important because they tell us whether our research is likely to provide useful generalizations about the behavior of future teachers.

There may be some question regarding how much can be learned from studying twenty-two student teachers. However, most significant medical research uses even smaller populations, and the research is of a very critical nature. Our study may later be replicated on a larger scale, but its comprehensiveness does not depend on its size as much as on the extent to which differences are fully accounted for. One fault of large statistical studies is that they fail to account for other dimensions.

For example, if 25 percent of married women feel they have sexual relations with their husbands too infrequently, the conclusion that their husbands are not interested enough in sex could be very misleading. It may be that out of 100 women, 25 are from homes in which there is no compatibility between husband and wife, and thus both parties are dissatisfied. The point is that without understanding other conditions involved, a single statistic always appears out of proportion to its real significance. Thus we have attempted a comprehensive study in depth in which over 250 variables were considered, rather than studying a single dimension of student teaching.

Furthermore, in analyzing this data we have attempted to use the simplest kinds of statistical procedures, such as proportional differences, so that we can see what is going on within the individuals and groups we are dealing with and can put it together in a form which is visualizable as a whole. This is a search process and we are looking for large differences. We know that when differences between groups or in the way people respond get as large as 30 percent, they are likely to be significant and not chance occurrences. We are also interested in the order of differences. That is, whether time and time again on different variables, the same groups are high, in the middle, and low. Part of the validity of our study comes not from any specific figure, but from the consistent repetition in distribution patterns. We are looking for patterns rather than single findings.

A teacher's confidence while teaching may be the best indicator of his readiness to teach. The degree to which he is hesitant and fearful tends to indicate his uncertainty about his competence in the classroom. Most novices begin with considerable uncertainty; some learn to overcome their fear and hesitance, while others appear never to feel at ease with themselves in the classroom. This dramatic inner struggle results in actions that we as outsiders can observe in our student teachers.

The structure we are attempting to build here starts from the inside and moves progressively outward. Thus the inner dimension of self-confidence leads directly to the outer dimension of actions, and through them to the interactive dimension of talk which takes us outside of ourselves to others.

FINDINGS: LOW, AVERAGE, AND HIGH GROUPS

After two weeks of teaching, our students rated their inner reaction to classroom teaching as hesitant and fearful more than half the time. This inner struggle lasted the full eight weeks for our low group. They experience a sense of uncertainty and fear 63 percent of the time at the start, classifying 41 percent of these responses as hesitant and 22 percent as fearful. They lost none of their fear and only a small portion of their hesitancy, so that after eight weeks their negative reactions consumed 58 percent of their energy. Teaching for them is clearly a trying experience in which their lack of confidence is a key factor. They feel confident only slightly over a third of the time, and they gained only five percent in confidence during this entire experience. This lack of self-confidence is a problem that reveals itself again and again in everything they do.

Though our average teachers reported being uncertain 56 percent of the time during the first two weeks, they managed to lose 20 percent of these negative reactions. At the conclusion of our study, they considered themselves confident 65 percent of the time, hesitant only in 21 percent of their reactions, and fearful in 14 percent. They felt uncertain about a third of the time (35%), and moved from uncertain to moderately confident in their patterns of internal reactions.

In the first three weeks of instruction, the high group student teachers felt fearful a *quarter* (26%) of the time, and hesitant a *third* (32%). However, they succeeded in channeling their fears into positive responses, and so reduced their fears to only five percent of their total responses. They cut their hesitancy to 17 percent of their reactions, and so were able to respond with confidence 77 percent of the time. They were able to face their fears and uncertainties more effectively than either of the other groups, especially the low group which arrived after eight weeks at the beginning confidence level of the high group (42%).

What is impressive about these figures, especially to those who have long since forgotten their initial reactions as novice teachers, is that such a frantic inner struggle is occurring. We shall next discuss some outward signs of these inner tensions and their resolutions: the kinds of action patterns that they foster. However, it is pertinent to point out that this internal affective dimension of teaching is far more important than the brief consideration (if any) that it is usually given in the preparation and guidance of student teachers. Our evidence indicates that the inner struggle involved in becoming a teacher is of real consequence and certainly most difficult.

An insight into the origin of the fears of the various groups can be derived from their self-reports relating to stress they felt while teaching the four lessons in the Improvement Series. All student teachers reported stress related to their own internal reactions; however, the highs, as compared with the low group, addressed themselves more to ideas, while the lows were more concerned with feelings. Most important, however, was the teachers' awareness of pupil stress. The evaluation form did not ask for this information, but the high group reported 27 responses relating to awareness of pupil stress, while the average group reported only 13, and the low only two. These responses indicate that the high group is aware of other people's reactions, but the low group is so involved with their own feelings that they are unaware of pupils' problems. Possibly the high group was able to reduce their fears and make significant gains in confidence as compared with the low, because being more at ease with themselves, they concentrated on the problems of others. Put simply, they spent less time thinking about themselves.

Gaining control of their classes and getting pupil interest were two main problems for the low group student teachers in the first three weeks. Only 20 percent of their hand and facial expressions seemed integrated with what they were saying. While 17 percent of their actions were alternating or emphatic in appearance, they too were often gestures of desperation or last-ditch attempts to keep their classes from getting completely out of control. A large part of their problems with pupils probably resulted initially from pupil boredom with having to hear and watch a teacher whose actions were disassociated, repetitive, or nervous during 63 percent of the class period.

By the end of eight weeks, the low student teachers had learned to become considerably more emphatic. They gained 15 percent in alternating actions which were, we will see later, accompanied by an increase in directive statements, and gained 10 percent in integrated actions for a concluding rating of 30 percent. The kind of full personal mobilization required for integration appears very hard for the lows to achieve, possibly because of their inner lack of self-confidence. Nevertheless, they were able to learn to reduce their disassociated actions from 63 to 38 percent of their general patterns of response, for an overall gain of 25 percent within this dimension of teacher learning—their area of greatest gain.

From listening to their peers' descriptions, the low group student teachers did learn *not* to appear as repetitive and nervous in their gestures as they may have inwardly felt. Perhaps this is a useful step in learning to become more genuinely self-motivating or personally integrated.

The average group made even slighter gains (+4) in integration, but they began with a rating of 43 percent, rather than at the 20 percent level of the lows. From the start they appeared to be more involved in what they said. During the eight weeks, they heightened their sense of personal involvement by dramatizing more of what they had to say, as is seen in the increase in their alternating actions from 24 to 33 percent, or to a third of their body movements.

The average group began student teaching with only a third (33%) of their action rated as disassociated, compared with an initial rating of the low group of 63 percent. By the end of the eight-week period, only one-fifth (20%) of the average group gestures revealed any disassociation. Their actions appear to be an area of some strength for the average student teacher.

Only a third (32%) of the high student teachers' actions were integrated at the beginning, but their final rating was 63 percent, as compared with the average group's standing of 47 percent. Most important is the fact that they gained 29 percent, almost doubling their initial rating. They also increased their alternating actions from 21 to 27 percent, for a total gain of 35 percent in these positive qualities.

This meant a reduction from 45 to 10 percent in their disassociated gestures. What is important is that in their teaching there is a relationship of about two to one in integrated to alternating actions, suggesting a reflective and relaxed atmosphere interwoven with dynamic stimulation. Their classrooms are, therefore, not overly theatrical. This atmosphere seems to provide the pupil with an increased opportunity to be self-motivative and evaluative. Integrated teaching appears to give an integral quality to the entire class.

What is communicated through the teachers' hands, face, and body probably determines in large part the atmosphere of readiness of pupil learning in the classroom. However, this necessary dimension of teacher education has been largely neglected. Still, the information gained here tends to indicate that in this area considerable learning can occur in students of widely varying abilities. Further, learning to communicate effectively by using our bodies meaningfully enhances the sense of integration in our daily lives.

While actions may establish pupil readiness to learn, talk probably determines their preparedness. The four types of talk *(now, what, how,* and *if)* form a logical cycle. Part of preparedness involves *directing* or ordering—telling our pupils when to do what. "Now, do this!" talk dominates in every content area. It appears that many teachers spend most of their time saying, "Sit down, open your book, read paragraphs 2 through 12, close your book, stand up, and leave the room in an even line " This, however, is possibly less true in art than in other content areas. But beginning student teachers in art all appeared to *need* to say "now" quite often. On a 100-point scale divided into thirds—*many* (100 to 67), *some.* (67 to 34), *few* (33 to 1)—the student teacher in the high group made the most "now" statements from the start (57 points). They increased only a little

(2 points) during the eight weeks and apparently found sufficient the number of directive statements they made.

The average pupils were weaker in this respect, starting with a rating of 41 and moving to a final standing of 52 points. They were the least directive as a group, for the low group started at 51 and moved to 61 points. All groups learned to make a few more directive "now" statements while teaching, and concluded by making a moderate but reasonable number of them. It is possible that the literature here and the edicts of progressive education have not been helpful for beginning teachers in distinguishing between the need for good class management statements and those other kinds of statements which make classes interesting, but not necessarily orderly.

We have seen again and again that an orderly classroom need not be a *dictatorial* one, but it is frequently a *directed* one. A good teacher is necessarily good at management, since pupil preparation and involvement in learning activities usually require teacher directions.

Once control is established, the teacher may introduce some concept or subject matter as the lesson topic. His statement concerning these topics is necessarily made in the form of "what" questions. Most topics need enrichment or filling out, so a number of these statements are essential if pupils are to develop their subject matter ideas fully. While a moderate number of "now" statements is sufficient for classroom direction, *many* "what" statements seem needed for adequate development of the topic. The major consideration here is the teacher's ability to *elaborate* upon a single idea. To elaborate does *not* mean to *repeat,* but rather to develop an idea's implications fully. Elaborative ability is one of the characteristics of highly creative individuals.

Since this capacity to elaborate was measured by the Torrance Creativity Tests before student teaching, it is possible for us to look at the high, average, and low student teacher groups to see what this and other verbal factors predict about their talk in the classroom. The tests showed the low group lower than the average group on *four* out of *five* sub-tests, and the average group lower than the high group on four of the five tests. The prediction then was that the low group would ask fewer "what" questions than the average, and the average fewer than the high. But in the first three weeks, the average group tended to ask *more* "what" questions (56) than both the lows (47) and highs (45).

However, by the end of student teaching, these three groups had changed their order. The highs appeared to be asking many more "what" questions than the average or lows. Moreover, the highs gained 27 points in this capacity. These scores suggest that the Torrance tests (in student teaching) measure *learning capacity* rather than immediate level of performance. Further confirmation lies in the fact that, after student teaching, the high group scored highest on all five of the sub-tests and outdistanced the other two groups in gains in four out of five tests, even though their scores were higher than the others to begin with.

The large gains made during student teaching were apparently directly transferred to, and reflected by, high students' increases in elaborative capacities. This conclusion is supported also by the fact that the next gains on the Torrance tests were made by the lows, and they ranked second to the high group in their increases on "what" talk in the classroom. These data suggest that the self-evaluative approach to student teaching, not only depends upon, but also promotes rather specific kinds of verbal-creative capacities.

When the teacher had dealt with the topic of the lesson fully, he needed to explain to pupils "how" to do the work connected with the lesson. In art, it is often necessary when dealing with individual pupils' expressive problems to aid them in the development of *unusual* uses of their materials so that they may improve their products. "How" questions or statements serve this purpose. This capacity is also measured by two of the Torrance tests, "Unusual Uses" and "Product Improvement," both of which are measures of procedural flexibility.

All groups had the same order of achievement in *flexibility scores* in their Product Improvement and Unusual Uses ratings. The order, however, is different from that involving elaborative "what" statements. The high group is still first, but the low group is second and the average is last. The three groups were only three points apart to start, but they again ended in exactly the order predicted: high 71, low 58, average 51 points. Again, the high group gained the most, 21 points, and they outdistanced the other groups in gains on four out of five of the scales relating to product improvement. The low group had the second largest gain on this test. Both these tests and the student teacher's classroom talk show that "how" talk involves method "flexibilities."

Since these processes are essential in art instruction and thus frequently employed, it is not surprising to note that the total gain across all groups on the "Product Improvement" scale represented a 52 percent increase over the original scores.[1] This is strong evidence that the student teaching experiences in this program did much to promote increased capacities for creativity. Though student teaching has been sometimes considered training in "social adaptation," it can become a period of extraordinary personal growth and development.

A number of forces in our society are now making "if" (or *suppositional)* talk a part of our daily lives. The first is, of course, our space program which is stretching our cultural imaginations so that we can conceive of flying without wings, and living and working without gravity in places without water or food, within extreme ranges of temperature.

Moreover, our ability to think in "if" terms has also been made elastic by new communications media. There is a "tomorrow" spirit about today which allows us to speculate in entirely new ways. We can see a movie about what it would be like "if" we were reduced to the size of virus and sent through the blood stream

---

[1] These gains were made on alternate forms of the Torrance tests. Student teachers given the A form pretest were later given the B form posttest, and vice versa. Other experiments using these tests show that such marked increases are unusual. See E. Paul Torrance, *Torrance Tests of Creative Thinking, Norms-Technical Manual*, Personnel Press, Princeton, N. J. 1966.

in a minute submarine. We see the whole body this way; we fall into a lung and are exposed to its giant winds; the walls of our submarine are nearly shattered by the sound of a pair of dropping scissors as we pass through the inner ear. We are attacked as enemies, foreign invaders, by the protectors of our nervous system, and our submarine is digested by white corpuscles.

This *Fantastic Voyage* is not science fiction for a class in human biology; it was made to entertain the general public. We thus are not only capable of thinking in tomorrow's terms, but we have as a public become used to watching TV programs based on what our lives *could* have been in the past. So it does not now surprise us to hear a history teacher ask the suppositional question: "What would be different in your lives today if, apart from the question of slavery, Grant had *lost* the war?" Somehow the consequences of the North winning thus become more important to us.

We are now getting used to the idea of thinking hypothetically about the values of the "merely possible" and are, therefore, more ready to entertain seriously the "seemingly impossible." Classroom and student teachers have thus been debating the values and virtues of what we call "Suppositional Education." This, of course, is only one aspect of successful teaching, but to many it seems the key to educational success in the contemporary classroom. Although our concerns are wider than the field of art, we take art to be the core of this revolution. Art has always been concerned with making the strange familiar and the familiar strange, with preserving and extending the imagination.

However, there are considerable differences in the number of "if" questions our student teachers are able to use in the classroom. The Torrance tests include a number of measures of this sort of thinking. One is called "Just Suppose," and the other deals with "Unusual Questions" in which the student is asked to "project yourself into a new world, or to project yourself into or become an object." These and other scales measure capacities for originality in pupils' work, and to maintaining their interest during instruction.

Our highs are consistently the strongest on these tests before and after student teaching. The low group is superior to the average except in two very important aspects. The average group is much stronger in the ability to elaborate on a single suppositional topic, which is the purpose of the "Just Suppose" test, just as they are stronger in elaborating "what" questions. Secondly, the average group makes fewer factual statements when they are trying to develop original ideas than do the lows. A classroom teacher must be able to do more than supply new ideas; especially when employing "if" questions, he must be able through discussion to fully develop possibilities.

Thus it is not too surprising to find that from the start the highs asked slightly more "if" questions than the average group, and the lows asked the fewest of them. The differences here at the end of student teaching are the more extreme than in any other area of "talk." The lows concluded with a rating of 39 (few); the average had 53 (some); and the highs had a concluding rating of 77 (many).

All groups gained in this capacity, but the highs increased nearly three times as much as the other groups.

The average group, because of their elaborative power and avoidance of common and factual responses in developing an imaginative theme, are not only a clear second in their classroom performances, but are very strong gainers in these suppositional capacities on the Torrance tests. The increase in suppositional thinking for all groups was 36 percent, with the low group making some gains on their elaborative capacities. However, it is important to recognize that both the tests and the classroom estimates of the talk show that the high group is twice as strong as the lows in these capacities which are central to the promotion of originality in pupils' work and maintaining their interest during instruction.

The interest in these new forms of imaginative instruction suggests that a major change is occurring in our classrooms. Student teachers' creative capacities for promoting pupil originality need to be trained now. The Torrance tests can help us diagnose the particular strengths and weaknesses of our student teachers, prior to classroom service.

Positive as the outlook is for the improvement of teacher training in the "talk" dimension, some major difficulties are evident, stemming from the interactive deficiencies in student teachers' capacities to learn with others. The problem of sharing in our culture is possibly the most critical one for our school systems and our society. Here there is no evidence that a cultural revolution is occurring. There is, however, much clear evidence that in shared evaluation, the differences between our groups are very significant. However, the clarity of the findings, and there are a number of them, makes them no easier to explain. Rather, it raises some difficult questions about the problems of developing character in the modern world.

Interactive evaluation begins with the designation of those criteria which each student teacher perceives as pertinent to developing a clear picture of his strengths and weaknesses in the classroom. The clarity of this picture depends, in part, upon the applicability of the criteria students suggest for themselves. While the other groups were able to develop criteria considered applicable to their teaching by their peers and cooperating teachers, nearly half (43%) of the lows' criteria were not considered applicable. They actually lost six points on the postratings, while both of the other groups gained.

The picture the lows created of themselves using their own criteria was also a minimal one. It indicates that they conceived of themselves as increasingly average in most respects. At the beginning, they rated themselves "poor" *less frequently* than the other groups, and "excellent," *as frequently*. Near the end of student teaching, they conceived of themselves as poor in only four respects rather than their initial seven, and excellent in only six rather than in their starting nine areas of accomplishment. They described themselves as being weak or strong in only ten qualities, as compared to 29 for the high student teachers. This not only makes for a much less varied description, but it suggests something about their level of aspiration which is not so much concerned with the development of strengths, as with personal acceptability and conformity as a primary goal. Their cumulative grade-point averages range from 2.36 to 2.19 for all courses, and are composed predominantly of Cs.

This lack of strong areas points to a missing depth of purpose and competency in over three years of college work. It would be easy to conclude that they are simply weak students who lack competency and creativity. However, their problem-solving capacities on the Torrance tests are generally greater than those of the average group. Though they lacked suppositional elaborative power, they were *more able* to ask unusual questions than the average students, but they asked fewer of them in the classroom. They did ask more "how" questions. Indications are that they have creative capacities which they continuously fail to utilize. They apparently have an unclear idea of their purposes as individuals, apart from their desire to pass.

This lack of involvement in depth resulted in pronounced inability to share evaluation, both with their peers and their cooperating teachers. Their shared evaluative responses consume only slightly more than a third (39%) of their interactive relationships during their lesson conferences; by the conclusion of student teaching, they are defensive 27 percent of the time, and privately preju-dicial 39 percent of the time with their cooperating teachers, and 42 percent with their peers. Two-thirds of the time they have a negative response to others concerning evaluation of their teaching.

The low group ratings might give the impression that the atmosphere is heated. It isn't: it is dull and resistant, characterized by their feelings that others are unable to get to know them. They just don't expose themselves. This lack of personal and outward involvement seems to stem from their difficulty in deter-mining what their purposes and standards are with respect to themselves as teachers. By not establishing goals, they avoid the problem of being judged or of having to evaluate themselves.

Their lack of strong purposes is even more damaging in that it eliminates any basis for sharing their directions or desires with others. By not making any investment, they have unknowingly eliminated the basis of sharing with others which occurs through the recognition of commonly held goals. Without goals, there is seldom any significant learning. But the consequences go beyond this point. When we have no positive commitments to support interaction, we are simply unable to identify with each other and feel socially isolated.

It is clearly only through our identification of the purposes and capacities of others that we come to know them. But, most important, it is through their identification of our purposes and capacities that we come to know ourselves. Others, therefore, constitute the mirrors for the development of our concept of our individualized, non-conforming identity. These mirrors remain non-reflective, however, until they are illuminated by the light emanating from the strength of our purposes.

What we are considering here is a lack of personal values and a corresponding sense of self-doubt. What is required for the development of character is the emergence of that form of courage which enables us to face our doubts about ourselves. The penalty for failure to do so is not so simple as to be ineffective or uninteresting to others; it is to live without any sense of our identify being reflected back to us from others. The penalty for being without purpose is loss of self-identity.

The attitude of the average group toward self-evaluation is very different by the conclusion of the student teaching from that of both the low and high group. First of all, they are capable of providing a number of criteria (74%) that are considered applicable to their instructional activities in the classroom. The kind of criteria they use is also suggested by the differences in their self-ratings on the lesson improvement series during the middle and later weeks in student teaching.

Initially, they rated themselves as "poor" in 17 respects as compared to seven such self-ratings for the lows and ten for the highs. They saw many things they considered to be wrong or wished to correct about their teaching. They rated themselves as "excellent" in approximately the same number of criteria (10) as the other groups. They apparently took a very critical look at themselves, and since they didn't like the impression they got, they eliminated 15 of these 17 areas as "undesirable" instructional behavior. This accomplishment is even more startling when we consider that the average group concluded with only two poor ratings as compared to the 11 concluding poor ratings the highs gave themselves.

The average student teachers conceive of themselves as having far fewer "faults" than the highs. This is because their target is to eliminate "negative" behavior, while they appeared not to be greatly concerned with adding more positive qualities. They rated themselves as "excellent" in only one additional criteria beyond the ten they originally employed. Their strongly critical attitude toward their first lessons resulted in a kind of increased openness to self-evaluation.

Though they started much like the low group in being privately prejudicial nearly a third of the time (30%) and critically defensive slightly more than a third (36%), they altered these attitudes, particularly the latter one. Because they were so self-critical, they reduced their defensiveness some 14 points. This brought their evaluative interactions into a kind of fifty-fifty balance—slightly more positive (52%) than negative through eliminating negative elements. Their idea of "self-perfection" appears to be "no faults."

This "I shall not" approach to self-fulfillment is a different kind of mirror than the "I wish to become better" approach suggests. The reflections of this negative mirror are always toward the need for "absence" rather than "presence." While it is nice to look average because we don't look bad, it is not very constructive or individual. The information relating to both their course achievements and their creativity shows a similar tendency. The average group is outstanding primarily in courses in which technical perfection is really important. They are weaker on the Torrance tests than either the lows or highs in discovering unusual insights or problem solutions.

It's easier and less creative to designate and correct what is "wrong" than discover a new form of "right." To recognize and correct our behavior is, of course, to be less subject to criticism, but as a preoccupation it can lead away from the development of significant self-identity. Something more is needed here.

The highs see themselves as clearly the poorest and the best of these three groups in their classroom behavior. What they see in this respect is also considered by others to be quite "applicable" to them. By the conclusion of student teaching, their peers and cooperating teachers felt able to give them ratings on 85 percent of their criteria—criteria which were realistic ones and both negative and positive.

The highs seem to accept the idea that to do something new means to make "new" mistakes. By the end of student teaching they rate themselves as poor in 11 criteria, compared with ten at the beginning; and they gain in excellence in 18, as compared to eight at the start. They are both self-accepting and self-assured and, therefore, began with more positive evaluative interaction with their peers and cooperating teachers. They started with a positive rating of 56 percent, which is above the concluding level of the average and low groups. They gained more than either of the other groups (25%), and thus concluded with a positive evaluative standing of 81 percent. This gain resulted from reducing their private prejudicial responses 21 to 8 percent, and their defensive ones from 23 to 11 percent.

The highs have a tendency in evaluative sessions to raise problems concerning things they are "poor" at or need to learn in order to reach their positive goals. Their attitude is one of self-challenge. They often initiate dialogue with their cooperating teachers and peers, probing for their ideas and suggestions. Their humor regarding their own dilemmas in the classroom is a little startling; it's as though they were looking quizzically at themselves. This attitude is not impersonal; it is rather one of skeptical wonder at seeing themselves in action through the eyes of others. This attitude may stem from considering their own character as a medium they wish to explore, in spite of the fact that it appears to them to be very uneven terrain. This disinterested pleasure in seeing the full range of themselves mirrored in the response of others is possibly what we mean by self-reflective inquiry. The landscape of any genuine individual would necessarily appear from an aerial view to be cratered with human error, but the error is a source of character. The creative person is clearly more capable of enabling others to become actively involved in looking with disinterested humanity at his own whole development as a creative problem.

Certainly the Torrance tests indicate that the highs are extraordinarily strong in all problem-solving capacities. Moreover, they grew much stronger during their student teaching experiences in their awareness of problem-solving processes. They seem to have discovered that reflective involvement in their purposes and direction allows them to assume an outside view of their humanness. This, in turn, permits them to act more fully on what they feel, exploiting any unexpected positive value that may be worth sharing with others.

Our experiment is probably the first in which cooperating teachers and their student teachers have both recorded and regularly rated their own evaluative attitudes toward each other. We were thus more than a little surprised by the honesty of their assessments and their readiness to identify the intensity of their emotional reactions toward each other. (This frankness, and the degree of differences in evaluation here are among our most significant findings.) The realities here are thus harder to deny. But everyone's need for internal honesty at every level is reassuring. If they had not been honest with themselves we would have found a far less consistent pattern of distinctions among these three groups.

That more self-deception didn't occur indicates an almost universal willingness to at least attempt self-evaluation and to engage in self-reflective inquiry with others. Thus students recognize that character development requires learning the self-imposed discipline of communicating positively with each other as members of a professional community. So it is not surprising that the problem-solving efforts across all groups resulted in a 41 percent increase (on Torrance tests) in students' capacities to raise problematic questions, and a 48 percent gain in their abilities to discover consequences. The time to learn problem-solving in student teaching is when problems are seen as personal and internal. Here evaluative sharing requires a real struggle to be honest with one's self, and a special concern for one's personal integrity. This suggests that accurate and inclusive self-knowledge promotes individuality; perhaps this is what education of character means—it means to become accountable.

Pupil-learning can be seen from the instructor's viewpoint, or from pupils' views of the instructor's contributions to his work. If we use both of these viewpoints, we can get a picture of the interactive learning experiences involved.

It may be useful to summarize briefly the four dimensions already discussed, so as to sense more fully the total event. The dimensions of *confidence, action,* and *evaluation* are like major countries that make up a larger continent. That is, they all fit together because they are concerned with emotional reaction of the teacher learner. These affective reactions are distinguished from cognitive ones, like those involving talk, because they fluctuate continuously between positive and negative poles of internal reaction.[2]

The student teacher's problem then is to move the emotional tone of his teaching toward the positive or "cooler" pole. Here the accumulative picture is

---

[2] These poles of reaction tend to characterize the extremes of responses in this affective world. The positive pole in this instance is "cool," and the negative one is "hot".

especially revealing when we consider how "hot" each group was to start and how "cool" they became, relative to their confidence, actions, and evaluative interactions during the program. The lows started "hot" or negative in 46 percent of their reactions, and moved (12%) to the temperate center zone to achieve a seesaw 48/52 percent hot-cool balance. The average group started at the central 48 percent point and moved (14%) to 62 percent on the positive cooler side. Thus both the average and low groups made moderate but important gains. The high group started at the center (51%) level in their affective reactions, but they gained nearly three times as much (35%) as the other two groups. Their concluding rating of 86 percent justified many of their pupils' views of them as "real cool".

The positive emotions of the high group not only enabled them to make proportionately larger gains in talk, but it also resulted in a more positive pupil attitude toward their lessons. For instance, by the conclusion of student teaching, their pupils gave them (on a 100-point "Interest in the Lesson" scale) a rating of 83 points. The average group received a rating of 73, and the low group one of only 57 points. The group gains here follow the same pattern as those reported earlier: 24 points for the high, 15 points for the average, and 10 points for the lows. The pupil estimates of their teacher's contribution show a similar 25-point spread: 75 to 65 to 49. Here there is a noteworthy difference. Pupils see the low group as making less of a contribution at the end than at the beginning of student teaching. They started with a score of 58 and lost 9 points.

The cause of the loss is indicated by other pupil ratings during this lesson improvement series. The 600 pupils in our student teachers' classes, at the end of each of the four lessons in the Lesson Improvement Series, indicated their satisfaction or dissatisfaction with the instruction of a 9-point scale. Ratings of one indicated extreme "dissatisfaction," perhaps outright frustration. We found that, in general, approximately 25 percent of the pupils feel very dissatisfied about *any* given lesson, regardless of how successful it may have appeared from our teaching viewpoint. However, "extreme dissatisfaction" was indicated by nearly half (100 of 200) of the pupils in the low group classes. The dissatisfaction rating rose from 43 to 47 percent of the class during these lessons, indicating decreased contributions by the student teachers.

It can be argued that pupil dissatisfaction is not a good index of pupil learning. After all, some dissatisfaction can be an incentive to learning. However, the evidence indicates that pupil learning appears to parallel pupil "interest" and "teacher contributions." The art achievements of pupils in these classes, as rated by the student teachers themselves, their peers, cooperating teachers, and college supervisors, provide the following standings in art quality: high group pupils, 79 percent; average group pupils, 69 percent; low group pupils, 58 percent. Pupils' art gains during this time for the high group were 33 points, for the average, 17, and for the low, 16.

All classes improved from unsatisfactory beginnings, but again the high group pupils gained twice as much as the other two groups. What accounts for these differences in gains? One aspect is the difference in the art achievement levels of the three groups of student teachers themselves, indicated best by their average grades in *Introductory Painting.* Averages are 85 (mostly As) for the high group, 77 (mostly Bs) for the average group, and 67 (mostly Cs) for the low group. The grades in Printmaking, Painting, and Drawing courses show the following parallels with their pupils' concluding ratings in art during student teaching:

	High	Average	Low
Teacher 2-Dimensional College Art Courses[3]	76	66	63
Their Pupils' Art Achievements	79	69	58

Competency in art is clearly a factor in successfully teaching art at any grade level.

A high level of competence and involvement in teaching parallels the ability to discover and state the cultural values for evaluating pupils' art products. In searching for an indicator of the differences in these student teachers' evaluative capacities, we found a major variant in their own ratings of their pupils' art work. The high group rated classes more systematically, and significantly they used between seven and eight titled art criteria each time they made a rating. The other groups employed from two to four criteria, or less than half as many. Again, as in their evaluation of *themselves as teachers,* the highs tend to employ a wider number of standards for judging their own or others' accomplishments. They consider success on twice as many criteria important for their classes.

Our first thought was that this would make their classes more difficult. However, in classes with many targets it is apparently easier to find something you can hit. In fact, the highs' lessons were rated as the least difficult by pupils. Moreover, the highs indicate on their lesson plans an expectation of a predominantly positive pupil response to their instruction. By contrast, the low group anticipates a predominantly negative response.

By the conclusion of student teaching, the high group lessons received a difficulty rating of 36, as compared to 48 for the lows and 57 for the average group. These ratings point up the difference between the average and high groups, because the average student teacher appears to be setting up a smaller number of targets and demanding greater perfection in marksmanship. Perhaps because they have succeeded best themselves in courses requiring technical know-how and high craftsmanship, such as Lettering, Mechanical Drawing, Design in Metal, and Photography, they appear to emphasize with their pupils, as

---

[3] Courses in which grades did not distinguish between the three groups are not included.

they do when evaluating themselves, the need for eliminating error and for perfecting the product. The tendency to judge others in the ways we judge ourselves is perhaps one key to the mystery of how others react to us as teachers.

Depth in content achievement and breadth in standards only account for some of the differences between these groups. Another important factor is interest and accomplishment in education courses prior to student teaching. The high group simply has higher grades, more As in their education courses. In "Introduction to Education" and in "Methods in Art Education" (Adolescent Art), they have a combined grade-average of 84, as compared to 70 for the average group and 72 for the lows. Their 89-point average in "Adolescent Art" is a partial reason for their success in instructing public school pupils. This achievement indicates considerable competency and involvement in teaching as a means of self-realization.

The total evidence here shows that the better student teachers (and incidentally the more creative on most of the Torrance tests) are superior in both art and education courses and find personal fulfillment in both areas. Teaching success would also appear to require at least moderate competency in content areas outside of studio art and education. The lows are weakest in these areas, having almost straight D averages in eight of the required academic courses, while the other groups were weak in no more than two such courses. There is some support here for the belief that the liberal arts also contribute something essential to the foundation necessary for teaching competence.

Awareness in the classroom appears then to be directly related to depth and breadth of interests and involvement. Learning to be a teacher thus requires a highly complex, multi-dimensional person, not a narrowly focused or an unfocused one. Consequently, teacher preparation and evaluation are also multi-dimensional problems. Fortunately, through inspection of these complex requirements, we can now predict student teaching potential. It is thus possible to give help where and when it will count most—before students get into the classroom. The Torrance tests are important here because they sort the highs out so clearly from the other groups. Superior grades in art, particularly in painting, printmaking and drawing, and high grades in education give us a second means of identifying potentially good teachers. They might be encouraged to teach early and be utilized as teacher-coaches in our method, participation, and independent study courses.

The Torrance tests blur the distinction between the average and low groups. But the low group is easy to locate because of its generally low grade-point average. So we can keep student teachers with GPAs of 2.5 or less out of student teaching until their senior year, and during their junior year give them help in place of their electives. The lows' only area of strength was introductory design and craft courses, and what they seem to require is more depth experiences in arts, greater exposure to the humanities, and intense participation training with public school pupils. Delaying student teaching until the last term of the senior year might help to achieve these objectives in part. The low group must be helped sooner to find and face their problems.

But perhaps our minimal standards also need to be raised, so that we don't have to go on inflicting incompetent student teachers on so many of our public schools. If colleges (and state laws) must protect mediocrity, perhaps the cooperating school could simply refuse to make anyone as a student teacher with GPA of 2.5 or less. This would help. If one fact stands out, it is simply that student teachers and their pupils both suffer as a result of the student teachers' many deficiencies and inability to learn through sharing with others. A revolution is needed so that teaching becomes a privilege rather than a last resort.

A much harder part of the problem is what to do about the narrow focused, white-collar image protecting the middle class values of our average teacher. One thing we know is that they need more training in procedural flexibility, risk-taking, and suppositional thinking. Here again, the Torrance tests could help us identify students who are particularly weak in product improvement and original · thinking. They might be helped by a course in "Creative Thought Processes and Their Application." They certainly need more training prior to student teaching, as do the lows, in the formulation of their evaluative criteria, both with respect to their own goals and purposes and those of their pupils. Thus it seems advisable to introduce an application course in evaluative practices prior to student teaching, as well as to require more work in art and to allow *fewer* narrowly-structured technique electives for average students.

We need not only a more flexible curriculum, but one that has a different purpose at its center. We need a college program in which shared evaluative dialogue is a normal transaction among students, as well as between students and their instructors. This is essentially a methodical change, not simply a curriculum change. How can a college educate its student teachers to become self-evaluative when their opportunities for classroom dialogue in relation to their own and others' work are so infrequent and lacking in guidance? If the development of character is a primary concern of our colleges, then we need more courses which provide feedback for students' interactive evaluative achievements. Then college students might feel less lonely and isolated. Colleges do foster students' feelings of isolation because they have failed to become interactive evaluative communities.

The criteria problem is the most critical of all, and is closely related to the confidence dimension. If students have no criteria, or inadequate or inapplicable criteria, they cannot develop a detailed picture of themselves—they cannot know their own strengths and weaknesses. Hence they have no legitimate basis for confidence.

The criteria underlying each dimension are pervasive and relatively stable; they limit the development which we permit ourselves in any dimension. Each of our student teachers seems to have built a different sort of structure for his own fulfillment. For three years prior to student teaching, we see the same pattern of activity in each student that occurred in student teaching. The eight-week program revealed a cross section of their whole lives, their characteristic life styles. What teachers are in the classroom is very much what they are outside the classroom. Character is the crucial variable; the structure of the student's life is determined by his criteria, and the drama lies in seeing what that structure permits or does not permit.

Our low student seems to be saying that he can build only a one-story house; he doesn't have the confidence to attempt anything more and doesn't see that being a teacher requires more. The average student wants a technically perfect house—an up-to-date one that other people will think well of—but particularly one other people won't criticize. The students in our average group thus are confident that they will be accepted, but do not have enough security to risk letting others see them as individuals. The stultifying, middle class value system characteristic of American teachers is probably the greatest single barrier to improving American education. Our teachers are afraid to be themselves. Good teaching requires individual integrity, but rather than risking distinction, our teachers prefer to look average by not looking bad.

Our high group of student teachers appears to have designed and built their own rambling personality structures; students are both curious and critical of their criteria and see their structures as both deficient and distinguished. They don't know whether or not to tear the structures apart, because they are not certain whether they are art or merely odd. But our high group character structures are interesting, and such a person has a right to feel confident in his individuality and his involvement in constructing a meaningful identity. For him, the process requires something more positive than mere reaction or revolt. The dramatic dimensions of teaching are revealed most clearly here because in this strange play each actor has a different quantity of character, but they all have the same task.

We wonder, of course, what teachers would be like if education as a whole ever seriously attempted to develop teacher learning in all five of these dimensions. In most colleges of education today, only conceptual "what" talk is considered an important aspect of learning (*how* and *if* are often neglected). The training of teachers can and needs to become multi-dimensional. The educational process depends absolutely on the balanced and fully developed character of the teacher who knows himself and who, by meeting his own fears and feelings of inadequacy, has achieved a significant and original integrity within his multi-dimensional self.

CHAPTER 16

Intellective, Non-Intellective, and Environmental Correlates of Mechanical Ingenuity[1]

W. A. Owens*

THE CONSTRUCTION of a special battery of tests designed to discriminate creative from non-creative or development engineers and their subsequent validation on an independent sample of 304 industrially employed engineers was reported by Owens, Schumacher, and Clark in 1957. The final form of the battery which survived cross-validation consisted of "The Personal Inventory" (PI), a quasi forced-choice inventory dealing with interests, attitudes, opinions, personal characteristics and experiences; "The Personal History Form" (PHF), a single sheet dealing with personal background; "The Application of Mechanisms Test" (AMT); solutions to "The Power Source Apparatus Test" judged to be workable (PSA–W); and total number of solutions to the PSA (PSA–T). Conclusive demonstration of the predictive efficiency of the battery, however, required a longitudinal design which would permit the accumulation of evidence of creative performance over a number of years. With this purpose in mind, the final battery was administered in 1955 to over 1500 juniors and seniors in the mechanically-related branches of engineering at 25 colleges and universities. The security of the test scores *was* maintained while criterion information was accumulating and what follows is essentially an account of the relationship between the predictions of 1955 and the actualities of 1964. An attempt has also been made to recognize some of the moderating influences involved.

PURPOSES AND HYPOTHESES

Specifically, attention has been directed to three questions:
1. What is the evidence regarding the predictive validity of the 1955 measures of creativity in machine design.
2. What are the personal (non-cognitive[2]) and environmental characteristics which have facilitated or inhibited the expression of this creativity in the meantime?

*William A. Owens is Professor of Psychology & Director, Institute For Behavioral Research, University of Georgia, Athens. He was formerly Professor of Psychology, Purdue University.

[1] The writer wishes to recognize the substantial contributions of the Drs. Maureen Kallick, Stephen P. Klein, Robert B. Means, and Mark Van Slyke, and of the graduate students, Michael Brodie and Richard Klimoski.

[2] Non-cognitive as used herein, is equivalent to non-intellective. Cognitive is likewise equivalent to intellective, including all the five intellective processes (operations) implied by such models as Guilford's "Structure of Intellect."

3. If we identify types of persons and types of environments, do they interact; i.e., is it true, that one type of environment is optimal for persons of type A and another for persons of type B?

Attendant upon and congruent with the preceding purposes, the following hypotheses were formulated:

1. The present cognitive tests are better predictors of creativity in machine design than a common mental ability (or scholastic aptitude) test; this is, at least in part, because the one places a premium upon a different cognitive pattern or style than the other (Guilford, 1959).
2. The creative individual is cognitively complex and can integrate more inputs than his less creative fellows; thus, tests which restrict or structure more, and which imply more inputs (PSA), will be superior to those which restrict or structure less (AMT).
3. Accepting the phenomenal nature and complex determination of creativity, prediction will be enhanced by appraising not only cognitive characteristics, but non-cognitive and environmental characteristics as well.
4. Since creative persons do not appear to respond to the same contexts or to function in the same way, an interaction between personal and environmental determiners of creativity is postulated. Thus environment "x" may be optimal for persons of type A and environment "y" for persons of type B.

METHODS

In overview, the methods adapted to the above purposes are as follows:

1. Correlational analyses were utilized to answer question one regarding the predictive validity of the 1955 battery.
2. To answer question two, inventories of personal (non-cognitive) and environmental characteristics were completed by the Ss in 1964; the items of each were factored, and factor scores were then correlated with the creativity criterion.
3. Question three was attacked by successively subgrouping Ss; first on the basis of the profile similarities of their job environment factor scores, and then on the basis of the profile similarities of their personal characteristics factor scores. The two classes of subsets then became the two criteria of classification for an analysis of variance in which the interaction would represent type of person x type of environment.

Subjects

The potential pool of Ss for the follow-up of 1964 consisted of 1537 students of 1955 who were, typically, originally tested as beginning upperclassmen in the mechanically-related branches of engineering. The vast majority were in civil, aeronautical, or mechanical curricula, and they were from all parts of the country and a wide variety of institutions. Alumni offices of the schools in question were able to supply 1268 addresses. Of these, 109 proved to be insufficient or incorrect and no forwarding address could be obtained. Thus 1159 Ss were actually contacted and 938 (81%) ultimately replied. Since seven returns were unusable, 931 Ss were involved in this study. These were assigned to one of the following three categories:

Group I was composed of 457 engineers employed in research and development (R&D).

Group II consisted of 104 former R&D engineers promoted into engineering management (EM).

Group III was composed of 370 Ss in two loosely defined subgroups; first, those not in engineering, per se, but in an engineering-related occupation, such as teaching engineering or sales engineering; second, those in an unrelated area, such as medicine, law, or the ministry.

Figure 1 essentially involves a comparison of the shapes of the test score distributions of the three groups of Ss on the single most valid measure. However, in speaking to the predictive purposes of the study, it must be clear that the Ss, by groups, have *not* had an equal opportunity to accumulate criterion evidence of their creativity. Attention has, therefore, been centered upon Group I (R&D).

Measuring Instruments

In the follow-up of 1964, two inventories and a covering letter were sent to each S. Many investigators have reported relevant and favorable experience with the biographical information blank, or BIB, as a predictor (Owens and Henry, 1966). Accordingly, the first inventory was a so-called "Life History Questionnaire" (LHQ) of 181 items dealing with the Ss demographic characteristics and experiential background, plus 10 criterion items (Klein, 1965). Pursuant to a suggestion by Taylor (1964), the second was a "Job Environment Survey" (JES) of 80 items covering the "research climate" in which the S worked (Kallick, 1964).

Criterion

The ten items of criterion information collected appear in Table I along with their means, standard deviations, and relative importance weights. These weights were assigned by five members of the engineering faculty at Purdue, all of whom had both academic and industrial experience of relevance to the design and development of products or processes. In the context of their importance to these activities, the weights were assigned to each criterion element by each judge in accordance with the Kelly "bids system" (Toops, 1944). The criterion score of a given S, then, was his standard score on the given criterion element, multiplied by the appropriate importance weight and summed across the ten elements.

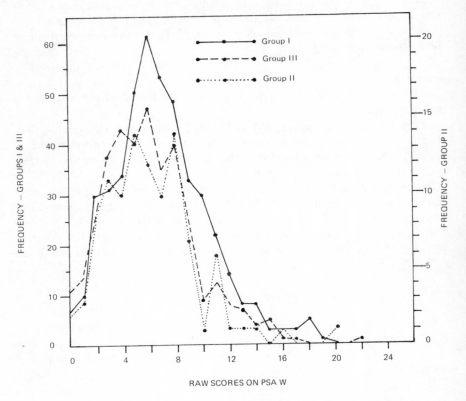

Fig. 1. A Comparison of the shapes of distributions on the PSA(W) Test
for Groups I, II, and III

Statistical Treatment

It is probably most intelligible to discuss the treatment of the data in the context of the three purposes originally stated. Thus the first purpose was to answer certain questions regarding the predictive validity of the creativity battery of 1955. As noted in the methods overview, these questions were answered in terms of correlational analyses of conventional character.

The second purpose was to identify some of the personal (non-cognitive) and environmental characteristics which have facilitated or inhibited the subsequent expression of the creativity measured by the battery of 1955. This purpose was served by factoring, independently, the items of the JES and the LHQ and by

TABLE I

Criterion Elements:
Their Means, Standard Deviations, and Relative Importance Weights

LHQ Item Number	Criterion Element	Mn.	Group 1 S.D.	Wght.
104. a.	Improving products or processes	5.28	11.44	1
104. b.	Developing products or processes	3.57	9.29	1
114.	Papers presented at professional meetings	1.27	0.68	2
121.	Papers published in professional journals	0.71	2.07	2
126.	The following are in the S's own name			
a.	Patents Held	0.06	0.32	3
b.	Patents Pending	0.21	0.81	3
c.	Patent Disclosures	0.42	1.50	4
127.	The following are in the S's own name but he made a contribution to them			
a.	Patents Held	0.12	0.68	1
b.	Patents Pending	0.11	0.62	1
c.	Patent Disclosures	0.14	0.65	2

relating factor scores on the factors obtained to the composite criterion of creativity. In the case of the JES, most of the items are answered as applying or not applying (1 or 0) to the given S's working situation. However, since some permit multiple responses, a total of 109 options were available for analysis. No continuum type items were included, and ten binary items were eliminated because they yielded response frequencies below ten percent, thereby enhancing the risk of obtaining difficulty factors. Thus 99 item-options (hereafter, "items") ultimately entered the factor analysis. Twenty-one factors were initially extracted from the matrix according to the method of principal components. A decision to rotate four of these was based upon a plot of the latent roots. Following an orthogonal rotation, all of the items which did not load at least 0.20 on one of the rotated factors were eliminated, as were most items which loaded nearly equally across several factors. This procedure was then repeated until nearly half of the original items had been dropped. The technique was adopted for two reasons: (1) it was felt that it would sharpen interpretations regarding the differential criterion relevance of various environmental influence factors; and (2) it was planned to fulfill purpose number three of this study by classifying Ss on their factor score profiles in a fashion requiring the independence of the basic dimensions. In anticipation of this next step, standardized factor scores were computed for each individual on each of the ultimate job environment factors.

With the following two exceptions, an identical procedure was utilized with the items of the LHQ:

1. The LHQ contains both continuum-type and binary items; however, the latter have several options under the same stem from which only one is to be selected. The options are, thus, not invariably independent, and only *one* from a common stem could be permitted to enter the factor analysis.

2. Since mixing binary and continuum type items leads to ambiguities, it was decided to factor the binary items first and to include binary factor scores, along with scores on continuum-type items, as entries in the matrix to be factored.

When the final set of three personal history factors had been identified, standardized factor scores were computed for each S on each factor. It was then a simple matter to fulfill purpose number two regarding the relevance of personal and environmental factors to creativity by correlating scores on each of the two sets of factors with the composite criterion.

Finally, purpose number three had reference to testing the possibility of a type of person by type of environment interaction. To test it required that Ss be subgrouped, successively, on each set of factors and assigned to appropriate cells in an analysis of variance design with two criteria of classification. On the job environment factors, for example, this was accomplished as follows. Each S's factor scores were regarded as comprising a profile. The similarity of each profile to each other profile was expressed in tterms of the D^2 statistic of Cronbach and Gleser (1953). Subgrouping was then accomplished through application of the hierarchical procedure of Ward and Hook (1963) to the obtained matrix of D^2 values. The technique essentially compares each profile with each other, combines the most similar pair, treats them as a unit, and repeats the process. The criterion is the minimization of within-groups variance, and the machine output indicates the increase in this variance which accompanies each reduction in the number of subgroups. Since the operation is sequential and the decision regarding the ultimate number of groups, judgmental, no claim is made that the overall solution is optimal.

For these reasons a special "affirmation program" was written (Brodie, 1966) to follow the Ward-Hook. Via the D^2 this program compares each S's profile with the mean profile of each potential subgroup and permits several important outcomes:

1. Ss may be reassigned to a new subgroup if this is indicated.

2. Ss who equally resemble two or more subgroups, within specified limits, may be placed in a residual group.

3. Errors made at several grouping levels may be used as one objective criterion for determining the optimum number of groups.

The affirmation program was applied to the present data and the results were used to serve the three purposes indicated.

When the Ss had been subgrouped in the indicated fashion on the basis of the job environment factors, the same procedure was repeated employing the life history factors. The former subgroups were then regarded as representing levels of a "job climate" factor, and the latter as levels of a "type of person" factor in an unequal cell-size, weighted means, analysis of variance design. Cell entries were composite criterion scores for a given type of S exposed to a given climate. An interaction between these two criteria of classification would then be identifiable, and would speak directly to the third purpose of the study.

RESULTS

In attempting to evaluate the predictive validity of the creativity battery of 1955, two preliminary issues arise. First, before examining the relationship of predictors to criteria *within* a selected group (R & D), it seems appropriate to inquire as to the distributions of the three groups on the single best predictor, PSA—W. Since the distributions concerned are skewed, their means and variances do not adequately define them, and the complete scatter plots have been included as Figure 1 (p. 256). It should be noted that two different scales are employed on the y axis in order to make the areas under the curves more nearly comparable. Given this, there is an apparent tendency for Group III to show the lowest scores and Group I the highest, in line with expectation. There may also be some tendency for Group II to score more like III than I, a result which might or might not have been anticipated.

Second, before examining in greater detail the issue of how well the creativity battery predicts, it seems a prerequisite that it predict with some uniqueness. The question most commonly raised concerns the independence of that which is measured by general mental ability tests from that which is measured by creativity tests. In the present instance, it was found possible to obtain scores on the American Council on Education Psychological Examination (ACE) for 167 of the 457 R&D engineers. The test had been administered to them as college freshmen some two years prior to the time when they completed the creativity battery. The top row of Table II contains the correlations of the ACE with the cognitive predictors of the creativity battery and with the composite criterion. It will be noted that none of the former is of substantial magnitude, and that the latter is near zero. On the other hand, those scores derived from the special battery are significantly, if modestly, correlated with the composite criterion. The result should not be overinterpreted, but it does suggest reasonable independence of creativity from general ability within the present sample.

To evaluate the predictive power of the creativity battery over time, reference is made to column five of Table II which contains *minimum* estimates of the relationships involved. It will be observed that only the PSA test and the PHF are effective predictors. Both the AMT, which looked promising in concurrent validation, and the PI, which had appeared to be making a marginal contribution, failed to correlate significantly with the criterion in the more demanding

TABLE II

Predictive Validities and Intercorrelations of the ACE and Several Specially Devised Predictors

(N = 457)				
	2	3	4	5
1. The ACE (N = 167)	.07	.32**	.20**	.01
2. Applications of Mechanisms Test		.14**	.40**	.06
3. Power Source Apparatus (PSA-W)			.63**	.25**
4. Power Source Apparatus (PSA-T)				.19**
5. Composite Criterion				
6. Personal History Form				.15**

* = 5% level, ** = 1% level

predictive context. At any event, the estimates of column five can, realistically, be increased if consideration is given to three qualifying influences.

First, unambiguous criterion data are available only for the R & D group. However, if the battery were administered as an employment test, immediately following graduation, the range of scores would be wider because both Groups I (R & D) and II (EM) would be included. If it were administered as engineering students became upperclassmen, to serve as a sectioning device, the range would be still wider because Group III would also be included. Even in the first case, the zero-order criterion correlations of Table II would be .02 to .03 points higher in the more variable sample (Thorndike, 1949).

Second, and for two reasons, the product-moment correlation provides a poor estimate of the critical predictor-criterion relationship for these data. This is because: (a) the criterion distribution is extremely positively skewed, with many values of zero or near zero; and (b) it is not the task of the present battery to discriminate throughout the range of scores, but only at its upper end. *A priori*, it seems clear that whatever fraction of engineers is to be regarded as truly creative, it probably does not exceed five to 20 percent. Accordingly, a decision was made prior to analysis of the data to examine several biserial cuts at several test score levels, vs. the continuous criterion. Levels selected were the highest 5, 10, 15, and 20 percent, with the middle two to be regarded as most critical. Scores selected were those on the single best predictor, the PSA—W test. Table III contains the results and shows the point-biserial correlation between test and criterion as a function of the level at which the former variable is dichotomized. It will be recalled that a correlation of 0.33 or 0.34 is .08 to .09 points above the minimum estimate of Table III.

TABLE III

Point-Biserial Correlations of PSA-W Score with the Composite Criterion

PSA-W Raw Score	Centile Level of Dichotomy	Biserial r	St. Error
19	95	0.24	0.09
12	90	0.34	0.07
11	85	0.33	0.07
10	80	0.29	0.06

Third, the zero-order estimates of the table just cited are really inappropriate because it was originally proposed to construct a battery to be *used* as a battery, and not as a series of separate subtests. Accordingly, it may be noted that combining the PSA—W and PSA—T with the PHF yields a shrunken multiple R of 0.28. This represents an increase of 0.03 points over the best zero-order validity coefficient of 0.25.

If the effects of the three influences noted were to be assumed to be additive, they would argue for an estimated correlation of the order of magnitude of 0.38 to 0.39 between the combined predictors and the criterion in (combined) Groups I and II, and with a selection ratio of 10 to 15 percent. To evaluate the reasonableness of this estimate, a random sample of 100 cases was drawn from the R & D group. The zero-order correlations were corrected for restriction in range; the PSA scores and the PHF score were combined into a single variate thru application of the "beta" weights derived from the multiple R; and this combined predictor distribution was dichotomized at the level of the top 10 percent of cases and the top 15 percent of cases. The resulting validity estimates were 0.41 and 0.37 respectively, giving support to the approximate accuracy of the additive estimate.

The second major purpose of this investigation was to identify those personal non-cognitive characteristics (measured by the LHQ) and those environmental characteristics (measured by the JES) which have significantly facilitated or inhibited the expression of creative potential by the present Ss between their initial testing in 1955 and the follow-up of 1964. Data pertinent to this purpose appear in Table IV which contains the names assigned to the LHQ factors ultimately identified, their intercorrelations, and the correlation of each with the composite criterion. All the factor validities are low, but the identification of factor 3 and its significant criterion correlation are worth a comment. The responses given by persons scoring high on this factor lead to the following characterization of the respondent: member of an honor society; high ranking in

TABLE IV

Intercorrelations and Validities of the LHQ Factors

$(N = 307)$ †			
	2	3	4
1. Socioeconomic background	-.02	-.07	-.09
2. Favorable Self-perception		-.03	-.13*
3. Academic achievement			-.19**
4. Favorable self-perception			---

* = 5% level, ** = 1% level, † = 150 cases "held out" to cross-validate multiple Rs

TABLE V

Intercorrelations and Validities of the JES Factors

$(N = 307)$ †				
	2	3	4	5
1. Utilitarian self-development	-.11	-.01	.03	-.13*
2. Supportive supervisory and peer relationships		-.15**	-.14	.08
3. Perception of success			.03	-.01
4. Professional and research orientation of supervision				.26**
5. Composite criterion				---

* = 5% level, ** = 1% level, † = 150 cases "held out" to cross-validate multiple Rs

class; a scholarship winner; and a joiner of professional organizations. As indicated by the criterion correlation of *minus* 0.19, the more creative Ss of this study could be so characterized a little *less* frequently than their fellows. It should, however, be born in mind that virtually all Ss of Group I hold engineering degrees and are professionally employed.

Corresponding data derived from analysis of the JES appear in Table V. Once more all of the correlations are low, but the criterion validity of factor 4 sets it apart as a variable of some interest and importance. The typical high scorer on this factor gave item responses implying the following characterization of his job environment: the head of his department publishes; his colleagues hold advanced degrees; the company provides out-of-hours laboratory facilities for personal research; the head of his department has contributed to patents pending or held; and the head of his department has an M.S. or Ph.D. in engineering. Score on this factor correlates as highly with score on the composite criterion as the best cognitive predictor and suggests the appropriateness of some subsequent discussion of its role and meaning.

Purpose number three relates to the task of evaluating the possibility of a "type of person" by "type of climate" interaction. The procedures described earlier were first employed to establish subsets of Ss with similar profiles on the four JES factors, and four subsets were identified. The same methods were then utilized to identify seven subsets of Ss having similar profiles across the three factors of the LHQ. The subsets then became levels of a job climate factor and of a type of person factor, respectively, in an analysis of variance design with two criteria of classification. Table VI contains the summary of the indicated analysis and reveals that the main effects associated with both sets of subgroups *are* significant, but that the desired interaction does not even approach significance. To test this result in yet another form, persons in the four quarters of the distribution of scores on the PSA—W were regarded as subsets, and as constituting four levels of a type of person factor based upon creative potential. A second analysis of variance was based upon this revised dimension vs. type of job climate. This summary appears as Table VII. Once again, no significant interaction emerged and it was, therefore, concluded that what constitutes the job environment most conducive to creativity may be generalized across all types of Ss or levels of potential represented in the present R & D group.

TABLE VI

LHQ vs. JES Defined Subgroups—Summary

Source	Sum of Squares	D.F.	Mean Sq.	F Ratio
JES Subgroups	2,309.77	3	719.92	9.79**
LHQ Subgroups	1,870.08	6	311.68	3.96**
Interactions	1,359.38	18	75.52	0.96
Error	30,210.96	384	78.87	

* = 5% level
** = 1% level

TABLE VII

PSA—W vs. JES Defined Subgroups—Summary

Source	Sum of Squares	D.F.	Mean Sq.	F Ratio
JES Subgroups	1,802.35	3	600.78	7.83**
PSA-W Subgroups	1,217.53	3	405.84	5.29**
Interactions	848.33	9	94.26	1.23
Error	31,996.11	417	76.73	

* = 5% level, ** = 1% level

DISCUSSION

Before drawing any conclusions on the basis of the data presented, certain limitations in it, and in the analytical methods employed, must be pointed out.

Restriction in Range. Prominent among the methodological problems of this investigation is that of a conspicuous restriction in the range of talent employed. Clearly, within the available sample, only the R & D engineers of Group I had had an equal and substantial opportunity to produce tangible criterion evidence of their creativity. Yet, if training and employment have partially selected them for aptitude, they are restricted to an unknown extent on the PSA as compared with a population of all engineering graduates. If it is desired to draw even broader inferences regarding the relationship of intelligence to creativity in the general population, the data are obviously inadequate. For example, it may well be that there is some intellectual level beneath which creativity is seldom if ever seen. If so, the two variables are correlated to this extent. Given the present sample of graduates of a difficult and technical college curriculum, however, it is difficult to conceive of any direct test of the hypothesis.

Restriction in another sense exists because only one area of application was considered. No type of person by type of environment interaction was discovered. If one type of person is creative in music, another in art, another in literature, and still another in machine design, the finding may, clearly, be artifactual. That is, there may indeed *be* an interaction between type of creative person and type of optimum environment, but no evidence of it in this case because the area of machine design is occupied by only one type of creative person. In short, a limitation of this study is that it does not include the full spectrum of talent, and that conclusions must be qualified accordingly.

Temporal Interval. A second series of problems intrinsic to these data relates to the time elapsed between testing (1955) and the collection of criterion information (1964). If the interval had been shortened, criterion data would have been less complete and reliable. On the other hand, during a nine-year period there have, no doubt, been some true, intrinsic, and differential changes in the creative capabilities of the Ss. These, of course, attenuate and lower predictor-criterion relationships in a manner which is for many purposes unwarranted. A case in point may be a postulated differential effect by school attended, which would have occurred subsequent to testing during the junior and senior years. Thus, if evidence of short-term validity is desired, the present data probably provide an underestimate of it.

Measurement. Another sort of limitation of the present design is that it involves the mixing of concurrent and predictive data. For example, the JES provides the former, and the PSA the latter. To compare their validities implies that the procedures are equally exacting; whereas, it is well-recognized that such is not the case.

A second illustration of the same type involves the PHF and LHQ. The former involves only eight open-ended items and has been shown to have predictive validity. When the follow-up was undertaken, it was felt that many potential non-cognitive predictors of importance had been omitted and the LHQ was constructed accordingly. However, the potential validity of this latter device was surely underestimated, since proven and critical items already included in the PHF were *not* reintroduced into the LHQ.

Statistics. Since the D^2 statistic was employed as a measure of profile similarity, it seems in order to point out one limitation of this index, as used, which is that it involves an unweighted summing of squared deviations across all dimensions of a profile. It was known that these dimensions had differing criterion validities, and they might have been differentially effective as potential moderators as well. At any event, a given deviation entered the sum with the same weight regardless of its origin. The implication that each dimension is of the same intrinsic importance in the subgrouping is probably misleading.

Criterion Heterogeneity. Finally, it must be recognized that the Ss of this investigation were employed in a wide variety of industries, producing many differing products and employing a plethora of methods. It is a truism that the attempt to predict criteria embedded in these widely divergent contexts is fraught with inaccuracy. How much better prediction might be *within* one company is a matter for conjecture, but the concurrent phase of the present study (1957) suggests that the increment would be very substantial.

INTERPRETATION

An hypothesis, suggested by the writer in 1957, is that it is necessary to highly structure or control the associative process in the present area of utilitarian creativity in order to enhance or optimize the validity of measurement. For example, the AMT requires only that *S*s name machines of *any sort,* within which the given mechanism might function. On the other hand, the PSA test requires that one start with a *prescribed* power source and produce a prescribed motion sequence.

The entire matter is probably better conceived in terms of current theories of cognitive style (Schroder *et al.,*1967). Adopting this frame of reference, it seems clear that the individual who can accept numerous situational restrictions and who can still be creative is simply able to integrate more inputs than the one who cannot. Cast in this form, the discriminating dimension emerges as one of cognitive complexity.

The present finding of little relationship between mental ability and creativity test results is in accord with the findings of Getzels and Jackson (1962). However, the methodology in the two cases is so divergent as to argue for little real precedent. In the case of academic achievement vs. creativity, on the other hand, there is at least an apparently sharp contradiction in outcomes. It is the impression of the writer that this is more apparent than real. Getzels and Jackson (*ibid.*) present data which indicate that some cognitive measures beyond the IQ might be useful in the prediction of academic success. However, they present *no* evidence that their "creativity tests" actually measure any external, normative criterion of creativity of any character. Thus, when they conclude that their high creativity-lower IQ group does as well in secondary school as their high IQ-lower creativity group, they are, in fact, only comparing selected groups which differ in their performances on two types of cognitive tests. In the present study, on the other hand, score on a cluster of LHQ items implying academic under-achievement has been correlated with an external criterion of creativity and found to be significantly associated with it. Here, creativity is defined not in terms of test performance, but in terms of such external evidence as patents and patent disclosures. Undoubtedly each type of finding has value, but they are contradictory in name only.

A result of greater import concerns the relationship of JES factor 4, Professional and Research orientation of supervision, to the composite criterion. Going back at least as far as the work of Adamson (1952) on "functional fixedness," there has been considerable, understandable ambivalence as regards the character of leadership most appropriate to an R & D operation, and most facilitative of creativity in general. The conflict has had polar opinions ranging from, "If we expect people to be creative we can't tell them what to do," on the one hand, to "If we market products within a restricted range, all new ideas do not have equal utility and some guidelines *must* be prescribed," on the other. A resolution has often led to a quite permissive philosophy of leadership. The present data, in another vein, suggest the appropriateness of something quite different. As indicated by the high loading items of Table V, the optimum environment for the present *S*s was one in which they were led by *example*—the example of not only their head, but their colleagues. It seems to be clearly implied that leadership from one who has *done* is not only tolerable, but that it probably constitutes a stimulus to do likewise.

In a related way, it is clear that the treatment of Ss with the optimum environment is far from uniform, and that this absence of uniformity tends to confound the relationship of predictors to criterion. Accordingly, adding JES factor 4 to the multiple correlation of PSA–W and PHF with the composite criterion increases the relationship by 0.03 correlation points. This operation is equivalent to asking, "If we knew in advance the sort of environment in which our Ss would function, would a correction for its favorability or unfavorability not enhance prediction?" Both rationally and empirically the answer is "yes."

Finally, in speaking of the complexity of creativity, it may be of interest to observe the results of combining both predictive and concurrent validity coefficients as though they were comparable and of identifying the three best measures. This task was accomplished by introducing into a "tear-down" multiple regression analysis all ten potential predictors of the composite criterion of creativity (4 JES factor scores, 3 LHQ factor scores, 2 PSA scores, and score on the PHF). Predictors were then dropped out in inverse order of their contribution until only three remained. Among these, the largest independent contribution was made by JES factor 4, Professional and Research orientation of supervision; the second largest by PSA–T; and the third largest by LHQ factor 2, Favorable self-perception. It is at least intriguing to note that one is a measure of the environment, one a cognitive measure, and one a non-cognitive. Complex determination of creativity seems clearly implied.

CONCLUSIONS

1. The PSA test *was* found to be a better predictor of the composite criterion of creativity in machine design than a well-regarded mental ability or scholastic aptitude test. Hypothesis number one may thus be regarded as supported.
2. The PSA test *was* found to be a better predictor of the present criterion than the less structured AMT. Hypothesis number two, and the implications of this finding for the relevance of the cognitive complexity dimension, therefore, may be regarded as sustained.
3. Since both non-cognitive and job environment measures were found to be significant predictors of the present creativity criterion, and to enhance prediction when added to that of a cognitive measure, hypothesis number three also may be regarded as sustained.
4. Since *no* significant interaction between personal and environmental determiners of creativity could be detected, hypothesis number four must be regarded as rejected in this context.
5. With respect to the predictive validity of the battery of 1955, it is estimated that, in a sample of graduates of schools of engineering, the best linear com-

bination of measures should correlate 0.35 to 0.40 with a composite criterion of their subsequent creativity in machine design. A qualification is that the battery predicts better if scores are realistically dichotomized at a high level than if they are employed as a continuous variate.

NOTE: This chapter, initially produced for presentation at this conference and for publication in this conference report, has also been submitted separately, essentially in identical form and with mutual concurrence, as an article which appeared in the *Journal of Applied Psychology,* 1969, Volume 53, 198-208, entitled "Cognitive, Non-Cognitive, and Environmental Correlates of Mechanical Ingenuity." Reproduced by permission.

CHAPTER 17

Creativity Research Program: A Review

Morris B. Parloff*

THE INVESTIGATOR who attempts to conduct research in the area of creativity may take comfort from the certain knowledge that he has associated himself with a problem of unequivocal significance. It is important that he experience this satisfaction since it may have to sustain him over rather long fallow periods.

Equally unequivocal is the fact that the investigator in this area will have difficulty in satisfying himself and others that the specific problems he has selected for study and that the methods he has employed are indeed pertinent to that mysterious, awesome, and thoroughly ambiguous area covered by the word "creative." Its imprecision is well-reflected in the definition offered by Fowler's *Modern English Usage:*

> Creative is a term of praise much affected by the critics. It is presumably intended to mean original, or something like that, but is preferred because it is more vague and less usual. . . .It has been aptly called a 'luscious, round, meaningless word,' and said to be 'so much in honor that it is the clinching term of approval from the school room to the advertiser's studio.' (1965, p.114)

I do not propose to dwell on this and other research difficulties inherent in the area of creativity, but shall instead go on to review the specific aims and directions of our research in this miasmic field.

Our primary interest in the problem of creativity stems from two basic aims: (1) to identify personality patterns associated with creative functioning, and (2) to advance current theories of personality development. Much of the current theory of personality development is derived from clinical and experimental investigations of the ineffectively and inadequately functioning individual. It seems plausible that the study of the highly effective and creative individual might yield new data and thereby provide opportunities for the extension of current theory. Since the clinician—among others—is called upon to assist individuals to utilize their creative capacities more fully, it seems appropriate that we attempt to discern what personality patterns are, in fact, conducive to creative performance "in real life." Such knowledge would be of assistance in aiding us to set relevant goals for intensive psychotherapy and for personality change efforts.

---

*Morris B. Parloff is Chief, Section on Personality, Laboratory of Psychology, National Institute of Mental Health, Bethesda.

Let it be perfectly clear at the outset that we need not assume that personality factors are the sole or even necessarily the most important correlates of creative functioning. We do assume, however, that creative performance is a function of a complex interaction among such factors as personality structure, environmental influences, and cognitive capacities. We further assume that it is tactically wise, in approaching a problem of such complexity, to identify those aspects of the interaction that are most relevant. This may then permit a rigorous and systematic study of a limited number of variables.

Our creativity research program has taken two major directions. The first concerns a series of experimental studies aimed at investigating the conditions relevant to facilitating creative performance. The second deals with a naturalistic, longitudinal study of the development of "creative scientists." A review of the variety of approaches we have taken may suggest that this report should be subtitled "Confessions of a Haphazard Obsessive."

Since our experimental studies concerning enhancement of creative performance have either been published or are soon to be published, they will not be reviewed now. However, there are two studies that will be described here informally, since I am unlikely ever to wish to do so formally. One study concerned the use of dreams in creative problem-solving. The other research investigated the effect of hypnotic suggestion in facilitating performance on some Guilford's tests of divergent thinking.

Our interest in problem-solving during sleep was stimulated by a report of Dement's work summarized in an esoteric technical journal—*Time* magazine. Dement found that subjects to whom he had presented a problem prior to their going to sleep frequently reported dreams which suggested that they had been working on the problem while asleep. On occasion they even hit upon or appeared to be very close to the solution, frequently without being aware of it. One of the problems which Dement used was the following sequence of letters followed by two blanks: O, T, T, F, F, , . The subject was informed that when the relationship between these letters was understood, he would be able to fill in the two missing letters. As many of you may have recognized, the letters are the first letters of the words One, Two, Three, Four, and Five. The missing letters should be "S" for Six and "S" for Seven. We undertook to administer this problem to subjects who were participating in dream studies at NIMH in the research program directed by Dr. Frederick Snyder. As the subject slept, EEG, respiration, and eye movement patterns were studied. When there was evidence that the patient had concluded a dream, he was awakened and asked to report the dream fully. In this manner, progressively irritable subjects reported their dreams throughout the night. The research went on for a period of months. We obtained clear evidence that the subjects had been dreaming during REM periods, but we found very little evidence that the subjects had been dreaming about the problem. My hopes for success dimmed considerably. One evening while addressing a class at a local university, I presented them with the O, T, T,

F, F, , , problem and urged that on the following morning they submit summaries of their dreams. Although a number of students reported their dreams, none of the dreams appeared to be related to the solution of the problem. However, one student reported that on awakening he had the strong conviction that he had indeed solved the problem. He stated that the letters O, T, T, F, F represented the first letters of words comprising the following tortuous sentence: "Only those that feel fine sleep soundly." Naturally, we terminated the project. I suspect that the subject may perhaps have been pulling my leg, but what worries me even more is that perhaps he wasn't.

The second study concerns the use of hypnosis to induce increased self-confidence in one's ability to solve a specific set of problems. We hypothesized that high self-confidence would increase the individual's willingness and/or ability to perform effectively on specific cognitive measures which investigators believe are associated with the creative capacities. It was assumed that self-confidence was a relevant variable in that it may increase the subject's willingness to undertake a problem and to persist in working on it and that it may cause him to evaluate the solutions that occur to him, instead of immediately dismissing them as trivial.

Our subjects were a group of college students who had been found to be good hypnotic subjects. The design required that each subject serve as his own control under three experimental conditions: (1) the normal waking state, (2) the hypnotic state, and (3) the hypnotic state with the positive suggestion of increased self-confidence. The self-confidence suggestion was aimed at improving the individual's attitude toward working on the types of tasks on which he was to be tested. The seven verbal tasks consisted of tests devised by Guilford and his associates: Word Fluency, Associational Fluency, Ideational Fluency, Expressional Fluency, Alternate Uses, Sensitivity to Problems, and Explanations of Problems.

Roughly equivalent forms of each test were constructed. Since each individual was to perform under each of three conditions—normal wakefulness, the hypnotic state, and the hypnotic state plus positive suggestion—it was anticipated that as each subject became increasingly familiar with the tests, serious "practice" effects might result. To counter such practice effects, the design of the experiment called for (1) the induction of amnesia at the end of each test condition, and (2) the restriction of the order of presentation of the test conditions. It was decided that the most rigorous test of any possible facilitating effects of the "hypnosis-plus-the-positive-self-confidence suggestion" would occur if this condition was always presented first to the subject. Performance on tests taken under subsequent conditions might show benefit from earlier experience with similar forms of these tests. If, however, the hypnosis with suggestion was indeed powerful, its enhancement of performance should exceed that of all other conditions even though the other conditions might have the advantage of practice effects.

Of the six subjects who were tested under these conditions, five demonstrated the effects precisely as predicted; i.e., their performance on randomly presented test forms under the conditions of normal wakefulness and hypnosis was inferior to their performance under hypnosis with the suggestion of increased self-confidence. The sixth subject invariably awakened from the hypnotic state whenever the suggestion of increased self-confidence was made. Subsequent interviews with this subject indicated that these instructions had a highly personal significance to her, but this need not detain us now. The results, then, were shockingly good. I am not accustomed to having unequivocally positive results. Like Mort Sahl, I am not "geared for total acceptance."

After brooding about these findings, I realized that, in my great concern to avoid the possible confounding influence of practice effects, I had inadvertently given our hypnotic subjects the opportunity to provide us with the results we desired, not so much by *enhancing* their performance under the experimental conditions as by *inhibiting* their performance in the control conditions. A good hypnotic subject is one who, among other things, is concerned with giving the experimenter the desired response. Since hypnosis with the "increased self-confidence" suggestions was always presented first, each subject had the opportunity of discovering either from the researcher's manner or from the specific modifications of the instructions that he was not expected to do as well under the other conditions.

We thereupon repeated the study still using good hypnotic subjects, but now randomizing the conditions of presentation. This time no difference between the conditions was discernible. So much for my foray into hypnosis.

Now to turn to a somewhat more detailed presentation of an ongoing study concerned with identifying personality characteristics associated with creative potential in science. In this study, we wished (1) to determine whether personality characteristics reliably differentiated between two carefully selected samples of male high school seniors similar in age, socioeconomic background, intelligence, and scientific aptitude, but differing in rated creativity of independently conducted research project; and (2) to compare personality characteristics associated with creative performance in the adolescent with those characteristics found to differentiate between more and less creative samples of adults.

It was anticipated that personality characteristics associated with creative performance in the adults and adolescents might not coincide, since the creative adult who has achieved considerable recognition for relatively long periods might reasonably be expected to enjoy higher self-esteem, greater sense of autonomy, more self-assurance, etc., than would the creative adolescent. This assumption is consistent with the observation of William James that "a man . . . with powers that have uniformly brought him success with place and wealth and friends and fame, is not likely to be visited by the morbid diffidences and doubts about himself which he had when he was a boy. . . ." It appeared possible that some personality characteristics associated with creativity in adults may be more the consequence of recognition than the precondition for such recognition.

Our study required that we identify potentially creative young men who could be followed in a longitudinal study. The selection of our sample was based on a very simple assumption: evidence of current or previous creative performance is a predictor of subsequent creative performance.

We are concerned here with creativity as measured by the qualities of a product. One of the main advantages of using a product definition of creativity is that these findings can more readily be generalized to common usage of the term. Much that has been written about the personalities of adult creative individuals is based on samples identified by the formally and informally assessed qualities (novelty and effectiveness) of the products they have achieved.

The decision to restrict the sample of adolescents to those expressing interest in an area of science was based on the assumption that the standards for judging the creativity of scientific works are somewhat less ambiguous than those employed in the area of arts and letters. We do not accept the view that creativity is uniquely the province of the artist or the writer. We assume that the frequency and quality of creative performance is no greater in art than in science.

Since personality characteristics are associated not only with creativity, but also with a variety of variables, such as vocational choice, age, sex, intelligence, socioeconomic background, recognition, etc., the design required that we also identify a control group of young men comparable to the experimental group on all these variables, but differing on the judged level of the creativity of their research products.

SAMPLE CRITERION

This report is based on the analysis of data derived from a sample which initially included over 2500 male high school seniors who successfully completed all entrance requirements to the 1963 Annual Science Talent Search, an annual competition conducted by the Science Service, Inc., as part of the Westinghouse Talent Search. Candidates for our study were those who met the following requirements: (1) recommended by members of their high school faculty as having demonstrated considerable promise as a scientist, (2) passed the annually revised Edgerton Science Aptitude Test—above the 80th percentile, and (3) submitted an independently conducted research report to Science Service, Inc.

The creativity of the product of each candidate was then assessed on the basis of the report submitted to pairs of judges. The judges' evaluation of the creativity of the product was based on a shared general view. The creative product represented the formulation, testing, and presentation of an idea which satisfied two criteria: novelty and effectiveness. A product was novel to the extent that it represented concepts and hypotheses which were judged to be "original" in a given area of study at a specified point in time. Effectiveness was assessed according to judges' standards of usefulness, tenability, plausibility, elegance, etc. Neither novelty nor effectiveness alone was sufficient to warrant a product's classification as creative.

Each student project was independently rated on a scale ranging from A to E by two judges competent in the area of science represented by the project, e.g., mathematics, physics, chemistry, biology, etc. If the ratings of the pair of judges differed by more than one letter grade, the judges were required to reconcile their differences. On the basis of these ratings, subjects receiving the grades of A and B were placed in the "more creative" sample, and those receiving lower grades were placed in the "less creative" group.

Of the 572 male subjects who passed the science aptitude test above the 80th percentile and submitted an independently conducted science research project, 536—i.e., 93.7 percent of the eligible sample—agreed to participate in this study. On the basis of the judges' ratings of projects, 112 Ss were classified in the "more" creative category and the remaining 424 Ss fell into the "less" creative category.

PERSONALITY MEASURES

In selecting personality measures, we included only those instruments which had been found relevant in previous studies aimed at differentiating personality characteristics of the more and less creative adults. In addition, we required that the reliability measures be high and sufficiently robust so that the tests could be self-administered. The battery of tests included the California Psychological Inventory, the 16 PF (Form B), the FIRO-B, and four scales from the MMPI: "K" Scale, the Welch Anxiety and Repression Scales, and the Barron Ego-Strength Scale (KARE).

RESULTS

In comparing the identified "more" and "less" creative adolescent groups, we found no reliable differences on the following variables: age, science aptitude, Scholastic Aptitude Test—Verbal, high school grade—point average, socio-economic status, and Scholastic Aptitude Test—Math.

California Personality Inventory (CPI)

An inspection of the "profiles" of the mean scale scores of both the more and less creative adolescent samples indicates that each sample presents a similar but well-differentiated pattern. Both the more and less creative groups are high on measures of poise, ascendancy, self-assurance, intellectual efficiency, self-reliance, and perceptiveness, but are low on measures of conformity and conventionality. In comparing the CPI profiles of both the more and less creative samples with a CPI normative sample of 6000 males, we found that the more and less creative adolescent samples score below the test norms on scales measuring sense of *Well-Being, Self-Control,* and *Good Impression.* This suggests that our adolescent sample tends to be less inhibited and less concerned with the impression they make on others, to be more able to hold unusual views, and to admit to more worries than the male normative sample. The scores of our adolescent sample are above the test norms on all other scales. It is important to keep these base-line data in mind in interpreting the individual mean scale differences between the more and less creative samples.

To test the reliability of the obtained mean scale differences between the more and the less creative samples, a two-way analysis of variance (unweighted means) was performed on each of the 18 CPI scales. The analyses concerned the influence of two levels of creativity, seven vocational preference groupings, and the interaction between creativity and vocation. Main effects ($p < .05$) attributable to creativity level were found on eight scales and main effects ($p < .05$) associated with vocational choice were found on five scales. Since we are concerned here primarily with the personality characteristics associated with creative performance, we will not dwell further on findings concerning the personality differences between vocational preference groups. An interaction between creativity and vocation was found on only one scale (*Social Presence*), suggesting that, in general, the personality characteristics which differentiate between the more and less creative groups are independent of the personality differences associated with vocational preferences. The raw score means and related F ratios of the more and less creative groups on each of the CPI scales are presented in Table I.

Those subjects in the more creative sample are higher than those in the less creative sample on seven scales: *Capacity for Status*—possessing more of the qualities and attributes which lead to the attainment of social status; *Self-Control*—more disciplined, thoughtful, and deliberate; *Tolerance*—more accepting of a variety of social beliefs; *Good Impression*—more interested in making and maintaining a favorable impression on others; *Achievement via Independence*—more self-reliant, motivated to work independently; *Intellectual Efficiency*—more clear thinking, capable, resourceful; and *Psychological Mindedness*—more perceptive, intraceptive, aware of the needs and motives of others. The more creative group is significantly lower than the less creative group on the Communality scale, suggesting that they are more willing to recognize and hold views that are unusual and unconventional.

KARE Scales

Comparable statistical analyses were performed on the four scales derived from the MMPI. The more creative sample obtained significantly higher scores on two of the scales, the "K" Scale (Candidness) and the Ego Strength Scale, and obtained significantly lower scores on the third, the Anxiety Scale. No differ-

TABLE I

Raw Score Means for Adolescent Creative and Control Groups,[1] and Results of
Unweighted Means Analyses of Variance for 18 CPI and 4 MMPI Scales

	Mean		F–Ratio		
	Creative	Control	Creativity	Vocation	Interaction
Scale	$N = 112$	$N = 413$	$df = 1/511$	$6/511$	$6/511$
CPI Scales					
Dominance	29.65	29.15	.48	1.75	.72
Capacity for Status	22.12	21.29	4.14*	1.73	2.11+
Sociability	25.87	24.94	2.40	4.52***	1.13
Social Presence	38.01	36.70	3.63+	2.94**	2.20*
Self-Acceptance	22.99	22.38	1.73	3.53***	1.11
Sense of Well-Being	36.29	35.44	2.66	1.07	.61
Responsibility	32.80	32.09	1.50	1.08	1.13
Socialization	38.08	37.80	.18	1.55	1.20
Self-Control	28.91	27.05	4.59*	2.52*	1.64
Tolerance	24.97	23.81	4.96*	1.34	1.60
Good Impression	18.88	16.70	8.93**	.89	1.53
Communality	24.69	25.25	4.96*	2.64*	1.72
Achievement via Conformity	28.67	27.95	1.83	1.19	1.34
Achievement via Independence	23.55	22.58	4.93*	1.48	.70
Intellectual Efficiency	43.04	42.01	4.59*	.39	.26
Psychological Mindedness	14.52	13.64	8.47**	1.15	1.10
Flexibility	11.77	12.02	.28	1.17	1.66
Femininity	16.96	16.55	.88	1.47	.73
MMPI Scales					
K (Candidness)	15.12	13.82	7.23**	1.65	1.47
A (Anxiety)	9.79	11.79	5.27*	.87	.66
R (Repression)	16.47	15.46	3.30	2.61	.89
E (Ego Strength	49.45	47.79	6.93**	.38	.31

[1]Eight vocational interest groups represented: Mathematics, Physics, Chemistry, Biology,
Engineering, Biochemistry, Other Science, Non-Science.

$+ = p < .10$; $* = p < .05$; $** = p < .01$; $*** = p < .001$.

ences were found attributable to vocation, and no significant interactions were
obtained. On the basis of these analyses, the more creative adolescent Ss appear
to be more prepared to state negative things about themselves, to be less
anxious, and to have a greater ability to cope with daily stresses than the less

creative sample. The means and F ratios of the more and less creative groups on each of these four scales are also summarized in Table I.

Sixteen PF Scales

Analysis of variance performed on each of the scales of the 16 PF indicated that the more creative sample's mean scores were significantly higher ($p < .05$) on "E"—more dominant, assertive, self-assured, dependable; higher on "H"— more adventurous and spontaneous; higher on "M"—more bohemian, more intense subjectivity and inner mental life; higher on "Q-1"—more radical, more inclined to experiment with new ideas; and higher on "Q-3"—more self-controlled, persistent, and effective in thinking. The data also suggest ($p < .10$) that the more creative sample manifests more intellectual power—"B"; and is less anxious, neurotic, or depressed—"O," than the less creative sample. (See Table II.) Differences associated with vocation were found on eight of the 16 scales

TABLE II

Raw Score for Adolescent Creative and Control Groups and Results of Unweighted Means Analyses of Variance for Each of the 16 — PF Inventory Scales

Scale		Mean		F Ratio		
		Creative	Control	Creativity	Vocation	Interaction
		$N = 112$	$N = 413$	$df = 1/511$	6/511	6/511
A	Outgoing	6.37	5.87	1.38	2.26*	2.26*
B	Bright	10.85	10.58	2.72+	1.24	0.21
C	Mature	18.07	17.74	0.49	1.57	0.70
E	Competitive	13.59	12.66	4.24*	2.15*	1.47
F	Enthusiastic	12.71	13.24	0.88	1.17	0.64
G	Conscientious	12.18	12.54	0.82	1.56	1.46
H	Adventurous	13.47	12.01	4.39*	3.59**	1.41
I	Sensitive	10.78	10.79	0.00	3.49**	0.34
L	Suspicious	7.54	7.45	0.05	2.57*	0.63
M	Bohemian	13.69	12.57	4.53*	3.98**	0.85
N	Sophisticated	9.90	9.61	0.40	2.75*	2.37*
O	Guilt Prone	11.06	12.01	2.91+	1.77+	1.86+
Q1	Radical	13.55	12.14	15.63***	0.63	0.31
Q2	Self-Sufficient	12.02	12.07	0.02	2.25*	0.77
Q3	Self-Controlled	11.90	11.09	5.53**	0.82	0.97
Q4	Excitable	11.56	11.68	0.06	1.97	2.95**

$+ = p < .10;$ $* = p < .05;$ $** = < .01;$ $*** = p < .001.$

and significant interactions were found on three scales: A (outgoing), N (sophisticated), and Q4 (Excitable).

FIRO-B

This measure consists of three scales indicating the degree to which the S "includes" others, "controls" others, or "expresses affection" toward others, and three scales which measure the degree to which the S wishes others to "include," "control," or "express affection" toward him. Analyses of variance on each scale indicated that only the affection scales differentiated the more and less creative groups: the more creative Ss indicated that they offer less and desire less affection than do the control Ss (see Table III). Although differences attributable to vocation were found on three scales, there were no significant interactions.

TABLE III

Means for Adolescent Creative and Control Groups, and Results of Unweighted Means Analyses of Variance for Six FIRO-B Scales

Scale	Mean		F Ratio		
	Creative	Control	Creative	Vocation	Interaction
	N = 112	N = 413	df = 1/511	6/511	6/511
Exercised inclusion	4.34	4.63	1.39	4.18**	0.89
Wanted inclusion	4.69	5.01	0.76	1.85+	0.66
Exercised control	4.50	4.22	1.02	1.73	0.66
Wanted control	4.27	4.61	2.27	2.18*	0.74
Exercised affection	2.89	3.59	5.21*	1.72	0.35
Wanted affection	3.80	4.48	4.92*	2.49*	0.47

$+ = p < .10$; $* = p < .05$; $** = p < .01$.

In brief, the more creative adolescent is differentiated from his less creative control in that he appears to be a more efficient thinker who is capable of and willing to experiment with new and unusual ideas; he has a better appreciation of reality and is more able to utilize fantasy in a constructive manner; he is more persistent, self-reliant, productive, and independent in his thinking; he is more attracted by the unusual or the unknown; he copes better with the world in which he lives; he attaches more value to his own ideas and is more willing to disagree with others; he is more aware of the impression he makes on others and will use this knowledge in order to facilitate the achievement of his own goals and interests; he is more discriminating and selective in deciding whose opinion matters to him; he does not view life as a popularity contest, for there are only a few individuals whom he empowers with the capacity to offer either positive or negative reinforcement for his ideas; he has strong preferences and is able to mobilize his skills and resources in achieving his goals, less encumbered by distracting anxieties than his less creative colleagues.

These findings suggest an affirmative answer to our first question: the more and less creative adolescent samples are differentiated on personality dimensions. I wish now to turn to the second major concern of this study, namely, to determine whether the personality scales which differentiate the adolescent samples similarly differentiate the more and less creative adult samples.

We hypothesized that if such substantial similarities were found, then it could be concluded that personality characteristics associated with creative performance seem to develop relatively early and remain relatively stable. A further implication of such a finding would be that those interested in the early identification of potentially creative individuals might be guided by the personality differences which characterize the creative man. If, however, different personality characteristics were found to differentiate the adult and adolescent more creative subjects from their less creative peers, then early identification might best proceed by establishing age-specific standards.

In order to obtain relevant data on creative adult samples, data derived from studies conducted by investigators at the Institute for Personality Assessment and Research (IPAR) were reanalyzed. The research of the IPAR group appeared to be particularly appropriate since those investigators had given careful attention to the selection of the experimental and control samples and had employed comparable personality measures with each of four vocational groups. Although researchers at IPAR had independently studied groups of more and less creative mathematicians, architects, writers, and research scientists, no effort had been made to perform overall analyses in terms of levels of creativity, vocational affiliation, and the interaction of the two variables. As a consequence, the reported differences among the more and less creative individuals within a particular field may theoretically confound the personality characteristics differentially associated with level of creative performance with those associated with success in a particular vocation.

The IPAR staff generously furnished raw data for each of 200 Ss, 101 of whom were identified as "more creative" and 99 as "less creative." The personality data for each subject included scores on 22 scales (CPI and the KARE) employed in our study of adolescent groups.

The adult *mathematician* sample consisted of 56 Ss of comparable age and education who had been studied by Crutchfield; 27 were judged to be "more creative" and 29 to be "less creative." Data on 81 *architects* were obtained from a study conducted by MacKinnon. Panels of judges nominated 40 individuals as among the most creative architects in the country and 41 (Control Group III) as somewhat less creative. (Control Group II was not included in our study as the mathematician and writer samples had no comparable control group.)

Information regarding *research scientists* was provided by Gough. The sample initially consisted of 45 industrial research workers: primarily, physicists, mathematicians, and electronic engineers. Each subject was rated by two supervisors and by at least four of his fellow scientists. Our analyses were restricted to 15 who were classed as "high" and 15 rated as "low."

Barron furnished material based on a sample of male *writers:* poets, novelists, and essayists who had been nominated by a panel of judges drawn from the English and Drama Departments of the University of California. The judges were asked to nominate writers who had a conspicuously high degree of originality and creativeness. The control was composed of less creative, yet successful and productive writers who had clearly "made their mark" in the field of writing. Nineteen of the sample were classed as "more creative" and 14 were identified as "less creative."

The average age of the 200 adult subjects was 45.1 years—ranging from 35.5 for the research scientists to 52.0 for the writers. The mean ages of the "more" and "less" creative groups were not reliably different (44.7 and 45.5 respectively).

The data for these four vocational groups were combined, and two-way analyses of variance were performed on each of the 22 personality scales. As shown in Table IV, five of the CPI scales differentiated between the two creativity levels at the .05 level of confidence, and an additional five scales differentiated at less than the .10 level of confidence. The fact that personality characteristics are clearly associated with vocational interest is demonstrated by the finding that 17 of the 22 scales showed differences significant at the .05 level of confidence attributable to vocational interest and an additional four scales differentiated among vocational groups at the .10 level. Of particular importance is the fact that on only one scale did the interaction between creativity and vocational interest reach the .05 level. It is apparent then that in the adult, as in the adolescent sample, personality factors associated with creativity are found to be independent of vocation and that, moreover, the direction of the difference between more and less creative samples was the same for each of the vocations represented.

The more creative adult sample was significantly higher than the controls of the following CPI measures: (1) *Social Presence,* i.e., more poised, spontaneous and self-confident; (2) *Flexibility,* i.e., more adventurous, humorous, rebellious, assertive, and egoistic; and (3) *Self-Acceptance,* i.e., more self-confident and self-assured. The more creative sample was lower on (4) *Good Impression,* i.e., less concerned with making a favorable impression; and (5) *Self-Control,* i.e., less disciplined, and less deliberate than the less creative adult sample. None of the MMPI scales differentiated the two creativity groups at either the .05 or .10 levels.

For purposes of identifying trends, CPI scale differences significant at the .10 level were also considered. It was found that compared to the less creative

TABLE IV

Raw Score Means for Adult Creative and Control Groups, and Results of
Analyses of Variance (Unweighted Means) for 18 CPI and 4 MMPI Scales

Scale	Mean		F Ratio		
	Creative	Control	Creativity	Vocation	Interaction
CPI Scales					
Dominance	30.25	29.25	1.42	4.18**	0.10
Capacity for Status	23.12	22.31	2.90x	2.54x	0.38
Sociability	25.32	24.27	2.04	3.91**	1.90
Social Presence	39.57	37.25	9.18**	6.44**	0.39
Self-Acceptance	23.21	21.54	8.63**	2.62x	0.32
Sense of Well-Being	37.51	38.20	3.08x	7.79**	0.99
Responsibility	32.92	32.72	0.12	6.30**	2.02
Socialization	35.54	36.18	0.75	5.99**	1.26
Self-Control	29.19	31.71	6.14*	2.86*	2.52x
Tolerance	24.93	24.67	0.19	4.87**	2.60x
Good Impression	16.00	18.30	7.05**	2.33x	1.93
Communality	24.99	25.52	3.70x	1.55	0.68
Achievement via Conformity	28.49	29.10	1.02	2.16x	2.10
Achievement via Independence	24.32	23.41	3.23x	11.74**	0.10
Intellectual Efficiency	42.32	41.44	2.03	10.79**	1.55
Psychological Mindedness	15.21	14.52	2.07	8.15**	1.82
Flexibility	13.15	11.34	8.96**	6.65**	0.28
Femininity	18.85	17.98	3.38x	4.58**	2.82*
MMPI Scales					
K (Candidness)	16.26	16.28	0.00	3.71*	0.72
A (Anxiety)	8.38	8.39	0.00	2.81*	0.01
R (Repression)	18.82	18.06	1.12	7.85**	0.73
E (Ego Strength)	49.95	50.02	0.01	15.21**	1.05

$*p = <.05$; $**p = <.01$; x $p = <.10$.

adults, the more creative adults were lower on *Communality,* i.e., they were able
to entertain more unusual ideas; they appeared more *Feminine* in their interests,
i.e., they showed greater breadth of interests and sensitivity; they were higher on
Achievement via Independence, i.e., they were more self-reliant and more
strongly motivated to succeed by independent action; they were lower on *Sense
of Well-Being,* i.e., they admitted to more difficulties; and they were higher on
Capacity for Status, i.e., they possessed more of the qualities that accompany

leadership and the achievement of social status. These findings are consistent with those previously reported by IPAR.

The demonstrated differences between the more and less creative adult samples suggest that, as with our adolescents, a set of personality characteristics independent of vocational affiliation is associated with creative performance. We can now compare the personality scales which differentiate the more and less creative adolescents and adults (see Table V).

Of the 22 personality scales (CPI and KARE) completed by both the adult and adolescent samples, the more and less creative adolescent groups were differentiated at or beyond the .10 level of confidence on 12 scales while the more and less creative adult groups showed reliable differences on 10 scales.

Six personality scales discriminated between the more and less creative samples in both the adult and adolescent samples. The creative adult and adolescent groups are both significantly lower than their respective control groups on *Communality* and are significantly higher on scales measuring *Capacity for Status, Social Presence, and Achievement via Independence.* On two scales, *Self-Control* and *Good Impression,* the mean scores of more creative adults and adolescents are reliably different from their respective controls, but the direction of the discrimination is reversed for adults and adolescents. While the creative adult group is lower than its control on *Self-Control* and *Good Impression,* the more creative adolescent group scores significantly higher than its control group on these scales. A similar trend is found for the *Sense of Well-Being* scale.

Scales which uniquely discriminate between more and less creative adults but not between comparable adolescent groups include: *Self-Acceptance, Flexibility,* and *Femininity.* Scales which uniquely discriminate between the more and less creative adolescent groups, but not between the comparable adult groups include: *Tolerance, Intellectual Efficiency, K, Anxiety,* and *Ego Strength.*

These findings suggest that personality may be a relevant dimension for the identification of the creative and potentially creative individual; however, a number of cautions must be kept in mind. The criterion used in this study involves not simply the formulation of a creative idea but also its development, its testing, and finally its forceful promulgation. The sets of personality variables conducive to each of these distinct activities are very likely different. The personality dimensions associated with the integration of a novel and effective idea need not be identical to those required for the rigorous testing of hypotheses or to those necessary for the effective communication of the ideas. As a consequence, investigators who limit their interest to the identification of personality characteristics associated with the capacity to produce innovative and effective ideas may find a different set of personality variables than that reported here.

In comparing adult and adolescent samples, one cannot assume that the absolute level of creativity represented is indeed equivalent. One can assume only that meaningfully different levels of creativity are represented between the more and less creative groups within each age sample. Whether the relative

Comparison of Adult and Adolescent Samples with Respect to Differences Between
"More" and "Less" Creative Group Standard Score Means on 18 CPI and 4 MMPI Scales

Scale	Adults			Adolescents		
	Mean		P Level of Difference[1]	Mean		P Level of Difference[2]
	Creative $N=101$	Control $N=99$		Creative $N=112$	Control $N=413$	
CPI Scales						
Dominance	57	54		56	54	.05
Capacity for Status	60	58	.10	57	55	
Sociability	52	50		53	51	.10
Social Presence	60	55	.001	57	55	
Self-Acceptance	61	57	.001	60	59	
Sense of Well-Being	50	52	.10	47	45	
Responsibility	54	53		54	52	
Socialization	48	49		52	52	
Self-Control	47	51	.05	47	45	.05
Tolerance	54	53		54	52	.05
Good Impression	43	47	.01	48	44	.01
Communality	49	52	.10	48	50	.05
Achievement via Conformity	52	53		52	51	
Achievement via Independence	64	61	.10	62	59	.05
Intellectual Efficiency	57	55		58	56	.05
Psychological Mindedness	65	63		63	59	.05
Flexibility	61	57	.001	58	59	
Femininity	57	55	.10	52	51	
MMPI Scales						
K (Candidness)	57	57		55	53	.01
A (Anxiety)	45	45		47	50	.05
R (Repression)	57	55		52	51	
E (Ego Strength)	59	59		58	56	.01

[1] Derived from unweighted means Analysis of Variance of 2 levels of Creativity and 4 Vocations; df for main effect of Creativity = 1/192.
[2] Derived from unweighted means Analyses of Variance of 2 levels of Creativity and 7 Vocational Interest groups; df for main effect of Creativity = 1/511.

creativity difference existing between the more and less creative adults is equivalent to the relative difference in creativity levels of the more and less creative adolescents is unknown. However, hypothesized differences in absolute levels of creativity represented in the adult and adolescent samples would not explain either the reversal in direction of discrimination of two scales or the fact that a number of scales mutually differentiate between the more and less creative groups independent of age.

It appears likely that creative performance is associated in both age groups with a shared set of personality characteristics; it is also likely that creative performance is associated with some personality variables unique to adolescents and others unique to adults.

Within the limitations of the instruments employed in this study, it appears that creative adolescents and adults, independent of the specific areas in which they are working or plan to work, show personality characteristics which differentiate them from their less creative colleagues. It is stressed that, although these discriminating personality variables show considerable overlap for both age groups, they are not identical for the adults and adolescents. Some of the personality variables which discriminate between the more and less creative adults may represent personality modifications in response to success and recognition rather than predisposition to creative performance. Some personality variables may be more relevant and "useful" in providing conditions for creative performance for the adolescent while other personality characteristics may be more appropriate for the creative functioning of the adult. The data suggest that the same personality characteristics may be useful at one period in the scientist's development and inhibitory at another period.

Since the design of this study involved cross-sectional rather than longitudinal investigations, it cannot be demonstrated which personality characteristics remain stable across age periods and which vary systematically. If it is assumed that the more creative adolescent sample comes from the same population as the more creative adult sample, it would appear that personality patterns of assertiveness, self-confidence, vigor and ambition, self-reliance, and independence in thinking may be conducive to creative performance in both adolescence and middle age. However, such personality variables as concern with one's impact on others and efforts to control one's overt behavior may be facilitating of creative performance in the adolescent, but inhibiting in the adult. This conclusion is plausible since the environment of the adolescent is typically far less supportive or tolerant of unmodified self-assertion, arbitrary demands, or seeming disregard for the opinions of authorities than is that of the acknowledged creative adult. It is also possible that the performance of the adolescent is, in fact, facilitated rather than inhibited by the self-discipline which is consistent with learning the basic information and the fundamentals of his discipline prior to his attempting to reorganize and restructure his field.

Efforts to identify personality characteristics which enhance the likelihood of creative performance must take into account such age-environment related phenomena. The study suggests that the creative adolescent cannot be identified simply by using as criteria personality standards derived solely from the study of creative adults and their controls.

These results have encouraged us to undertake a further study with a comparable sample in order to test the stability of these findings and to determine the backgrounds and parent-child relationships associated with varying levels of creative performance. The subjects in these samples will be studied as they complete their education and pursue their careers. Of particular concern will be the interaction of environment and personality over time, as it relates to creative performance in the "more" and "less" creative groups.

CHAPTER 18

A Holistic Approach to Creativity

A. H. Maslow*

IT HAS BEEN interesting for me during this research conference to compare the present-day situation in the field of creativeness with the situation about 20 or 25 years ago. First, the amount of data that have been accumulated—the sheer amount of research work—is far beyond that which anybody might reasonably have expected then. A second impression is that, in comparison with the great accumulation of methods, of ingenious testing techniques, and of sheer quantity of information, theory in this realm has not advanced very much. It seems to me that I could be most useful in raising the theoretical questions, that is, what disturbs me about the conceptualizations in this field of research, and the bad consequences of these disturbing conceptualizations.

The most important thing that I would like to communicate is my impression that the thinking and the research in the field of creativeness tends to be too atomistic and too *ad hoc,* and that it is not as holistic, organismic, or systemic as it could be and should be. Now, of course, I don't want to make any foolish dichotomies or polarizations here, that is, to imply any piety about holism or antagonism to dissection or atomism. The question for me is how to integrate them best, rather than choosing between them. One way of avoiding such a choosing up of sides is to use Spearman's discrimination between a general factor (g) and specific or special factors (s), both of which enter into the makeup not only of intelligence, but also of creativeness.

As I read the creativeness literature, it seems terribly impressive that the relationship with psychiatric health or psychological health is so crucial, so profound, so terribly important, and so obvious, and yet it is not used as a foundation on which to build. For instance, there has been rather little relationship between the studies in the field of psychotherapy, on the one hand, and of creativeness, on the other. One of my graduate students, Richard Craig, has published what I consider to be a very important demonstration that there *is* such a relationship (1966). We were very much impressed with the table in Torrance's book, *Guiding Creative Talent* (1962), in which he pulled together

---

*Deceased. The author died just a few days after returning corrected proof for this final overview chapter on the field of creativity. At the time of his death, he was Senior Fellow, Laughlin Foundation, Menlo Park, California. Prior to that, he was Professor of Psychology at Brandeis University.

and summarized the evidence on all the personality characteristics that have been demonstrated to correlate with creativeness. There are perhaps 30 or more characteristics that he considered sufficiently valid. What Craig did was to put down these characteristics in a column and then, in another column beside them, to list the characteristics that I had used in describing self-actualizing people (Maslow, 1954), which overlaps considerably with the lists many other people have used in describing psychological health (i.e., Rogers' "Fully Functioning Person" or Jung's "Individuated Person" or Fromm's "Autonomous Person" and so on).

The overlap was almost perfect. There were two or three characteristics in that list of 30 or 40 which had not been used to describe psychologically healthy people, but were simply neutral. There was no single characteristic which went in the other, opposite direction, making, arbitrarily, nearly 40 characteristics, or perhaps 37 or 38 which were the same as psychological health—which added up to a syndrome of psychological health or self-actualization.

This chapter is cited as a good jumping-off point for discussion because it is my very powerful conviction (as it was a long time ago) that the problem of creativeness is the problem of the creative person (Maslow, 1963) rather than of creative products, creative behaviors, etc. In other words, he is a particular or special kind of human being, rather than just an old-fashioned, ordinary human being who now has obtained new extrinsic possessions, who has acquired a new skill like ice skating, or accumulated some more things that he "owns" but which are not intrinsic to him, to his basic nature.

If you think of the person, the creative person, as being the essence of the problem, then what you are confronted with is the whole problem of transformation of human nature, the transformation of the character, the full development of the whole person. This, in turn, necessarily involves us in the question of the *Weltanschauung,* the life philosophy, the way of living, the code of ethics, the values of society, and so on. This is in sharp and direct contrast with the *ad hoc,* causal, encapsulated, atomistic conception of theory, research and training implied so often: e.g.: "What is *the* cause of creativity?"; "What is *the* most important *single* thing we can do?"; "Shall we add a three-credit course in creativity to the curriculum?" I half expect to hear someone ask soon, "Where is it localized?", or to try implanting electrodes with which to turn it on or off. In consultations with research and development people in industry, I also get the strong impression that they keep looking for some secret button to push, like switching a light on and off.

What I would propose in trying to achieve the creative person is that there could be hundreds and, almost literally, thousands of determinants of creativeness. That is, anything that would help the person to move in the direction of greater psychological health or fuller humanness would amount to changing the whole person. This more fully human, healthier person would then, epiphenomenally, generate and spark off dozens, hundreds, and millions of differences in behaving, experiencing, perceiving, communicating, teaching, working, etc., which would *all* be more "creative." He would then be simply another *kind* of person who would behave in a different way in *every* respect. And then instead of the single secret push button or trick or three credit course which will presumably, *ad hoc,* produce more creativeness, *ad hoc,* this more holistic, organismic point of view would suggest the more likely question: "And why should not *every* course help toward creativeness?" Certainly this kind of education *of the person* should help create a better *type* of person, help a person grow bigger, taller, wiser, more perceptive—a person who, incidentally, would be more creative as a matter of course in *all* departments of life.

One example comes to mind. A colleague, Dick Jones, did a doctoral dissertation (1960) which I thought was terribly important from a philosophical point of view, but which has not been noticed enough. What he did was to run a kind of group therapy course with high school seniors and then found that, at the end of the year, racial and ethnic prejudice had gone down, in spite of the fact that for one full year he had made it his business to avoid ever mentioning these words. Prejudice is not created by pushing a button. You don't have to train people to be prejudiced, and you can't really directly train them to be "unprejudiced." We have tried and it doesn't work very well. But this "being unprejudiced" flies off as a spark off the wheel, as an epiphenomenon, as a by-product, simply from becoming a better human being, whether from psychotherapy or from any other influence that improves the person.

About 25 years ago, my style of investigation of creativeness was very different from the classical scientific (atomistic) method. I had to invent holistic interviewing techniques. That is, to try getting to know one single person after another as profoundly and as deeply and as fully as possible (as unique, individual persons) to the point where I felt I understood them (as whole persons). It was like getting very full case histories of whole lives and whole people *without* having particular problems or questions in mind, that is, without abstracting one aspect of the person rather than another; i.e., I was doing it idiographically.

And yet it is *then* possible to be nomothetic, to *then* ask particular questions, to do simple statistics, to come to *general* conclusions. One can treat each person as an infinity, and yet infinities can be added, percentages made, just as transfinite numbers can be manipulated.

Once you get to know a sample of people profoundly and deeply, and individually in this way, then certain operations become possible that are not possible in typical classical experiments. I had a panel of about 120 people, with each of whom I had spent an awful lot of time just simply getting to know them in general. Then, *after* the fact, I could then ask a question, go back to the data and answer it, and this could have been done even if all the 120 people had died. This contrasts with *ad hoc* experimentation on a single problem in which one variable would be modified and all others presumably "held constant" (although, of course, we know very well that there are thousands of variables which are presumably, but not actually, controlled in the classical experimental paradigm and which are very far from being held constant).

If I may be permitted to be bluntly challenging, it is my firm opinion that the cause-effect way of thinking, which works pretty well in the non-living world and which we have learned to use more or less well to solve human problems, is now dead as a general philosophy of science. It shouldn't be used any more because it just tends to lead us into *ad hoc* thinking; that is, of one cause producing one specific effect, and of one factor producing one factor, instead of keeping us sensitive to *systemic* and organismic changes of the kind that I've tried to describe, in which any single stimulus is conceived to change the whole organism, which then, as a changed organism, emits behavior changed in *all* departments of life. (This is also true for social organizations, large and small.)

For instance, if you think of physical health, and if you ask the questions, "How do you get people's teeth to be better?" or "How do you get their feet to be better?" or their kidneys, eyes, hair, etc., any physician will tell you that the best thing to do is to improve general systemic health. That is, you try to improve the general (g) factor. If you can improve their diet and mode of living and so on, then these procedures, in one single blow will improve their teeth and their kidneys and their hair and their livers and their intestines and *everything else;* their entire systems will be improved. In the same way, general creativeness, holistically conceived, emanates from the whole system, *generally* improved. Furthermore, any factors that would produce a more creative person would also make a man a better father, or better teacher, or better citizen, or a better dancer, or a better *anything,* at least to the extent that the "g" factor is strengthened. To this is then added, of course, the specific (s) contributions that differentiate the good father from the good dancer or good composer.

Recently, I read a pretty good book on the sociology of religion (Glock *et al.,* 1965), and I would recommend it as a rather intelligent and competent picture of this type of atomistic and *ad hoc* thinking. *Ad hoc* thinkers, S-R thinkers, cause-effect thinkers, one-cause-to-one-effect thinkers, when going into a new field start the way these writers do. First, of course, they feel they must define religion and, of course, they have to define this in such a way that it is pure and discrete, not anything else. Then they proceed to isolate it, cut it and dissect it away from everything else. So they wind up with the old Aristotelian logic "A" and "Not A." "A" is all, "A" and nothing but "A." It's just pure "A"; and "Not A" is pure everything else, and so they have no overlap, no melting, no merging, no fusing, and so on. The old possibility (taken very seriously by all profoundly religious people) that religious attitudes can be one aspect or characteristic of practically *any* behavior—indeed of *all* behaviors—is lost on the very first page of the book. This enables them to go ahead and get into an absolute and total chaos, as beautiful a chaos as I have ever seen. They get into a blind alley—and stay there—in which religious behavior is separated off from all other behavior, so that all they deal with through the whole book is the external behavior—going to church or not going to church; saving or not saving little pieces of wood; and bowing or not bowing before this or that or the other thing. Thereby they leave out of the whole book what I might call small "r" religion, entirely; that is, the religious attitudes and feelings and emotions of profoundly religious people who may have nothing to do with institutions or with supernaturals or with idolatry. This is just one good example of atomistic thinking among plenty of others, I assure you. You can think atomistically in any department of life.

We can do the same with creativeness if we wish. We can make creativeness into a Sunday behavior also, which occurs in a particular room in a particular building, such as a classroom, and at a particular separated off time, e.g., on Thursdays. It's just creativeness and nothing else there in that room and at that time, and at no other time or place. And only certain areas have to do with creativeness: painting, composing, writing, but not cooking or taxi driving or plumbing. But I raise the question again of creativeness being an aspect of practically any behavior at all, whether perceptual or attitudinal or emotional, conative, cognitive, or expressive. If approached in that way, you might get to ask all sorts of interesting questions which wouldn't occur to you if you approached it in this other dichotomized way.

It's a little like the difference in the ways you would try to learn to be a good dancer. Most people in *ad hoc* society would go to the Arthur Murray School where you first move your left foot and then your right foot three paces and, bit by bit, you go through a lot of external, willed motions. But I think we would all agree, and that we *know,* that it is rather characteristic of successful psychotherapy that there are *thousands* of effects, among which might very well be good dancing, i.e., being more free about dancing, more graceful, less bound up, less inhibited, less self-conscious, less appeasing, and so on. In the same way, psychotherapy, where it is good (and we all know there is plenty of bad psychotherapy too) and is successful, then psychotherapy, in my experience, can be counted on to enhance the creativity of a person without the therapist ever trying to, or mentioning the word.

I can also recall a relevant dissertation one of our students has done, which turned up most unexpected kinds of things. This started out to be a study of peak experiences in natural childbirth, ecstasies from motherhood, and so on. But it shifted considerably because what Mrs. Tanzer discovered is that all sorts of *other* miraculous changes come about when childbirth is a good or great experience. When it's a good experience, many things in life change for the woman. It may have some of the flavor of the religious conversion experience, or of the great illumination effect, or the great success experience which changes radically the woman's self-image and, therefore, changes all her behaviors.

This general approach seems to be a much better, a more fruitful way to talk about "climate." Yesterday, we tried to pin down in the Non-Linear Systems organizational set (Maslow, 1965) what was the cause of all the good effects there. All I can say is that the whole place was a climate of creative atmosphere. I couldn't pick one main cause as more important than another. There was freedom of a *general* kind, atmospheric, holistic, global, rather than a little thing that you did on Tuesday—one particular, separable thing. The right climate, the *best* climate for enhancing creativeness would be a Utopia, or Eupsychia, as I prefer to call it; a society which was specifically designed for improving the self-fulfillment and psychological health of all people. That would be my general statement, the "g" statement. Within and against that background, we could *then* work with a particular "figure," with a particular *ad hoc,* the "s", or specific factors that make one man a good carpenter and another a good mathematician. But without that general societal background, in a bad society (which is a general systemic statement), creativeness is just less likely, less possible.

I think that the parallel from therapy can also be useful to us here. We have much to learn from the people who are interested in this realm of research and thinking. For instance, we must face their problem of what identity means, of what is the real self, and of what therapy does and what education does, by way of helping people move toward identity. On the other hand, we have a model of some kind of real self, some kind of characteristic which is conceived biologically to some extent. It is constitutional, temperamental, "instinctoid." We are a species and we are different from other species. If this is so, if you can accept this instead of the *tabula rasa* model, the person as pure clay which is to be molded or reinforced into any predesigned shape that the arbitrary controller wants, then you must also accept the model of therapy as uncovering, unleashing, rather than the model of therapy as molding, creating, and shaping. And this would be true also for education. The basic models generated by these two different conceptions of human nature would be different—teaching, learning, everything.

Is then creativeness part of the general human heritage? Half a dozen people in the last few days here have said, "Yes"; they thought so. It does very frequently get lost, or covered up, or twisted or inhibited or whatever, and then the job is to uncover what all babies are, in principle, born with. Well, I think that this is a very profound and very general philosophical question that we are dealing with, a very basic philosophical stance.

One aspect of it is that I see myself here as really challenging the classical model of science and everything that goes with it: the classical model of the experiment, the controlled experiment, the cause-effect relationships, the nature of objectivity, prediction, control, precision, and so on and so on. With the kind of work that you do in this field, I am sure that these questions, this clash in philosophy of science is unavoidable now because there are several books available or will be soon. I have a book on *Psychology and Science* (1966), but the *great* book, the revolutionary one, a big fat thing that you will have to sweat your way through, if you haven't already—it's a new era in scientific thinking in my opinion—is Michael Polanyi's *Personal Knowledge* (1958). It's a big, difficult, hard book. After four months spent sweating my way through it, now I will have to go through it again because I don't think I quite got it. It's a different way of looking at our data, our science, research, and so on.

Finally, I would like to make one last point which is an "s" point, not a "g" point. I would like to ask, when do we *not* want creativeness? Sometimes creativeness can be a horrible nuisance. It can be a troublesome, dangerous, messy thing, as I learned once from a "creative" research assistant who gummed up a research that had been underway for over a year. She got "creative" and changed the whole thing in the middle without even telling me about it. She so gummed up all the data that a year's work was lost completely. On the whole, we want the trains to run on time and, generally, we want dentists *not* to be creative. A friend of mine had an operation a couple of years ago, and he still remembers feeling uneasy and afraid until he met his surgeon. Fortunately, he turned out to be a nice obsessional type of man, very precise, perfectly neat with a little hair-line moustache, every hair in place, a perfectly straight, controlled and sober man. My friend then heaved a sigh of relief—this was not a "creative" man. Here was a man who would do a normal, routine, pedestrian operation, not play any tricks or try any novelties or experiments or do any new sewing techniques or anything like that. This is important, I think, in our society where, with our division of labor, we ought to be able to take orders and to carry through a program and be predictable. It is also important for each of us, not only in our capacity as creative workers, but also as students of creativeness with a tendency to deify the one side of the creative process—the enthusiastic, the great insight, the illumination, the good idea, the moment in the middle of the night when you get the great inspiration—and of underplaying the two years of hard and sweaty labor that then is necessary to make anything useful out of the bright idea.

In simple terms of time, bright ideas really take a small proportion of our time. Most time is spent on hard work. My impression is that our students don't know this. It may be that these dead cats have been brought to my door more because my students so frequently identify with me, because I have written about peak experiences and inspirations and so on, that they feel that this is the only way to live. Life without daily or hourly peak experiences, that's no life, so they think they can't do work that is boring.

Some student tells me, "No, I don't want to do that because I don't enjoy it," and then I get purple in the face and fly up in a rage—"Damn it, you do it, or I'll fire you"—and he feels I am betraying my own principles. In making a more measured and balanced picture of creativeness, we workers with creativity have to be responsible for the impressions we make upon other people. Apparently one impression that we are making on them is that creativeness consists of lightning striking you on the head in one great glorious moment. The fact that the people who create are good workers tends to be lost.

REFERENCES

Adamson, R. E. Functional fixedness as related to problem solving: A repetition of three experiments. *Journal of Experimental Psychology,* 1952, 44, 288-02.

Barlow, J. A. Aspects of programming, learning and performance. Unpublished paper presented at American Psychological Association, Chicago, 1960.

Barron, F. *Creative Person and Creative Process,* New York: Holt, Rinehart & Winston, 1969.

Barron, F. The inheritance of aesthetic judgment and creative thinking abilities. *Acta Geneticae Medicae et Gemellologiae,* 19,, (1) Rome, Italy, January, 1970.

Barron, F. & Egan, D. Leaders and innovators in Irish management. *The Journal of Management Studies,* No. 1, February 1968, 5, 41-61.

Brodie, W. M. A program to affirm the reality of hierarchical grouping. Unpublished manuscript, Computer Sciences, Purdue University, 1966.

Brooks, G. W. & Mueller, E. Serum urate concentrations among university professors. *Journal of the American Medical Association,* 1966, 195, 415-18.

Bruner, J. S. *On Knowing.* Cambridge: Harvard University Press, 1962.

Cattell, R. B. & Butcher, H. J. *The Prediction of Achievement and Creativity.* New York: Bobbs-Merrill, 1968.

Christensen, P. R., Guilford, J. P., & Wilson, R. C. Relations of creative response to working time and instructions. *Journal of Experimental Psychology,* 1957, 53, 82-9.

Conant, J. B. *The Education of American Teachers.* New York: McGraw-Hill, 1963.

Cowen, E. L. Stress reduction and problem-solving rigidity. *Journal of Consulting Psychology,* 1952, 16, 425-8.

Craig, R. Trait lists and creativity. *Psychologia,* 1966, 9, 107-10.

Cronbach, L. H., & Gleser, G. Assessing similarity between profiles. *Psychological Bulletin,* 1953, 50, 456-73.

Cunnington, B. F. & Torrance, E. P. Eyes at their fingertips. Minneapolis: Bureau of Educational Research, University of Minnesota, 1963. (Mimeographed)

Cunnington, B. F. & Torrance, E. P. *Imagi/Craft Series.* Boston: Ginn, 1965a.

Cunnington, B. F. & Torrance, E. P. *Sounds and Images.* Boston: Ginn, 1965b.

De Simone, D. V. *Education for Innovation.* Elmsford, N. Y.: Pergamon Press, 1968.

Drucker, P. *The Practice of Management.* New York: Harper-Row, 1954.

Ellison, R. L., McDonald, B., James, L., Fox, D., & Taylor, C. W. *An Investigation of Organizational Climate.* Greensboro, N.C.: Richardson Foundation, 1968.

Folger, A. & Gordon, G. Scientific accomplishment and social organization: A review of the literature. *American Behavioral Scientist,* 1962, V, 51-8.

Fowler, H. *Modern English Usage,* Oxford. Clarendon Press, 1965.

Galanter, E. (Ed.) *Automatic Teaching, the State of the Art.* New York: Wiley, 1959.

Getzels, J. W. & Jackson, P. W. The highly intelligent and the highly creative adolescent: A summary of some research findings. In C. W. Taylor & F. Barron (Eds.), *Scientific Creativity: Its Recognition and Development.* New York: Wiley, 1963.

Ghiselin, B. (Ed.) *The Creative Process.* New York: Mentor Books, 1955.

Gibb, J. R. Communication and productivity. *Personnel Administration,* 1964, 27, 8-13.

Gibb, J. R. Fear and facade: Defensive management. In R. E. Farson (Ed.), *Science and Human Affairs.* Palo Alto, Cal.: Science and Behavior Books, 1965.

Gibb, J. R. The effects of human relations training. In A. E. Bergin & S. L. Garfield (Eds.), *Handbook of Psychotherapy and Behavior Change.* New York: Wiley, in press.

Gibb, J. R. Group experiences and human possibilities. In H. A. Otto (Ed.), *Human Potentialities: The Challenge and the Promise.* St. Louis: Green, 1968.

Gibb, J. R., & Gibb, L. M. Humanistic elements in group growth. In J. F. T. Bugental (Ed.), *Challenges of Humanistic Psychology,* New York: McGraw-Hill, 1967.

Gibb, J. R., & Gibb, L. M. Emergence therapy: The TORI process in an emergent group. In G. M. Gazda (Ed.), *Innovations to Group Psychotherapy.* Springfield, Ill.: Thomas, 1968.

Gibb, J. R., & Gibb, L. M.   Leaderless groups: Growth-centered values and potentials. In H. A. Otto & J. Mann (Eds.), *Ways of Growth: Approaches to Expanding Awareness.* New York: Grossman, 1968.

Glock, C. & Stark, R. *Religion and Society in Tension.* Skokie, Ill.: Rand-McNally, 1965.

Gough, H. C. *Manual for the California Psychological Inventory.* Palo Alto, Cal.: Consulting Psychologists Press, 1957.

Guilford, J. P. Three faces of intellect. *American Psychologist,* 1959, **14**, 469-79.

Guilford, J. P. Letter to S. J. Parnes. University of Southern California, October 31, 1961.

Guilford, J. P. Motivation in an informational psychology. In D. Levine (Ed.), *The Nebraska Symposium on Motivation 1965.* Lincoln, Nebr.: University of Nebraska Press, 1965. Pp. 313-32.

Guilford, J. P. Intelligence: 1965 model. *American Psychologist,* 1966, **21**, 10-26.

James, B. J., Guetzkow, H., Forehand, G. A., & Libby, W. L. Jr. Education for innovative behavior in executives. Chicago: Cooperative Research Project No. 975, University of Chicago, 1962.

Jex, F. B. Negative validities for two different ingenuity tests. In C. W. Taylor & F. Barron (Eds.), *Scientific Creativity: Its Recognition and Development.* New York: Wiley, 1963. Pp. 299-301.

Jones, R. *An Application of Psychoanalysis to Education.* Springfield, Ill.: Thomas, 1960.

Kallick, M. Organizational determinants of creative productivity. Unpublished doctoral dissertation, Purdue University, 1964.

Klaus, D. J. Letter to B. J. Decker. American Institute of Research, April 27, 1961.

Klaus, D. J. & Lumsdaine, A. A. Some economic realities of teaching machine instruction. American Institute of Research, Pittsburgh, 1960.

Klein, A. (Ed.) *Grand Deceptions.* Philadelphia: Lippincott, 1955.

Klein, S. P. Life history and ability correlates of mechanical ingenuity. Unpublished doctoral dissertation, Purdue University, 1965.

Kuhn, T. S. *The Structure of Scientific Revolutions.* Chicago: University of Chicago Press, 1962.

Kuhn, T. S. & Kaplan, N. Environmental conditions affecting creativity. In C. W. Taylor (Ed.), *The Third (1959) University of Utah Research Conference on the Indentification of Creative Scientific Talent.* Salt Lake City: University of Utah Press, 1959.

Lindquist, E. F. *Design and Analysis of Experiments in Psychology and Education.* Boston: Houghton Mifflin, 1956.

Lumsdaine, A. A. & Glaser, R. *Teaching Machines and Programmed Learning—A Source Book.* Department of Audio Visual Instruction, NEA, 1960.

MacKinnon, D. W., Block, J., Crutchfield, R. S., Gough, H. G., Hall, W. B., & Helson, R. *Proceedings of the Conference on "The Creative Person,"* University of California Extension, Berkeley, Calif.

Maier, N. R. F. *Problem-Solving in Creativity.* Belmont, Calif.: Brooks Cole, 1970.

Maltzman, I., Simon, S., & Licht, L. The persistence of originality-training effects. Los Angeles: University of California, Department of Psychology, Technical Report 4, Prepared under contract Nonr 223 (50) for the Office of Naval Research, August, 1959.

Maslow, A. H. *Motivation and Personality*. New York: Harper & Row, 1954.

Maslow, A. H. The creative attitude. *The Structurist*, 1963, No. 3, 4-10.

Maslow, A. H. *Eupsychian Management: A Journal*. Homewood, Ill.: Irwin-Dorsey, 1965.

Maslow, A. H. *Psychology of Science: A Reconnaissance*. New York: Harper & Row, 1966.

McPherson, J. Environment and training for creativity. In C. W. Taylor (Ed.), *Creativity: Progress and Potential*. New York: McGraw-Hill, 1964.

Meadow, A. & Parnes, S. M. Evaluation of training in creative problem solving. *Journal of Applied Psychology*, 1959, 43, No. 3, 189-94.

Meadow, A., Parnes, S. J., & Reese, H. Influence of brainstorming instructions and problem sequence on a creative problem-solving test. *Journal of Applied Psychology*, 1959, 43, No. 6, 413-16.

Mednick, S. A. The associative basis of the creative process. *Psychological Review*, 69, No. 3, 221.

Miles, M. B. Changes during and following laboratory training: A clinical-laboratory study. *Journal of Applied Behavioral Science*, 1965, 1, 215-42.

Moustakas, C. (Ed.) *The Self*, New York: Harper & Row, 1956.

Muller, H. J. *Freedom in the Modern World*. New York: Harper & Row, 1966.

Myers, R. E. & Torrance, E. P. *Invitations to Thinking and Doing*. Boston: Ginn, 1964.

Myers, R. E. & Torrance, E. P. *Can You Imagine?* Boston: Ginn, 1965a.

Myers, R. E. & Torrance, E. P. *Invitations to Speaking and Writing Creatively*. Boston: Ginn, 1965b.

Myers, R. E. & Torrance, E. P. *For Those Who Wonder*. Boston: Ginn, 1966a.

Myers, R. E. & Torrance, E. P. *Plots, Puzzles, and Ploys*. Boston: Ginn, 1966b.

Nielsen, E. Factor analysis of a biographical information inventory. Doctoral dissertation, University of Utah, 1963.

Olton, R. M. A self-instructional program for the development of productive thinking in fifth and sixth grade children. In F. E. Williams (Ed.), *First Seminar on Productive Thinking in Education*. St. Paul, Minn.: Creativity and National Schools project. Macalester College, 1966.

O'Sullivan, M., Guilford, J. P., & de Mille, R. Measurement of social intelligence. *Reports Psychological Laboratories*, No. 34, University of Southern California, 1965.

Owens, W. A., & Henry, E. R. *Biographical Data in Industrial Psychology: A Review and Evaluation*. Greensboro, N.C.: The Richardson Foundation, 1966.

Owens, W. A., Schumacher, C. F., & Clark, J. B. The measurement of creativity in machine design. *Journal of Applied Psychology*, 1957, 41, 297-302.

Parnes, S. J. *Creative Behavior Guidebook*. New York: Scribner's, 1967.

Parnes, S. J. Effects of extended effort in creative problem-solving. *Journal of Educational Psychology*, 1961, 52, No. 3, 117-22.

Parnes, S. J. *News and Reports*. OE-34002-4, U. S. Office of Education, Washington, D.C., March, 1961.

Parnes, S. J. & Meadow, A. Effects of "brainstorming" instructions on creative problem solving by trained and untrained subjects. *Journal of Educational Psychology*, 1959, 50, No. 4, 171-6.

Parnes, S. J. & Meadow, A. Evaluation of persistence of effects produced by a creative problem-solving course. *Psychological Reports*, 1960, 7, 357-61.

Polanyi, M. *Personal Knowledge*. University of Chicago Press, 1958.

Price, P. B., Taylor, C. W., Richards, J. M., & Jacobsen, T. L. Measurement of physician performance. *Journal Medical Education*, 1964, 31 (2).

Runner, K. R. & Runner, H. Manual of *Interpretation for the Interview Form III of the Runner Studies of Attitude Patterns.* Golden, Colo.: Runner Associates, 1965.

Schramm, W. *The, Research on Programmed Instruction.* Washington, D.C.: U. S. Department of Health, Education and Welfare, 1964.

Schroeder, H. M., Driver, M. J., & Streufert, S. *Human Information Processing.* New York: Holt, Rinehart, & Winston, 1967.

Sherwin, C. W. & Isensen, R. S. Project Hindsight: A Defense Department study of the utility of research. *Science,* 1967, **156,** 1571.

Simpson, R. M. Creative imagination. *American Journal of Psychology,* 1922, **33,** 234-43.

Skinner, B. F. Letter to B. J. Decker. Harvard University, February, 1961.

Spearman, C. *Abilities of Man.* New York: Macmillan, 1927.

Taylor, C. W. Some educational implications of creativity research findings. *School Science and Mathematics,* November, 1962, **62,** (8), 593-606.

Taylor, C. W. Clues to creative teaching. Series of ten articles appearing in *The Instructor Magazine,* September, 1963 to June, 1964, Dansville, N.Y.

Taylor, C. W. Productive thinking in science education. Supported by AFOSR Project No. AFOSR-11-63 and AF-AFOSR-144-63. Rowena Swanson, Monitor. (Mimeographed)

Taylor, C. W. *Widening Horizons in Creativity.* New York: Wiley, 1964.

Taylor, C. W. Cultivating creativity within the new curriculum. Speech given February 5, 1966 to National Association of Secondary-School Principals. (Mimeographed)

Taylor, C. W. Nearly all students are talented—Let's reach them! *Utah Parent Teacher Magazine,* February, 1968, 9-10.

Taylor, C. W. Multiple talent approach. *The Instructor,* April, 1968, **27,** 144, 146.

Taylor, C. W. Talent—Waving good-bye to the "average" man. *PACE Magazine* June, 1969, 22-3.

Taylor, C. W. The highest talent potentials of man. *The Gifted Child Quarterly,* 1969, xiii (1), 9-30.

Taylor, C. W. Be talent developers as well as knowledge dispensers. *Today's Education,* December, 1968, 67-8.

Taylor, C. W. (Ed.) *Creativity: Progress and Potential.* New York: McGraw-Hill, 1964.

Taylor, C. W. (Ed.) *Creativity Across Education,* Salt Lake City: University of Utah Press, 1972.

Taylor, C. W. & Barron, F. *Scientific Creativity: Its Recognition and Development.* New York: Wiley, 1963.

Taylor, C. W., Ellison, R. L., & Tucker, M. F. Biographical information and the prediction of multiple criteria of success in science. Supported by the National Aeronautics and Space Administration Research Project NASw-105, 1965.

Taylor, C. W., Ghiselin, B., & Wolfer, J. Bridging the gap between basic research and educational practice. *National Education Association Journal,* 1962, **51,** 23-5.

Taylor, C. W., Ghiselin, B., Wolfer, J.A., Loy, L., & Bourne, L. E. Jr. *Development of a Theory of Education From Psychological and Other Basic Research Findings.* University of Utah, 1964, Cooperative Research Project No. 621, report to U. S. Office of Education.

Taylor, C. W., Ghiselin, B., & Yagi, K. Exploratory research on communication abilities and creative abilities. Supported by Air Force Office of Scientific Research, AF–144–63. Rowena Swanson, Monitor. (Forthcoming)

Taylor, C. W., Lewis, E. G., Nelson, E. D. Loughmiller, G. C., & Price, P. B. Synthesis of multiple criteria of physician performance. *Journal of Medical Education,* 1969, **44,** 1063-1069.

Taylor, C. W., Neilsen, E., Clark, B., Sponberg, R. A., *et al.* Talent awareness training. *The Instructor,* May, 1969, 61-8.

Taylor, C. W. & Williams, F. E. *Instructional Media and Creativity*. New York: Wiley, 1966.

Taylor, C. W., Yagi, K., DeMik, G., Branum, J., Tucker,   F., & Wight, A. R. *Development of Situational Tests for the Peace Corps,* University of Utah, 1967.

Thorndike, E. L. Intelligence and its uses. *Harper's Magazine,* 1920, 140, 227-235.

Thorndike, E. L. Restriction of range. In *Personnel Selection*. New York: Wiley, 1949.

Thurstone, L. L. *The Nature of Intelligence*. New York: Harcourt, Brace & World, 1924.

Toops, H. A. The criterion. *Educational and Psychological Measurement,* 1944, 4, 271-97.

Torrance, E. P. *Guiding Creative Talent*. Englewood Cliffs, N. J.: Prentice-Hall, 1962.

Torrance, E. P. Explorations in creative thinking in the early school years: A progress report. In C. W. Taylor & F. Barron (Eds.), *Scientific Creativity: Its Recognition and Development*. New York: Wiley, 1963. Pp. 173-83.

Torrance, E. P. *Rewarding Creative Behavior*. Englewood Cliffs, N. J.: Prentice-Hall, 1965a.

Torrance, E. P. *Mental Health and Constructive Behavior,* Belmont, Cal.: Wadsworth 1965b.

Torrance, E. P. *Gifted Children in the Classroom*. New York: Macmillan, 1965c.

Torrance, E. P. Preliminary guide for scoring dot-squares test for originality. Minneapolis: Minnesota Studies of Creative Behavior, 1965d. (Mimeographed)

Torrance, E. P. *Torrance Tests of Creative Thinking. Norms-Technical Manual* (research ed.). Princeton, N. J. Personnel Press, 1966.

Torrance, E. P. *Preliminary Manual for the What Kind of a Person Are You? Test.* Minneapolis, Minnesota Studies of Creative Behavior, 1966b.

Torrance, E. P. Epilogue: Creativity in American education, 1865-1965. In J. C. Gowan, G. D. Demos, & E. P. Torrance (Eds.), *Creativity: Its Educational Implications*. New York: Wiley, 1967.

Toynbee, A. Is America neglecting her creative minority? In C. W. Taylor (Ed.), *Widening Horizons in Creativity*. New York: Wiley, 1964. Pp. 3-9.

Ward, J. H., Jr., & Hook, M. E. Application of an hierarchical grouping procedure to a problem of grouping profiles. *Educational and Psychological Measurement,* 1963, 23, 69-81.

Whitehead, A. N. *The Aims of Education*. New York: Mentor Books, 1929.

INDEX

Volumes from the six previous national research conferences in this series are:

1955   The Identification of Creative Scientific Talent,
            University of Utah Press (multilithed), 1956

1957   The Identification of Creative Scientific Talent,
            University of Utah Press (multilithed), 1958

1959   The Identification of Creative Scientific Talent,
            University of Utah Press (multilithed), 1959

———   *Scientific Creativity: Its Recognition and Development,*
            Wiley, 1963, (Selected papers from 3 conferences above).
            Hardback and paperback (with Frank Barron, co-editor).

1961   *Creativity: Progress and Potential,* McGraw-Hill, 1964.

1962   *Widening Horizons in Creativity,* Wiley, 1964.

1964   *Instructional Media and Creativity,* Wiley, 1966.
            Hardback and paperback (with Frank E. Williams,
            co-editor).